JUSTICE, LAW AND CULTURE

Justice, Law and Culture

by
JAMES K. FEIBLEMAN
Tulane University

1985 **MARTINUS NIJHOFF PUBLISHERS**
a member of the KLUWER ACADEMIC PUBLISHERS GROUP
DORDRECHT / BOSTON / LANCASTER

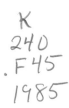

Distributors

for the United States and Canada: Kluwer Academic Publishers, 190 Old Derby
Street, Hingham, MA 02043, USA
for the UK and Ireland: Kluwer Academic Publishers, MTP Press Limited,
Falcon House, Queen Square, Lancaster LA1 1RN, UK
for all other countries: Kluwer Academic Publishers Group, Distribution Center,
P.O. Box 322, 3300 AH Dordrecht, The Netherlands

Library of Congress Cataloging in Publication Data

```
Feibleman, James Kern, 1904-
   Justice, law, and culture.

   1. Justice.  2. Law--Philosophy.  3. Social
contract.  4. Culture.  I. Title.
K240.F45  1985        340'.1        84-22671
ISBN 90-247-3105-4
```


ISBN 90-247-3105-4

PRINTED IN THE NETHERLANDS

The People should fight for the
Law as if for their city-wall.

                    Heracleitus

Let us abide awhile and see
injustice done.

                    A.E. Housman

TABLE OF CONTENTS

INTRODUCTION   IX

PART ONE. THE THEORY OF JUSTICE

I   THE PROBLEM OF JUSTICE   1
II   JUSTICE AND LEGAL THEORY   5
III   EMPIRICAL EVIDENCE FROM THE
        ADMINISTRATION OF JUSTICE   11
IV   EMPIRICAL EVIDENCE FROM INJUSTICE   17
V   A DEFINITION OF JUSTICE EXPLAINED
        AND DEFENDED   23
VI   THEORETICAL EVIDENCE FROM ETHICS
        AND MORALITY   31

PART TWO. THE THEORY OF LAW

VII   THE LAW: ORIGINS AND DEVELOPMENT   39
        1. What is Law?   39
        2. Origins   47
        3. Development   53
VIII   THE LEGAL SYSTEM   59
        1. Pandects and Peregrines   59
        2. Legal Systems as Partial Orderings   61
IX   MORALITY   65
        1. Morality and Legality   65
        2. Rights and Duties   72
        3. The Outcome in Social Morality   77

viii

X   HUMAN NEEDS, MORALITY AND THE LAW   79
        1. The Situation in Actual Practice   80
        2. The Situation as It Ought-To-Be   86
        3. From What-Is to What Ought-To-Be   91

XI   INSTITUTIONS, LAW AND MORALS   97

XII   THE STATE AS LEGAL CUSTODIAN   111

XIII   THE OPERATION OF LAW   121
        1. How Laws are Framed   121
        2. Statutory Codification, Implementation and
           Interpretation   123
        3. Belief in The Law   128
        4. Legal Procedures   129
        5. Crime and Punishment   137

XIV   HOW THE LAW IS CORRUPTED   141
        1. The Miscarriage of Justice   141
        2. Evasion   143

XV   THE SPECIFIC LAWS   151
        1. Contract   151
        2. Persons   153
        3. Property   157

XVI   THE METAPHYSICS OF LAW   163
        1. The Two-Story World   163
        2. The Three Theses   166

            APPENDIX RIVAL THEORIES OF JUSTICE

XVII   SOME ANCIENT THEORIES OF JUSTICE   173
        1. Plato   173
        2. Aristotle   174

XVIII   SOME TRADITIONAL THEORIES OF JUSTICE   177
        1. Kant   177
        2. Hegel   179

XIX   SOME RECENT THEORIES OF JUSTICE   183
        1. Radbruch   183
        2. Del Vecchio   186

XX   SOME CONTEMPORARY THEORIES OF JUSTICE   187
        1. Rawls   187
        2. Hart   199

INDEX   203

INTRODUCTION

The following pages contain a theory of justice and a theory of law. Justice will be defined as the demand for a system of laws, and law as an established regulation which applies equally throughout a society and is backed by force. The demand for a system of laws is met by means of a legal system.

The theory will have to include what the system and the laws are intended to regulate. The reference is to all men and their possessions in a going concern. In the past all such theories have been discussed only in terms of society, justice as applicable to society and the laws promulgated within it.

However, men and their societies are not the whole story: in recent centuries artifacts have played an increasingly important role. To leave them out of all consideration in the theory would be to leave the theory itself incomplete and even distorted. For the key conception ought to be one not of society but of culture. Society is an organization of men but culture is something more. I define culture (civilization has often been employed as a synonym) as an organization of men together with their material possessions. Such possessions consist in artifacts: material objects which have been altered through human agency in order to reduce human needs. The makers of the artifacts are altered by them. Men have their possessions together, and this objectifies and consolidates the culture. Libraries for instance contain the collective memories of generations of individuals, and hold more information than any one brain can manage to contain and hold it longer — indefinitely, as a matter of fact.

A culture, then, is an organization of men and artifacts much broader than a society though containing society as one of its most important elements. That without men, without a society, there would be no culture, seems too obvious to argue; it seems so obvious, in fact, that it has misled men into confusing it with culture. But that would be to leave the artifacts out of consideration as an important set of elements. And I would submit that their importance is hardly less than that of the men who made them and who use them. Indeed the production and use of artifacts seems to be what the culture itself is all about. If this sounds too 'materialistic' in the oldfashioned sense of that word in which it was opposed to spirt, let me emphasize that I am talking about a new kind of scientific materialism in which values are included.

Justice and the laws are regulative, not constitutive, to use an old Kantian distinction. They define a set of relations but they are not substantive. They declare how men propose to deal with each other, how they propose to work together, and how they propose to use their artifacts. But it is at all times the inter-personal relations and the material possessions which are in question; culture, not society merely. To orchestrate the elements of such a vast scheme as a single human culture, requires a continual awareness of all the demands of its highly diverse parts. Surely a living human being is not to be understood in the same way as a tool, not even when that tool has the complexity which we find in a computer; and in turn a computer however self-dependent in its operation, is not to be considered anthropomorphically.

Artifacts are results of the behavior of man; they exist because men have discovered how to penetrate further into the material environment, how to alter and combine materials until something is constructed which can be turned against the environment to alter it in ways that man working only with his bare hands was never able to do. And these same artifacts, which have now become part of the immediate human environment, make their own demands upon human behavior and to some extent alter it. Men, in other words, are conditioned to a great extent by the artifacts for whose existence they were originally responsible; to give an example, scholars may be regarded as the "creations" of libraries.

Artifacts are designed by a very few individuals, manufactured by more, but become part of the environment for many and even for all. The telephone is a case in point. It is the product of a single company yet it has become part of the daily lives of most people even though they do not altogether understand its operation. The complexity of artifacts and their consequent power marks the degree of penetration of the material environment. Every additional degree changes all the values and calls for new systems of law. Consider the extent to which the new knowledge of matter has allowed for the production of new products and hence of new customs and even institutions. The television set has occasioned new habits. The light tensile metals made fast flight possible, and the new information about genetic engineering promises large increases in agricultural production.

Of course it can happen, and does more often than we commonly recognize, that the reaction to artifacts is the name of the game, that some artifacts were indeed made in order to produce in the individuals the kind of highly desirable reactions that could not otherwise be obtained. A plow was designed to turn over the soil, but a piano was designed for the effects which could be produced in a listener when music is played on it. The piano is no less an artifact than the plow, even though their aims are different. Hunger in the man is reduced, at long remove, by the effects which can result in the planting of crops by the use of the plow. A hunger of a different sort is also reduced in the man if the music which was written for the piano is played on it in his presence. He anticipates and welcomes the effects in both instances. Artifacts are not the whole story of human relations and the law but they are a large part of it.

From this perspective let us now look at justice and the laws. The laws are how men propose that they ought to behave toward each other and toward their artifacts, and justice is the measure of how well they behave toward the laws but more fundamentally also how well the laws fit. Given any culture, that is to say, any population of human individuals together with the artifacts they have succeeded in developing – and this theory would hold presumably for a primitive culture as well as for an advanced one – then the justice which prevails and the laws which are established must be precisely those which would best regulate the culture to the mutual advantage of the individuals.

The peculiarities of the culture, such as the particular environment, say arctic or tropical, and the peculiarities of the population, in terms of its inherited beliefs and aims, demand that the particular system of laws be appropriate. Different environment and different beliefs and aims, then different sets of laws. The overall demands of justice of course remain the same.

More precisely stated, what men know, what they feel and do, must be organized together into some system of society and of culture, regulated by the laws appropriate to the organization at the given stage. This must include of course a program for the future: what they propose to learn, what they propose to feel and what they plan to do. All are susceptible to regulation, and the only provision is that such laws must allow for the proposed developments and not merely hamper them. Laws should be conducive, not prohibitive, even as applied to the

xii

feelings, as for example innovative artists in painting and literature have often painfully been compelled to recognize. The censorship of literature by politicians is not unknown in many cultures. Yet it is the delicate technique of the ideal of administration that it should further developments rather than hamper them, otherwise there would be little beyond reliquaries to administer.

The raw material of a culture consist in the individuals, their institutions and their artifacts — a society, if you like, and its material possessions. But the influence is not all one way; it is necessary to think of a cohesive whole in which there are many mutual though asymmetrical interactions of men and their artifacts. In this amalgam the proper relations are recognized and preserved by the system of laws which the members of the society have agreed to establish and obey.

In traditional terms, the governing relation of the entire culture is provided by contract. The "social contract" of Hobbes and Rousseau has to be understood very broadly so as to include both the constitution of the state and the enacted laws which from time to time have to be revoked or amended. No contract, then no state, but also no ownership of property, no bills of sale, no compensation for services, nothing, in short, which could be recognized in the day by day operations of a going society.

I fail to see, however, why the enthronement of contract has to be understood as the abolition of all utilitarian considerations. That a society has a modus operandi does not relieve it of its central aim, which might well be the one stated by Bentham: the greatest happiness of the greatest number. Everything after all is done with something in view; few actions are purely random, certainly not those which promote the interests of the individual or even of society as a whole.

Perhaps the Bentham maxim could be improved on. Perhaps it would be better if we were to say that the aim of culture is to benefit society, and not merely to achieve the happiness of the greatest number. We need an objective criterion, not a subjective one, although in the larger conception the subjective one could be retained as an important part. And the welfare of society could be construed to mean not only the lofty considerations of thoughts, feelings and actions but also the wider and more inclusive components of knowing, doing and being, and in the future as well as in the present. But these questions must in the end be left to ethics. Here it should be sufficient to conclude that this is the direction in which all jurisprudence points.

Part One. "The Theory of Justice" was first published as Perspectives on Justice in the 1973 Rosenthal Lectures delivered at the North-western University School of Law and published by the Northwestern University Press (Evanston, Illinois, 1975). This material is reprinted with permission.

Chapter IX, "Sexual Behavior, Morality and the Law", first appeared under the title *Sexual Behavior and the Law*, Ralph Slovenko (ed.), (Springfield, Illinois, 1965).

Chapter X, "Institutions, Law and Morals", first appeared under that title in the *Tulane Law Review*, XXXI, 503-516 (April, 1975).

Chapter XX, section 1, first appeared as "Rawls' Theory of Justice" in the *American Journal of Jurisprudence*, vol. 18, 198-205 (1973).

Huntington Cairns and Stanley C. Feldman made many valuable criticisms and suggestions. For any shortcomings in the final result, however, I must hold both lawyers blameless; the faults are mine.

New Orleans
February 1982

PART ONE. THE THEORY OF JUSTICE

We must begin with an inquiry into the problem of justice, particularly as it concerns legal theory and administration but considering injustice also, and ending with some definitions and an examination of the relations of justice to ethics and morality.

CHAPTER I

THE PROBLEM OF JUSTICE

The search for the meaning of justice must begin with a decision concerning the method to be employed. Rational understanding begins with definitions.[1] In my efforts at understanding I propose a new approach to the idea of definition: definition by inference from assumptions, that is to say, from presuppositions. We must ask what the term, justice, has meant in some typical theoretical and practical contexts. I am aware of course that all definitions are limitations and so apt to prove inadequate. Actual material existence and abstract logical structures both have a way of escaping in depth and extent of complexity which puts them beyond all meagre formulations. But they do mark the first phase of a rationality on its way to full systematization by means of axioms, rules of inference and the proofs of theorems. Such later fully systematized stages stand or fall by the earlier. They are therefore vulnerable, and the more so since they are the more easily altered.

Before a definition can be discovered and adopted, I propose to obtain it from a combination of the rational with the empirical which is by the way, the only acceptable empirical technique since empiricism is incapable of standing alone as a finished product. In the case of justice, this means deriving the meaning of the term from its actual uses in legal theory and then resting that meaning twice: one for consistency with its necessary position in ethics, and once for completeness against the hard facts of the experiences encountered in law-making and law-enforcement by legislators, judges, administrators, lawyers and police.

1 I am aware of the arguments of those who insist that a definition of justice is not required (Bodenheimer) and that to attempt one would be futile (Lask). For the former see Edgar Bodenheimer, *Treatise on Justice* (New York 1967, Philosophical Library), p. 262; and for the latter see *The Legal Philosophies of Lask, Radbruch, and Dabin*, Kurt Wilk, trans. (Cambridge, Mass.: Harvard University Press 1950), p. 21.

What I hope to arrive at in this fashion is a universal meaning, which can then be checked back against another set of samples selected with the proper degree of randomness. Our access to facts for this purpose is strictly limited. When men speak of looking at a topic universally, what they mean of course is earth-wide and for the period of known history, which includes unfortunately only the last ten thousand years, a provincial view but at least one not limited to a specific date and place. The day is rapidly approaching when that will not do at all, but it will have to serve now.

If the definition of justice does not rise above the level of a captive concept in the hands of a single government, as when for instance men judge of what is just according to the American practice, then it can contribute little to legal theory. We want to be able to judge our own situations as well as others and for praise or blame, and this we cannot do without a conception which rises above them in some way. Those who charge that cultural relativism reduces all conceptions to functions of the society in which they were framed overlook the fact that their criticism is as culture-bound as the theory they are criticizing.

That there is a universal truth which transcends the laws of nations can be demonstrated to a secular and empirically-minded age through the common understanding of the demand for justice and the ancillary need for a universal comprehension of the term. We must have absolute principles though not for the erroneous purpose of making absolute applications but in order to know what we are modifying when we encounter extenuating circumstances.

In all of the thousands of years that such a question has been seriously considered there has been no agreement about the meaning of justice, no accepted definition. But I take it this does not mean that there has been no common understanding. Only its formulation is wanting, a lack which has serious shortcomings but also some advantages in allowing to the administration of justice the requisite flexibility. There need be no inconsistency between an inflexible definition and a flexible administration provided the true nature of definition be understood. Things can be properly related only when they have first been properly distinguished. Rationality is not aided by a muddy empiricism in which principles and practices are hopelessly confused. Principles first must be learned from practice but then firmly separated and properly interrelated as principles before being returned to practice with a greatly increased power over it.

Let me put this in another way. An interest in the law for practical reasons is the business of the practicing lawyer. It is not the same and it does not have the same results as an interest in the law for theoretical reasons. Law-makers no doubt must have both interests but they rely as much on the previous work of the theorists as they do on their knowledge of the practices to which the laws they enact will be applied. Behind every charter of government, written or unwritten, there stands a philosophy overt or covert.

In search of the theory of justice I plan to look first (II) at some of the empirical evidence which is to be found in the administration of justice, and next (III) at the same kind of evidence but from injustice. Then (IV) I shall propose my own definition of justice and try to support it (V) by theoretical evidence from studies of ethics and morality as these have related to the state.

CHAPTER II

JUSTICE AND LEGAL THEORY

In this book I offer a theory of justice and law. They are not the same. If they were, then the politics which determines power would also govern morality. It doesn't; if only because there is a distinction between enforcing the law and administering justice. As Lord Denning has observed, the judge aims at "preventing a party from insisting upon his full legal rights, when it would be unjust to follow him to enforce them."[1]

In my willingness to address myself to such topics I am aware that there must have been a large measure of temerity, for I do not profess to have the final word about anything, I have only some studied guesses which I favor over others, chiefly perhaps because they are mine. What aggravates the situation is that this marks a departure from my proper business which is to aid the inquiry into the true nature of things by discovering a whole way of looking at the world. Now however I find myself undertaking the employment of abstract theories in the analysis of practice. But I am aware that it is still true as Plato said that "the philosophers are apt to appear ridiculous when they enter upon public business,"[2] and more particularly, "when they enter the courts of law as speakers,"[3] although he did add that those who have trained as court orators since their youth are apt to be "always talking against time, hurried on by the clock," for there is always another party to the suit and "the other party does not permit them to talk about anything they please, but stands over them exercising the law's compulsion by reading the brief from which no deviation is allowed."[4] The philosophy of law

1 *The Discipline of Law* (London 1979, Butterworths), p. 207.
2 *Gorgias*, 484 D-E.
3 *Theaetetus*, 172 C.
4 *Op. cit.*, 172 D-E.

may be deemed firmly anchored when the same set of propositions concerning the legal system can be induced from the actual practice of law, which is concrete, and deduced from a speculative metaphysics, which is abstract. Jurisprudence is one of those intermediate theories which are neither fully concrete nor fully abstract and which therefore must look in both directions.

There is no pretense here that this book is complete. I have not touched on all the topics which such a vast enterprise would have to treat. I have not tried to be exhaustive, but merely suggestive, in an effort to show how the philosophy of law would look from the perspective of a particular system of philosophy. All that I have hoped to do is to indicate a point of view, to which others if they be any so inclined could add, yet I presume to hope one which may suggest a full philosophy of law of the kind suitable to support the maintenance and increase of the culture of a state.

The lawyer immersed in practical affairs has no time for abstract theory. Even a legal thinker like Pound, who is so excellent at getting down to cases[5] had, as he himself admitted, "little patience with analysis and definition and classification for their own sake."[6] He could not see evidently that at the foundations of legal systems, theory and practice are interdependent. Theories are designed to make workable practices possible, practices are applications of theories. Without systems of law no state could function, and systems of law are based on theories, often on deep metaphysical theories, such as the dialectical materialism of Marx, Engels and Lenin which supports the Soviet Union.

By and large the professor of law who is interested in jurisprudence does not operate at the level of the philosophy of law. Jurisprudence is in the hands of legal theorists who are working at the level of empirical generalization, one level below the philosophy of law, which is concerned with logical, metaphysical and epistemological interpretations. I will offer as examples for empirical generalizations, the question of whether a specific code, such as that given in Deuteronomy, can be called a set of laws or merely a collection of rules and precepts, and for the philosophy of law, the question of whether positive law can be called nominalistic. To some extent the ethical level is employed by both groups. Both levels are legitimate and necessary objects of study, and I do not mean to imply that they are not; but they are at the same

5 Roscoe Pound, *Justice According to Law* (New Haven: Yale University Press, 1951), p. 47 f.
6 *Ibid.*, p. 52 ff.

level of abstraction. It may be indeed that philosophers of law have looked too closely at the actual legal procedures in terms of the men and events involved and not closely enough at the empirical generalizations. Again, if one were to compare the relative merits of the English common law and the Roman law, this might be considered a question for study in jurisprudence; but if one were to compare the metaphysical assumptions behind the English common law with those behind the Roman law, this could be a question for the philosophy of law.

In a very disturbed period in western civilization, when all of the values and institutions by means of which most of us have lived out our lives are threatened not only by proferred alternatives but also by anarchy, it requires a great deal of fortitude for a man to turn away from practice, ignoring the degree of risk of survival involved in order to devote speculative thought and productive imagination to pure theory. But this is what the culture of the future must rely on when the time comes that the present has joined the past. This work is based on the theory of the unity of material culture, from which no human activity is exempt. Cultures are the work of speculative and imaginative thinkers but are operated on a day-to-day basis by practical men who seem able blandly to forget how the cultures in which they work were ever produced. They do not tolerate happily the presence of abstract ideas in their midst, and the more abstract the ideas the more scornful the tolerance. It is not an easy thing to watch practice deteriorate and yet to think only how theory could be improved, and yet the ones who did are those we have the best reason to remember.

I need, therefore, in the interest of the general argument made in this book, to enter a plea for irrelevance. The cry of the day in academic and intellectual circles is for relevance; so much is happening so fast, and there are so many challenges and changes in the arena of the day-to-day life of practical events, of struggles and controversies, that the individual tends to get lost and so look to his leader for guidance: what, he asks, does it all mean? And yet he himself tends to disregard pure mathematics and logic, ancient history, the literary and artistic classics, yes and even the pure theory of politics, out of a conviction that it will tell him nothing about his own times and problems.

The paradox is that what he says is true and yet he is wrong. He is right in thinking that immediate problems have to be solved immediately and without reference to theory, and so it becomes the work of the leaders of the present to guide him. But at the same time all civilization is the accumulation of the achievements of the past: if there are to be any advances in the future, they must be made now. And to make them, we have to provide the requisite isolation for productive people: they must be free to speculate *in abstracto* and not called out of their ivory towers to aid in settling practical issues, at which they would in all events not be very good, anyhow.

In short, we must see to it that society makes an investment in its own future and that it does so here and now. Its investment, that for which probably it will be remembered if it is remembered at all, lies just there, in the work of men who are concerned not with the here and now but with principles which can be held and applied to all times and places. Theirs is the arena of irrelevance, a dedication to undertakings specifically chosen for their lack of relevance to the burning issues of the day.

The philosopher of law ought to concern himself not with correcting the injustices which have not yet been righted, not with calling attention to wrongs which otherwise might be slighted, but with the being of truths respecting the theory of law and justice, truths which he suspects exist to be found but which are as yet unknown. Yet he ought to be empirical enough to know what is going on and what such goings on mean in terms of the assumptions they generate and the theoretical considerations they call into play. Tomorrow's practice comes out of today's theory, not out of all theory but out of some of it; and the necessity to speculate upon what is the preferred theory is the work of men who are at least somewhat removed from the hurly burly of the world but at the same time well aware of its nature and indeed even acquainted with something of its details.

I have endeavored to advance chiefly three theses. The first is the importance of material relations, the second is the interpretation of justice as the demand for a system of order, and the third is the centrality of contract.

(1) What I have in mind throughout is not Marxist materialism, which is sadly out of date even in terms of its own criterion, but the new materialism as discovered by the physical sciences. Moreoever, material relations are *relations* as much as any other kind.

(2) The search for a unified legal order, though it remains just out of reach of theory, continues to be the prevailing if often unacknowledged aim of all studies in jurisprudence.

(3) The centrality of contract is the substance of the community and has been since other fixed norms were swept away. The contract represents material interests and itself functions as a material object because it has the force of law.

The material bearing of all contracts and the dependence on them of property relations as well as their dependence in turn on a unified system of order will emerge from these studies if I have done my work well.

CHAPTER III

EMPIRICAL EVIDENCE FROM THE ADMINISTRATION OF JUSTICE

We need to glance first, then, at some examples of what the administration of justice as practiced seems to indicate concerning the meaning of justice. These examples, we will discover, offer empirical evidence for a particular kind of definition.

To begin with, it can be pointed out that laws are neither made in a vacuum nor administered in one. According to some, justice is binding on magistrates as well as on offenders, and so the concept needs to be defined in order to set goals for law-makers and law-enforcers as much as for law-breakers. Again, when a particular theory of justice has been adopted, this does not mean that practice will always conform to it. Too often men depart from that behavior which they know to be most comfortable to the set of values to which they subscribe. This happens for instance when an action taken by an officer of a state differs from that morality which governs its citizens, and does so with their implicit or even express approval.

It is evident from an examination of the laws in effect in any western nation that they are intended to cover every possible contingency and to do so in a perfectly consistent fashion. Whether they ever did so is another question. In private business as well as in public order, in the civil as well as the criminal law, care has been exercised over the years by those in authority to see that no situation can arise in which the legal requirements are not spelled out and the penalties not prescribed for any infractions. The requirement of consistency was met when the rules governing the duties of common carriers were applied to the railroads *in the same way* as they had been to the stage coaches. The requirement of completeness was met when there were no longer any common carriers to which the governing rules did not apply.

Constitutions are written by men who do not always have the aim of total provision in mind, but law-makers sit as a body and make them-

12

selves available, so that as the society develops and unforeseen eventualities arise, new statutes can be enacted to provide for them. It was for this reason, for example, that the Sherman Anti-Trust Act and later all of the law governing civil aeronautics were considered necessary. In short, there is always a determined effort to make the law complete with respect to the activities of a given society, although the requirement of completeness for the laws has never been codified.

Another version of this requirement shows up in quite a different way. In actual law practice there is always present the appeal to an abstract principle of justice, and its applications are engineered through a series of adjustments which are continually being made. An unacknowledged effective legal version of the principle which has come to be known as Occam's Razor calls for there to be no more laws than are necessary. People are unhappy with superfluous laws which make them feel restricted in a way which is not beneficial to them nor to the society, but there is a counterbalancing equally acknowledged but also effective principle announced by Kant, and which I have named Kant's Shaving Bowl, the legal version of which requires that there be as many laws as are necessary.[1] But without laws to regulate the new situations there would be more unhappiness.

Laws and law-making machinery arise in the simple response to needs. Witness the federal regulative agencies which have sprung up in the last couple of decades: the Civil Aeronautics Board and the Nuclear Regulatory Commission, for instance. The laws tend to expand to cover whatever activities emerge which are potentially at least threats to the common good. There are laws now for example governing the securities business, the insurance companies and labor relations, which had formerly been relatively free of regulations. The adjustments which are found necessary in order to keep the legal system a workable affair include those designed to preserve or restore consistency and those intended to keep pace with the requirement of completeness.

Justice may occur in practice simply as a response to the demand for order. This can even happen by chance, as it were. In England, the East India Company, which was chartered by Queen Elizabeth in 1600 to trade in what is now Indonesia, and which returned its first revenues from Sumatra by looting a Spanish galleon, ended by founding an empire; and when in 1858 Disraeli relieved the Company of its responsibilities and gave India to Queen Victoria, the English legal system had become so entrenched and so valuable that even after India obtained its independence from England it retained the English system of law and law practices.[2]

1 *Critique of Pure Reason*, A 656; B 684.
2 See *e.g.* Brian Gardner, *The East India Company* (New York, 1972, McCall).

The demand for order may make itself felt where a legal system already exists. Confusion results when laws are enacted which are more complex than the citizens can comprehend. No one in the United States is free from taxation but few can understand the tax statutes. Too complex a structure is not an order but in the end amounts to a new and contrived kind of disorder. The enormous proliferation of laws in the United States at both the federal and state levels amounts itself to a kind of confusion. Laws which remain on the books after they have ceased to be enforced could always be revived and sometimes are, with the result that in many instances the citizens do not know exactly where they stand with respect to the law.

Government bureaucrats tend to forget that all of the revenues of the state eventually derive from the productivity of agriculture and manufacture much in the same way that business men and farmers tend to forget that all of the property rights they enjoy and the enforcement of contracts upon which their profits depend rely entirely upon the stability of the state in which they hold citizenship. The enormous intricacy of the modern scientific-industrial nation often temporarily blinds men to the true state of affairs. Justice reaches upward at this point to insist that the legal order be a system. In human affairs, since injustice does occur, this works out to the demand for the restoration of that order to which the administration is already devoted.

But it may lead also to the demand for an essentially new order. The legal system thus far has been in every case a limited order. If a universal social order does exist, and there is every reason to hope that it may, it has not yet been discovered. There are at the present time insuperable obstacles in the way. There has never been any question of concrete universals, since they will not be proved to exist until it is possible to ransack the universe; the question is only whether or not they are known, for they could exist and yet not be known. If justice be a universal, then we can say that universal standards of justice may exist but cannot be verified with certainty. The assumption of their existence, however, provides a background for less general instances of justice.

The point made by Charles S. Peirce, the classic American philosopher, about the necessary vagueness of generality[3] is supported in many common law interpretations and indeed in the promulgation of most legislation. What is the "due process of law" referred to in the 5th and 14th Amendments of the Constitution of the United States? There is certainly evidence of its vagueness in some of the judicial decisions

3 *Collected Papers of Charles Sanders Peirce*, C. Hartshorne and P. Weiss, eds. (Cambridge, Mass.: The Belknap Press of Harvard University Press, 1960), 6 vols., vol. V, paragraphs 450 and 505 ff.

14

which have issued from it. There is a kind of principle of indeterminacy at work here which is akin to the principle of the same name in atomic physics: in a given legal procedure, such as in statutory interpretations, one part of a statute can be rendered precise only by allowing other parts to remain uncertain. The legislature for example can formulate a law with accuracy but then leave open the question of just how far its effectiveness extends, or it can state a law in general terms but then leave open the nature of its application.

Such a demand for order, however, must be distinguished from any particular order, for if too rigidly administered under rapidly changing circumstances, one particular order could function as a disorder. Back of such a situation there is an assumed requirement of justice, which can be as much abrogated by a narrow order as by a wide disorder. If it develops that laws need to be enlarged and extended, restricted or eliminated, or indeed modified in any way which a developing society may make necessary in order to eliminate inconsistencies which may have arisen in the body of laws under the wear and tear of practice, this does point to a hidden constant, an ideal parameter behind the limited formulations of the legal code.

That so many legal codes are provided with built-in self-corrective techniques is evidence for the existence of the law as an open system. An open system in the legal sense is one which is left free to exchange conditions with the rest of the society in which it exists to provide order; free, that is to say, to modify and be modified by material conditions. The laws of a society exist as its effort at self-regulation, and so they in turn are regulated by the society as it develops and changes. For no society is fixed forever; it is always under the necessity to interact with the human and non-human elements of its environment.

The law-makers in a state endeavor to frame the laws in a perfectly coherent manner and one which covers every contingency. That a system of order is what is being interpreted in the administration of justice is shown by the three principles contained in Dicey's famous definition of the rule of law.[4] The supremacy of the law, the equality of all before the law, and their rights as defined and enforced by the courts, makes of the legal system a single inclusive and irrefrangible body of doctrine and procedure. This works out in practice to a facilitative rather than a restrictive, a regulative rather than a punitive, over-all effect. It aims to promote the welfare of individuals in such a way that they do not interfere with each other.

4 *Law of the Constitution*, 9th edition (Wade, ed.), p. 202.

In laying down guide-lines for what can and cannot be done, there is a consistency sought which suggests the grounds for a general assumption of justice. That laws are also brought into operation when they are not violated indicates a certain allowable behavior from which all conflict is eliminated. Since conflict may be defined as the material analogue of the logic of contradiction, a certain consistency is implied and since the aim is to specify violations for all laws and to stipulate penalties for all violations, a certain completeness is implied also.

CHAPTER IV

EMPIRICAL EVIDENCE FROM INJUSTICE

We turn next from a consideration of justice to that of injustice. What is it that the phenomenon of injustice may be said to indicate with respect to the meaning of justice? Injustice is a variety of disorder, it may be defined as disorder in society. The basis of disorder may be connected with the facts of genetic injustice: that individuals were not born equal with respect to anything but their sheer humanity; in terms of the potentials for abilities of any sort, whether physical or mental, they are not equal. Society ignores this difference when faced toward systems of justice and law. As a consequence disorder may be considered, loosely enough, as the absence of order; but a more precise definition may be useful here. Cairns has in fact defined jurisprudence as "the study of human behavior as a function of disorder."[1] Elsewhere I have defined disorder as the extent to which the elements of a given order are distributed outside that order among the elements of other orders.[2]

I propose to argue here that as a matter of practical exigency injustice always has been a function of justice, requiring of necessity the administration and enforcement of the laws. The *Corpus Juris Civilis* promulgated by the Roman Emperor Justinian about A.D. 535 conceived of law in terms of remedies, not as a matter of rights and duties but of liabilities to certain actions. Injustice could occur only within the confines of the acceptance of a legal system.

I am speaking of justice here of course in the limited sense in which it describes adherence to a particular order. Injustice in the universal

---

1 Huntington Cairns, *The Theory of Legal Science* (Chapel Hill: University of North Caroline Press, 1941), p. 1.
2 "Disorder" in Paul G. Kuntz (ed.), *The Concept of Order* (Seattle: University of Washington Press, 1968), pp. 3-13.

sense of the term is another matter, and would have to have a wider meaning. The very existence within a social order of an established set of procedures and a trained set of men to administer them is evidence enough that with the establishment of a system of laws goes the assumption that some of the laws will be disobeyed on some occasions. The recognition of an offense, whether a crime, a misdemeanor or a tort, negatively affirms the existence of law; and the number of statutes intended to cover all offenses affirms that it is the nature of the law to be complete.

With regard to a society in the round, the demand for a system of order makes itself felt most strongly in revolutionary situations. The systems of legal order presently prevailing in France and the Soviet Union were born of violent revolutions. Anarchy cannot serve as the basis for the stability of a society. One important consequence of this is that while every revolution takes place to bring to an end a particular system of order it is always followed by the establishment of another system of order and often by one which is even more intolerable than the one it replaced. If justice is a system of order, injustice is disorder; but while injustice on a small scale can be purely random, in terms of our definition of disorder injustice on a large scale, as the organizations of pirates and brigrands in the Mediterranean and the Caribbean in the late nineteenth century graphically illustrates, can be a system, too; and yet we shall have to say that injustice is the property of a lesser system of order, one less inclusive than that which is provided by justice.

That there will always be a need for the administration of law depends upon a number of factors. In the first place, law is not always punitive, it is also regulative and facilitative; so that if no laws were ever broken there would still be a need for administration. But there is little danger of that, for in the second place, no matter how law-abiding a society may be there is always a minority of law-breakers. Anyone may infract a law through thoughtlessness, carelessness or ignorance, but in a more deliberate way there is always a very considerable percentage of willful law-breakers and of pathological cases; habitual criminals will never cease to exist.

Even more dangerous situations will continue to occur. As we have just seen, injustice as well as justice may be organized and indeed often is. Most criminals who have acted in any consequential way have persuaded themselves and sought to persuade others that to the contrary it was they who were moving against injustice and that in so doing they were preserving a system of justice Robin Hood was neither the first nor the last to claim that in robbing the rich to give to the poor he was righting a wrong, and Al Capone could insist that by breaking the prohibition against alcohol he was helping to satisfy a legitimate need. Injustice, as a matter of fact, tends to keep pace with justice. The awesome power of organized crime in the United States today illustrates clearly that as a society becomes complex it often is matched in its complexity by criminal systems of subversion.

There are more factors which indeed must be taken with extreme seriousness. The first of these is that men by nature have ambivalent drives, only one set of which is peaceful and constructive. The evidence of pre-history, which has been greatly expanded in recent decades through the findings of fossil man and of his artifacts, shows that we have inherited from our remotest ancestors, the hominids, a deep physiological as well as psychological aggression, which I here define as the alteration of the material environment both organic and inorganic for the purpose of somatic need-reduction. This has been the inevitable result of hundreds of thousands and even millions of years of hunting culture, which included cannibalism, and of nomadic existence, in which men had to kill to live. In a mere ten thousand years of settled civilization we have not lost the habit, to which our slaughter houses and wars offer mute but vivid evidence. The need for destruction at this stage in the history of the human species probably lies deep in the genes.

Perhaps this may explain somewhat — if not altogether — the romantic admiration which is so widely held for the criminal: for the highwayman, the bandit, the bushranger and the pirate, and now to some extent for organized crime, the Mafia. The plight of victims is either forgotten or in some perverse way included in the admiration.[3]

The somatic need to continue existence is carried out, then, by an aggression which takes two forms: destructive and constructive, both of which are necessary. In order to exist together, men have had to organize their societies into states, and it has become the business of the state to limit the destructive form of aggression internally by means of laws. In this way the state has grown into a community of law, and a well-ordered state into one possessing a system of law. Externally it has become the business of the state to expand the destructive form of aggression. There are not many states, if indeed there are any, which

---

3 Cf. Hilary and Mary Evans, *Hero on A Stolen Horse* (London 1977, Heinemann).

20

can claim no injustice in foreign relations.[4] Lawlessness at this level is all but officially acknowledged.[5]

Added to this picture is an even more distressing fact, and that is the frequent success of injustice. Plato was a great dramatist of the truth and so he allowed his adversaries to present eloquent arguments in their dialectical debates with Socrates. In *Republic I*[6] and in the *Gorgias*[7] both Thrasymachus and Callicles expatiate at length on the rewards of injustice. Granted that they dealt only in half-truth, I remind my readers that 'half-truths' though half-false are also half-true. It is bound to be a temptation to profitable wrong-doers to remember that virtue is not always rewarded and vice not always punished. Too many of our captains of industry have stolen and butchered their way to fortunes, only to die peacefully at the end of long lives in their hospital trundle beds. The attractiveness of law and order and justice will have to rest on other grounds if it is to succeed at all.

That injustice does succeed in large measure is evidence that there may be other grounds for it, although this tends to have more weight at some periods of history than at others. In periods of relative social stability feelings of personal obligation and fears of sanction cooperate to insure compliance with the law, but in such periods, when the stability of the social fabric is threatened from without as well as from within, the fear of social chaos operates with increased force. All responsible citizens are aware of the consequences of the breakdown of order and − what is the same thing − of law.

Short of the parolled mental patient with a homicidal intent and a gun, and like situations which would call out the instinct of self-preservation with its resultant violence in even the most peaceful and law abiding of citizens, coercive law enforcement need only be held in the background to serve as a deterrent to the average citizen. But there is always the criminal who by his behavior insists on its exercise. Given the makeup of a large population, the ideal of perfection contained

4 "Injustice" is used questionably here since there is no established system of international law. However, there are tentative signs of one in the making: there is an International Court of Justice and there is the United Nations. Fishing rights, telecommunications and air travel all depend upon treaties between nations.
5 Examples in modern history are not hard to find. The United States wrested Texas from Mexico. The Soviet Union overran the Baltic States, Latvia, Lithuania and Esthonia, and invaded Hungary and Czechoslovakia. Communist China seized Tibet.
6 336B–354C.
7 482C–486E.

in the theory of justice and its rule of law can never be absolutely attained in practice.

However, what is true of individual man in little, that he is by nature a fighting animal, extends to his society in large. States are permitted to do what individuals are not permitted to do unless acting for the state. This has confused many a simple-minded citizen who has at different times in his life been called upon to act in different capacities. What the state would punish him for doing in private life — murder, for instance — it is prepared to punish him for *not* doing when he finds himself a soldier and in battle.

The violence of a society is a function of its total energy. This may make it a necessary precondition for relative calm in a society that its aggressive drives be allowed full scope beyond its borders. Societies famous for having been "law-abiding" in their day, such as England was in the nineteenth century, may have been so because the aggressive drives of the citizens were allowed and even officially encouraged abroad. A *Pax Britannia* was established throughout the world by means of wars of conquest conducted on four continents, but this may have been what made possible so much adherence to law and order at home, just as several millennia earlier the widespread "Roman peace" was based on the readiness of the Roman legions to fight. Similarly, in the United States in the same period the western frontier was the scene of the exercise of violence, as our artists and writers as well as our historians have been at pains to tell us.

Man alone among the animals is capable of doing things wrong because he alone has a choice. It is because of the existence of disorder that the administration of order is needed. There are few people who have not at some time or other broken the laws but all laws are not equally important except *as* laws and few offenders have ever voluntarily submitted to punishment or correction for the infraction of laws which even they considered just. The probability of the occurrence of injustice is therefore very high, and so justice must be founded on the use or the threat of force. The general assumption that an abstract justice has concrete demands is the reason why the laws for all their supremacy within the state must still face the requirements of equity. Justice may come into conflict with other goods, for it sometimes happens that goods conflict. We speak of just and unjust laws, which would seem to indicate that justice is higher than law. Central to justice is the respect for the individual as both rational and responsible, and the law distributes its sanctions accordingly.

There is an appeal to the meaning of justice as defined by the actions of men when they defy a court injunction on the plea that the law they are disobeying is not a valid law. Presumably they mean that under a higher notion of justice the law itself is unjust. This has occasionally been the case with the leaders of labor unions who rely upon the numerical strength of their supporters as measured by union membership to uphold them against the authority of the courts. Justice implies the rule of law not only over men but also over laws. There is a suggestion here too of the laws as forming a system in which some particular law does not consistently belong.

How is a government to keep the activities of its various branches consistent when it is compelled to delegate its powers as a matter of practical necessity? Thus in 1971 we had the spectacle of a Surgeon General doing everything possible to discourage the sale and use of tobacco and at the same time of a Department of Agriculture subsidizing tobacco farmers. That inconsistencies in bodies of laws do arise may be due in part to the proliferation of federal agencies whose operation is semi-independent without anyone being responsible for their coordination. There are inconsistencies too in the order of importance of law enforcement procedures. Issuing tickets for parking in no parking zones often takes up more of the policeman's hours than pursuing heroin pushers, rapists or murderers.

A final argument for the existence of injustice as part of the demand for a system of order is to be found in the position of the criminal. He has no conception at all of his dependence upon the stability of the social order he infracts. If the system were to break down altogether, the money he steals would be worthless and the influence he buys would be without the power to shield him. The value to him of his disobedience is a function of the obedience of most others. Everyone cannot afford to be a criminal, the system will not support it; but, on the other hand, everyone can be honest and obey the law, and this the system will support. I am reminded of the open letter a grateful reader once wrote to Dale Cargenie, author of *How to Win Friends and Influence People*. The reader said that he had found the book useful but that he hoped everyone would not buy it and follow its advice, because obviously this would cancel his advantage.

CHAPTER V

A DEFINITION OF JUSTICE EXPLAINED AND DEFENDED

Having, I hope, found some evidence for a definition of justice both in the actual administration of justice and in the gross facts of injustice, I turn next to a statement of my definition of justice; but first we must understand it in its most general sense. Justice as such is the demand for order: everything in its proper place or relation. It is the material analogue of the logical principle of identity.[1] In a certain sense then, the demand for order is a demand for unity, the proper fitting of parts in the whole.[2] But order quite simply means a one-to-one correspondence with the positive integers, and so it must be evident that what I am talking about here is no simple order. Justice would of course be impossible without social order, and the maintenance of social order rests upon social laws.[3] Thanks to the existence of law-enforcement machinery, the state intervenes directly when laws are broken (Criminal Law) or stands ready to intervene indirectly when appealed to (Civil Law). It is the laws which organize society and so make of society a state, though statehood rests not just on a collection of laws but on a

---

1 The idea that justice is not confined to the human domain is as old as Anaximander (circa 560 B.C.), who wrote that "the source from which existing things derive their existence is also that to which they return at their destruction, according to necessity; for they give justice and make reparation to one another for their injustice, according to the arrangement of Time" — Kathleen Freeman, *Ancilla to the Pre-Socratic Philosophers* (Oxford: Blackwell, 1948), p. 19. Although in what follows I shall be talking about justice as it exists in human society and material culture, it is the abstract idea of justice with a wider interpretation that is still assumed in the background.

2 That there can be a proper fitting of parts in wholes in domains other than that of the human species is amply illustrated by plate tectonics in geology.

3 The same thing can be said of law that was said of justice: "Over thousands of years the most powerful minds of all nations have been unable to agree on a universal definition of law." W. Friedmann, *Legal Theory* (London: Stevens & Sons, 1949), p. 421.

system of laws.[4] Justice, then, will be concerned with a system of laws.[5]

It is obvious that here we need a definition of system. A system in the broad sense may be regarded as a set of elements having a common property; in the narrow sense, as a set of sentences in which every sentence is either an axiom or a theorem, in which case there are the further requirements of consistency, completeness, and categoricity. I shall be talking here chiefly about systems in the broad sense, but when I refer to the system of laws which justice demands I shall find it necessary to raise the questions of consistency, completeness and categoricity.

A legal system is consistent if none of the laws conflict. A legal system is complete if all of the laws in the system can be shown to be laws of the system, and if all of the laws which could be laws of the system can be shown to be laws in the system. In other words, consistency requires that all of the laws in the system belong in the system, and completeness requires that all of the laws that belong in the system are in the system.[6]

Categoricity is more difficult to explain. Perhaps first it should be pointed out that when the concepts of logic and mathematics are applied to concrete systems it is always with appropriate modifications and interpretations. With this provision in mind a category may be defined as a class of sets with similar structure.[7] Categoricity uniquely determines the system it describes. If any two interpretations satisfying

4 Morris R. Cohen observed that "though the law may never become a completely logical system, it can never entirely dispense with the effort in that direction." — *Reason and Law*, Prologue. Those laws on which the state rests are axiomatic and are usually framed in a constitution or charter, written or unwritten.
5 In the sense that it is by means of a system of laws that justice is effected in human society, justice is prior to law. But in the empirical sense of the exigencies of society, justice is not the source of the law, as some have claimed. It was the medieval idea of law that justice is the source of law. See e.g. Walter Ullmann, *The Medieval Idea of Law*: As Represented by Lucas de Penna (London: Methuen, 1946), especially chapter III.
6 In mathematics, a consistent system is one which does not contain any contradictions, and a complete system is one in which every true sentence is a theorem. One of the favorite ways of proving the consistency of a mathematical system is to make a model of it, and when such a model consists in a concrete interpretation, as it so often does, the procedure implies the assumption of the consistency of the material universe.
7 More specifically, in mathematics these are called "objects"; and "structure-preserving functions", called "mappings or morphisms", are preserved between them. Cf. William S. Hatcher, *Foundations of Mathematics* (Philadelphia: W.B. Saunders, 1968), ch. 8, Sec. I, esp. p. 267.

the axioms are isomorphic, then the system can be said to be categorical. That the laws of a society are categorical is guaranteed by the fact that they all follow from the same theory of reality and all exist on the same level of analysis.

Understanding the terms 'justice', 'law' and 'system', then in the senses defined above, I am ready with my definition.

Justice is the demand for a system of laws.

Now a system of laws, like any system, must be made up of axioms and the theorems (in this case, the laws) which follow from them. But which axioms? Obviously, in a given society those which are constructions of the values whose preeminent reality the members of the society accept in their beliefs, embody in their artifacts, and aim at in their actions. Without a single consistent and comprehensive set of values, accepted by the members in feeling if not in principle, no society would be viable. The aim of a system of laws is to achieve in practice those values which the axioms represent.

Justice under the law proves to depend upon what theory of justice the laws embody. Thus Aristotle's criterion that "the just is the proportional"[8] would yet depend upon what it is that the society values most, upon what it is that is being proportioned.

When a state establishes a system of laws it does not do so arbitrarily nor by canvassing the wishes of individual citizens but always by looking to the embodiment of the ideal of justice, however vague such a conception may seem to be as it hovers in the background of more specific stipulations. Different legal systems such as are found in different states are partly the results of human choice; for man alone, it seems, has this option before him. But because much of what he does in a socio-cultural way is laid out for him by the exigencies of material conditions as these exist in a given date and place, his options are limited and his actions partly at least the result of necessity.

What we are dealing with in any society, then, is not mere laws but a system of laws, since a social order is a system. More specifically, justice is employed to guard against the assumption, often made in practice, that disorder can prevail. Logically, if justice is the material analogue of the principle of identity, injustice appeals to the truth of the *un*excluded middle. In social affairs justice would call for the making of laws and injustice for their administration. Thus justice is tied to the defense of social order and therefore to the restoration of order through the rejection of disorder or injustice.

8 *Eth. Nic.*, 1131b18.

I have been talking in ideal terms. Any actual legal system will tend to be a partially-ordered system, and a partially-ordered system is one which meets to some extent the requirement of consistency but not of completeness.[9] That is to say, not all of the laws in the system belong in the system and not all of the laws that belong in the system are in the system. Contradictions and incompletenesses occur, but not in sufficient numbers to cancel altogether the effectiveness of the system so far as the social order is concerned.

The definitions of justice which I have given in earlier works occurred in connection with ethics and politics and are congruent with partial ordering. In my ethics I have defined justice as the restoration of good,[10] and in my politics as conformity to the good.[11] The good is the name for a qualitative bond, and this is the typical kind of piecemeal affair which calls for a description in terms of partial ordering; but the good is also a combining force, a unifying property as Plato sugested when he placed it at the apex of his hierarchy of ideas.[12] But here I am looking to the broader meaning which both definitions imply.

In any social system there are too many variables to be calculated correctly by any of the means presently at our disposal. The demand for the *ideal* of justice is a demand for a well-ordered system, a perfect legal system which would be both consistent and complete. The *actuality* of justice is a partially-ordered legal system. The *direction* of justice is the movement from the actual to the ideal, present in the aims of those who would seek improvement in the legal system.

We might speak then of *ideal* justice as the ideal of a system of law; of *actual* justice as the actual system of laws, one which includes statutes, unwritten laws, courts, judges, lawyers, as well as administrative and enforcement officers; and finally of *directional* justice as the law-making machinery consisting of legislators and their authorization. I have talked about ideal justice as natural justice. Directional justice is what is aimed at by enactment. It is aimed at equally in the framing of constitutional law and statute law. It is intended to promote public utility, in Hume's sense.

But it is at this level of actual justice that my definition will be challenged, and so it will be well to say a few words in extension and explanation. An established system of laws is one which is in effect in an

9   In mathematics, a set of elements is said to be partially ordered with respect to a relation R if R is reflexive.
10 *Moral Strategy* (The Hague: Martinus Nijhoff, 1967), p. 131.
11. *The Reach of Politics* (New York: Horizon Press, 1969), p. 61.
12. *Republic*, VI, 509.

actual society and remains in force though perhaps changed from time to time until overthrown. It exists within the individuals who are the members of the society; it exists within the society as its established institutions regulating the individuals, their interest groups, their actions and their artifacts (or property); and it exists also in the external relations of the society. We may consider each of these briefly.

First as to its existence within the individuals. To say that an established legal order exists within the individuals in a society means that covertly it is the way in which they would wish to be governed. They have beliefs which are of a fundamental nature, and of the majority of these they are not conscious. This becomes most evident when they are called on for precipitate action, which is usually from beliefs not deliberately held. There are of course levels of belief, some lying much more deeply than others and hence harder to recall. Such are for instance the more fundamental beliefs concerning the nature of reality which the individual holds in common with his fellows in the society, beliefs which of course would differ from society to society. There are other beliefs which exist at the same profound level and which are private, but these are rare, and we shall not have to deal with them here. Meanwhile it is this consistency of the part within the whole which gives to the individual who obeys the law what Mill called "the sentiment of justice," the feeling of what is right.

Next as to the established system of laws within the society. For a legal system to be consistent it must be applicable and for it to be complete it must be compatible with the fundamental convictions of a majority of the citizens. To say that an established legal order exists between them means that overtly they have consented to be governed in this fashion. Such public beliefs are embodied in institutions, first and foremost in the institution of the state, with its administration of law.

Finally, we must consider the extension of the established system of laws outside the state. Justice requires that the social order be the largest possible under the circumstances. A lesser order, as we shall note later, can function as a disorder in international society. The established system of laws of a society cannot be too much in conflict with those of other states without damage to justice.

Against my definition it will probably be argued that it is too broad, that under it a tyranny is a social order and so meets the demand for order. "National Socialism," the order established by Hitler and the Nazis, would seem to satisfy my definition, it will be claimed, for it did meet the demand for a system of laws. To this criticism I can offer two denials.

Tyranny, however systematic, does not meet two of the requirements of order, the one within the individual citizens, and the other
outside the state, for the following reasons.

A state with an established tyranny in which the tyrant rules by
promulgation is still an orderly government, however undesirable it may
be from some points of view, since it satisfies the requirement of consistency which is set by the definition of justice. It satisfies this requirement, however, only at the expense of completeness. Order in the sense
in which I use the term includes order in the individual citizens as well
as between them. Order, as Plato said in the *Republic*, is order within
the soul as well as within the state. Toynbee drives a distinction between a dominant minority which rules by charm and has the approval
of those who are ruled, and a dominant minority which rules by force
and so operates despite the disapproval of most citizens.[13] The former
condition meets the requirements of my definition better than the
latter.

It is possible of course for an absolute monarchy to have the approval of a majority of the citizens, as when for instance the monarch
is believed to be divinely appointed and no other form of government
is known. This was probably the case in ancient Egypt when for many
long millennia no one seems to have questioned the right of the rulers
to rule. So much for conformity within the state, which is never perfect. With regard to the extension of the established system of laws outside the state, the prevalence of wars throughout the ten thousand
years of known history would seem to indicate that the requirement
of completeness is never altogether met and seldom met at all. The
situation in this regard grows worse rather than better, for in terms of
transportation and communication, the world is a much smaller place
than it was, and the requirement of completeness imposed by the
definition of justice as the demand for a system of laws extending outside the state lacks the needed conformity if many states are to exist
together. Put otherwise, in a projected global state, the demand for
completeness would turn into a demand for consistency.

Any political order can be disturbed as much from within as from
without. The preservation of order requires an equilibrium to be maintained without any disturbance which could challenge it as an order.
Thus one principle of order is that it must be wider than any contained
disorder. There are serious and even crucial issues in which practical

---

13 Arnold J. Toynbee, *A Study of History* (London: Oxford University Press,
    1935, vol. V, p. 29 ff.

exigencies take precedence over moral considerations. When the crime rate is low, it is possible to concentrate on the criminal and whether justice is being done him, and to complain, as Taft did when he was Chief Justice of the Supreme Court, that our criminal law was a disgrace. But when the crime rate reaches the proportions it has assumed today then the attention shifts to the protection of society. An order can be imposed by conflict but can be maintained only by consent. But an order may deliberately make provisions for the inclusion of lesser conflict, as is the case for instance when business competition exists within an economic order.

CHAPTER VI

THEORETICAL EVIDENCE FROM ETHICS AND MORALITY

Let us see finally how an ideal of justice, which exists within individuals as their beliefs, within the society as its institutions, and beyond the society as its relations with other societies, can be viewed when interpreted in terms of ethics.[1]

Human societies are not mere collections of men, they are organizations of men and materials, the addition to men of raw materials and artifacts: mere territories as well as formed materials which have been altered through human agency for human uses. Cultures are the most complex material organizations known, for they include human individuals with their brains and nervous systems, but they include also artifacts, interpersonal relations, and brain-artifact relations. They differ from time to time and from place to place, and their contents differ: different sorts of artifacts; and different sorts of people who, even though all belonging to the same species, lead different sorts of lives because of two variable factors: the peculiarities of the environment and the idiosyncracies of explicit ideals; and finally, as we should expect, different sorts of organizations and with them different sorts of laws and law practices. The key to what holds all these disparate parts together may be looked for in morality. A morality is the kind of behavior which is called for in a given environment in terms of a given set of stated ideals of the good. It is what happens to a given theory of ethics when confronted by an inescapable set of material conditions. A morality is a set of values by means of which the members of a society live together. When that society becomes a state its morality so far as this can be recognized is established by codification; laws are intended to be codified morality. The established laws and law practices

---

1 There is a considerable body of argument for justice as part of morality in Aristotle. See especially *Eth. Nic.*, Book V.

32

endeavor not only to particularize the accepted morality but also to enforce and defend it.

Individuals within a society retain two sets of schemes of beliefs which we can now recognize as moral, one set which they share with their fellow citizens and another set which they hold alone. The scheme which they share with their fellows is the public sector; it reflects the morality and guides the individual toward conventional behavior and the observance of laws. The private sector of the retention schemata may be aberrant or it may not. Since all activities are conducted in terms of beliefs the private beliefs may lead to aberrant behavior and to infractions of the laws. Not all such infractions are so rational, however; there are also infractions on impulse or from psychotic motives.

Conscience is the awareness on the part of an individual of an obligation to obey his beliefs. When these issue from the public retention schema they impel the individual toward obedience to the laws of his society, but occasionally the beliefs contained in the private retention schema cut across that impulse and thwart it. When Lieut. (jg.) D.L. Mendenhall, the bombardier-navigator of an F-4 Phantom reported that "whatever our feelings about the war, we're still dropping our bombs — and we enjoy it,"[2] he was admitting that his own misgivings with respect to the public morality were too slight to interfere with his actions. But when a man asks himself whether with a clear conscience he can obey a law that he considers unjust, he is appealing not to his conscience as such but to its contents, which may contain a different morality. When Oskar Schindler saved hundreds of German Jews from the Auschwitz extermination camp, through deliberate misrepresentations to the Nazi authorities, he was hearing a different drummer.[3]

Such moral difficulties occur within the individual more often when the society is changing, for change usually occurs in one institution before influencing the whole society, as in a new religious insight or a new political ideal, and individuals tend to be institutionally oriented.

Now allow me to recapitulate. Justice, you will remember, is the demand for a particular kind of order: for a system of order. And order is implemented in a system of laws. The laws themselves establish a particular morality. The morality follows from a theory of ethics and, when codified, is enforced by the state. Morality is the essence of society, and every society has a morality, but the moralities differ from society to society as the societies themselves differ. The morality of a

2 *New York Times* for January 9, 1972, p. 1.
3 *Ibid.*, p. 24.

society is the only kind of order which is suitable to that society and therefore the only kind which can satisfy justice. When the society changes, the morality changes with it. The administration of law is the carrying out of the kind of justice a particular morality requires.

According to my theory, then, the forging of the laws of a state together with its administration and revisions is the outcome of the encounter and resolution of two opposed forces: the morality, which is handed down from the deep-set convictions of the members of the society, and the peculiar material requirements, which are a product of the brute encounters of sense experience. The resultant legal system derives its consistency from the morality and its completeness from the experiences. It might be added parenthetically that the morality itself issues from a theory of reality, or ontology, which however implicit and unrecognized nevertheless stands behind it.

And just as ethics is anchored securely somewhere between the theories of ontology and the practical exigencies of concrete moralities, so laws are anchored somewhere between abstract morality and practical exigency; both change, and therefore so must the laws. It must be recalled, however, that laws are not mere collections, they are systems, and though operated by short-lived individuals they are legal systems within such long-lasting institutions as the state. The necessary continuity is preserved, but that is why the laws do not direct society, they only regulate it. But they regulate it in a particular direction, more specifically, in that direction which was the one selected when the laws were chosen in the first place. The laws implement a particular morality, but because they are laws and because they are established, changes in the laws are apt to lag behind changes in the morality. For the laws were chosen after the morality, and thenceforth they follow it at a safe distance. The laws forbidding abortion in the United States will have to be changed to conform to the morality permitting abortion if respect for the law itself is not to be injured.

That the laws follow the shifts in morality, even though at a discreet distance, is most evident perhaps in the changes which take place in the decisions of the Supreme Court of the United States. If the Court does not exactly follow election returns, as has been claimed, it does follow public opinion in its alternations of conservatism and evolution, and public opinion is a good index to the implicit and prevailing morality. The liberal policy of the Warren Court of the 1960s makes an interesting contrast with the Taft Court of the 1920s.[4] Morality is dictated by

4 Paul L. Murphy, *The Constitution in Crisis Times: 1918-1959* (New York: Harper & Row, 1972).

the ideals of the leading instituion, and business, in that interim period between the two Courts named, has been downgraded.

The police, the district attorneys and the local courts enforce some laws and allow others to remain unenforced. The decision to enforce or not is made on the basis of shifts which are left in the background morality. No one can name or describe it but its influence is felt no less strongly for that. Thus it may happen that those who are responsible for changes in the morality may run counter to the laws. Sometimes they make revolutions, though of course all revolutions, peaceful or otherwise, do not necessarily mark advances; they may lead retreats as well. To think that every change is a sign of progress is to commit what I have named the fallacy of *post ergo melior*.

Ever since the Greeks of the fourth century B.C. discovered the distinction between natural law and man-made or positive law, and even more intensively since the discovery of experimental science in the seventeenth century, men have dreamed of finding laws of society which would be as firmly rooted as the laws of nature. The Greeks did not mean by natural law what that phrase has since come to mean, but rather the necessary principles of a successful society. Unfortunately, men have often believed that they have found such laws, and they have backed up their claims with ontological justifications, usually of a theological variety, through the possession of a divinely inspired absolute truth. There may or may not be a god – I am not concerned with that question here – but the fact is that the absolute truths of the 'world' religions do differ widely. And the coming of cultural secularism has not altered that situation materially; secular truths may be held just as absolutely and indeed often are, as is the case with Marxism. Indeed there is nothing in the world cheaper or more prevalent than the absolute truth. Everybody has one.

No social laws can be held absolute in any final sense until all men agree as to their nature and establish them as the laws of a global society. In the meanwhile the best of viable ideals is to suppose that every society has laws which are natural to it given its ingredients and circumstances, and that natural laws applied in each case would give the same results as those which already prevail. But this conclusion serves only to reinforce the existing state of affairs, which must be wrong because of the fact of change. And so we are nowhere, unless we preserve the distinction made in the first instance between natural law and positive law.

Justice at the level of positive law is in the charge of the state and subject to it. But the fact that justice applies to the state as well as to those laws which were established by the state, is evidence for the belief in the universal ideal of justice at the level of natural law. That is why revolutions to overthrow the state may come in the name of a wider justice than the state administers even though it may happen that the revolution reduces rather than restores the level of justice. For Hans Kelsen nautral law theories have operated to justify the forces of conservatism and reaction, while for Max Weber they have served to defend change and revolution. But unless there is justice at the level of natural law there would be no protection of the individual's rights against their incursion by the state.

What I am proposing, I suppose, is a modification and combination of the two traditional theories which are usually conceived as opposed, natural law theory and positive law theory. Natural law which is contained in the ideal of justice becomes embodied in positive law, which is framed as an approach to it. Positive law reflects the expedient or short-range interests, natural law the long-range. Both serve the needs of the community; the former keeps it going, the latter keeps it on course. Positive law is contained in the organization of society as the morality directing its aims. This is what I have called ideal justice, with actual justice containing the direction toward the ideal.

A definition of social justice as the demand for order embodied in a system of laws places outside the state such capricious making and unmaking of the laws as occurs when an arbitrary sovereign or absolute dictator rules by decree. There can be an order under such circumstances, but there is no system of order. The Constitution of 1936 of the Soviet Union laid down certain individual rights, but these have since been abrogated by the state, and there is no legal machinery for their remedy. A system of laws implies a greater comprehensiveness and a greater degree of permanence. Systems of order have to be forged under the trials of experience and of those modifications which the successive repetitions of time call for.

The fact is that law-makers do not operate in a vacuum or impulsively *de novo* but in strict accordance with the morality which exists in the society and by which it must be regulated. They are morality-codifiers proceeding in terms of legal interests. The law essentially means accepting restrictions on individual freedom as the vehicle of accommodation with others. There are from time to time changes in the morality of the society which call for corresponding changes in the law; for instance the recognition of the right of privacy and the granting of legal rights to women in the latter part of the nineteenth century.

The principle of justice as the demand for order as embodied in a legal system has unlimited application to societies. And because systems are characterized by consistency and completeness we should expect to find efforts made to see that these requirements are met. It is possible to read the judge-made law which exists in the citing of precedence as evidence of the legal system reaching for consistency. And when the laws are extended to include areas formerly left relatively free for individual action, such as labor laws, laws regulating insurance, and laws concerning the issuance of securities, it is possible to see the legal system reaching for completeness.

It might be added parenthetically that the ideal of a perfect legal theory is one which would be in such complete equilibrium with its society that there would be no infractions and so it would not be needed. At this point order could become one with anarchy, only it would have to be a perfect order and a total anarchy. There is little danger that either will ever be attained.

PART TWO. THE THEORY OF LAW

We have looked at a theory of justice. We must next turn to a theory of law. Justice is not law nor law justice. The law is the way in which it has been thought that justice could best be executed. Law is the application of justice. All knowledge has a practical aim but first it has to be secure as knowledge. In the process of validating its claim the question of its eventual usefulness may have to be set aside temporarily.

In this Part I introduce three new ideas which must be counted in the understanding of my theory of law. They are: the organ specific needs, the importance of artifacts in society, and the existence of an implicit and dominant positive morality.

(1) All the activities of the human individual are made in response to his needs. These are the needs of specific organs and they are reduced by means of the aggressions of the organism as a whole.

(2) Societies consist in human individuals and social groups interacting with artifacts, which are material objects altered through human agency to serve human needs.

(3) And, finally, the organization of a society through its laws, is dominated by a positive morality which is held in the unconscious mind at deep levels of belief.

CHAPTER VII

THE LAW: ORIGINS AND DEVELOPMENT

1. What is Law?

The question of the traditional definition of law was raised in Chapter IV in connection with the explanation of justice. Here I want to look at the topic from a different angle, this time on its own. Just what is law, what is its purpose, what kinds of law are there, and how does the law operate? I shall take up these and other questions and seek to answer them, but it may be best to begin by stating my own definition.

If we may assume that a rule is a principle governing conduct, then a law is a rule everyone in a society is forbidden to break, more specifically, a law is an established regulation which applies equally throughout a society and is backed by force.

All laws are social and exist only within that framework. A law is a statement with a special kind of social position: all must respect it, many may need it, and everyone must be aware of its existence, despite the fact that few will be familiar with it personally. Though often possessed of a literary quality, particularly if framed by a gifted professional, it still is assumed to be valid only for its didactic properties. For it is usually expressed in a language which while designed to render it precise also reserves it to the understanding of professionals even though it was intended for all members of the population.

There are no laws that can be called laws outside the state. Agreements between states are thus far no exception because as laws they do not exist. With no way to compel compliance, they lack the force of law. A law is a command to behave or to refrain from behaving in a certain fashion, backed by penalties for non-compliance. A law may order a certain action or it may prohibit one; it may order those who drive cars to procure a license first, it may prohibit driving while drunk. There are specific penalties for infractions in both cases. The authoriza-

40

tion comes from the state regardless of whether its form is that of a monarchy, a democracy or a dictatorship. And it comes from the sovereign: a king, the elected representatives of the people, or the leaders of the ruling community. The connection between sovereignty and legislature is so intimate in Savigny's view[1] that he considered them convertible terms. Without the one there could not be the other.

Many other definitions of law exist of course, and I will for the sake of comparison choose the two which have perhaps received the most attention.

Hobbes attacked Coke by confirming a theory of law which was intended to render it so simple that every intelligent layman could understand it: "Law is the command of a sovereign".[2] And so it is, but it is more than that. The definition leaves the law as something altogether arbitrary. The whim of a sovereign could not be called a law simply because it was issued as a command. There have been states run in this fashion more often than not, but they could hardly be described as lawful. Nothing of establishment is contained in the definition and it could be changed every minute if the sovereign so chose, in which case it would not be a law because it was not a rule. John Austin later lent the rule theory powerful support when he added that "some laws are rules" which oblige to acts of forebearance.[3] This leaves the matter not too far from where I have presumed to take it.

The second well-known definition and one much preferred by hardheaded practitioners is Holmes' conception of the law as what the courts will do.[4] But this is to accept the end product of a process without taking into account the source of that process or its nature. My definition undertakes to spell out what the law in essence is, his reports only what it comes down to in practice. The two are not incompatible. But look behind any judge's decision and you will see the elements at work that brought him to it. Holmes' definition makes it sound very much as though what the courts do is arbitrarily decided. This is very far from being true. What is true is that the judge undertakes to fit the case before him under the proper class, and having done that endeavors to see how similar cases have been treated in the past. He is then better equipped to hand down a judgment.

The purpose of law is the establishment and preservation of order in

1 Friedrich Carl von Savigny, *The Vocation of our Age for Legislature and Jurisprudence*, 1814, Hayward trans. 1831, passim.
2 *Leviathan*, Part 2, chapter 21.
3 *Lectures on Jurisprudence*, 4th ed. (Campbell), vol. I, p. 86, 182-3.
4 Collected Papers, 173. Cf. also Jerome Frank, *Law and the Modern Mind*, 46.

the state for common good. Out of fear of receiving injury men are compelled to cultivate justice. Banded together they might hope to prevail against the forces making for disorder, where individually they could not expect to cope.

Laws were first established in response to the exigencies of material conditions. They were needed if men were to live together, and were intended to operate for the benefit of all citizens in so far as needs could be anticipated and arrangements formalized. Men have to cooperate if they are to obtain satisfaction for their many needs; for example water, food, sex, information, security, activity. The problem of law is a social question of arranging things so that men who have interests in common can be facilitated in their aims, and those whose interests are opposed can have them mediated. They are often opposed in many legitimate pursuits and require protection from each other's aggression. The law undertakes to regulate behavior in order that legitimate needs may be reduced without conflict.

As conditions change, so do the laws, though more slowly. They are in a certain sense the best ones that could be provided under existing conditions, and in that sense there is no distinction between positive law and natural law. Natural law, the laws of the physical sciences for instance, are of two kinds: those that operate continuously, and those that have to be brought to bear. Gravitation works continuously but the conditions which bring about the electrolysis of water have to be prepared in advance. Positive law is of the same two kinds. By analogy, laws prohibiting murder operate continuously, while traffic laws apply only to those driving cars, not to those who stay at home. Whether dealing with nature or with that segment of it called human society, the laws must eventually reach an accommodation or run into trouble. That is why the work of legislatures is never done.

There are many kinds of law covering the spectrum of social concerns, and I shall name here only a few. There are laws of persons, laws of things, laws of contract, laws of tort, private (or civil) law, commercial law, criminal law, prerogative (or royal) law, canon law, constitutional law, common law, and maritime law. Not all of these operate at the same time or in the same society, though some may be concurrent. Prerogative law and canon law were employed together in ninth century Europe. Martial law is often invoked in time of war to take precedence over civil law. In recent centuries in western Europe the tendency has been to reduce the old collection of civil, customary and canon law to enacted law. Codification is the rule, but there is also case law which continues to maintain its own position in the judiciary.

The purposes served by law are many and varied. Laws are employed to maintain a social or political order, to insure justice for the individual, to right a wrong, to settle a conflict, or to punish an offender. Laws exist to keep the peace and to prevent that war of all against all which Hobbes believed to be the true state of man. Many laws are concerned with acts, and acts involve aggression of some sort: something material altered by force either as a matter of construction or destruction. The laws allow for the permissible acts and set limits to the impermissible ones. If every man exercised at will such power as he had, there would be mutual destruction and eventual chaos, and human life would be rendered impossible. Therefore his capacity for violence is transferred to the state, while he exercises the remainder within the rules.

Laws in their effects are facilitative or restrictive, and sometimes they are both. They allow something to be done which could not be done without them, or they restrict specific actions. Traffic laws are facilitative, the 14th Amendment of the Constitution restricts State actions but facilitates the rights of the citizens of the States. One test of a law is whether it permits more than it forbids. The law against arson saves lives as well as property. Laws properly speaking are regulations and thus facilitate the ways in which men go about seeking the reduction of their needs. Needs do not change so much as do methods of need-reduction, and these call for fresh regulations as new conditions are encountered.

Laws are universal statements while actions are particulars. Laws follow the actions of men and seek to make them mutually acceptable. The laws of a given society set forth what may and what may not be done as well as what must be done. What each citizen asks of the law is to preserve order in the state and protect him without laying on too many restrictions while he obtains his own and enjoys its use. The law defines rights and duties, and thus specifies and implements the morality. It consists in commands to act, in accordance with what is held to be right, and to refrain from those actions held to be wrong. For example one *must* pay taxes, one *may not* commit mayhem. In addition to the twin ideas of right and wrong there is also that of remedy: enforcing a right and redressing a wrong, providing restitution and damages.

Language, both oral and written is very important in law. Lawyers argue in court, codes are recorded, all of course in language. And yet there is more to law than language, there are legal acts: property changes hands, the police are active, people are arrested and jailed, statutes are adopted involving permissions and restraints on actions. Language is an instrument, not an end. It promotes order by its prescriptive nature.

Anglo-American philosophy, following the Oxford-based Austrian, Wittgenstein, and his many followers both in England and America, currently stresses the meaning of language, which can be both expressed and explained in language. There is more to language than that, however; language in addition to meaning has reference, and reference lies outside language. The moon may be defined as a word defined by other words; yet the reference of the word is not another word but a material object which may be seen often at night and has been visited by astronauts, a thing and not a word.

J.L. Austin introduced the term, 'performatives', for expressions which brought about states of affairs instead of merely describing them.[5] A performative utterance is one which executes the action it describes. Austin gave as examples "I apologize", "I congratulate you".[6] I would argue, however, that even these are not what he claimed. They are descriptive language, and refer to personal feelings and attitudes which are not in themselves linguistic. They communicate information rather than bringing about what it conveys. Olivecrona was concerned that performatives, or, in his phrase "performative imperatives", as for instance in the marriage ceremony, "I take this woman to be my lawful wedded wife",[7] do much more than merely cognitive language does. He is correct of course. But speech acts are not to be confused with other kinds of acts. There is a great deal of difference between saying and doing. Saying to a man "I kill you" is not the same as killing him. All laws are not commands, either, though some are; more often they lay down conditions.

Human beings are material organizations, organisms living in a world of other human beings, raw materials and artifacts with all of which they interact and must therefore reckon. The life of man is a series of aggressions of one sort or another, and it must be recalled that I have counted among aggressions the constructive as well as the destructive varieties of altering material objects in the immediate environment by means of force. This is the primary fact of human existence, and law must reach an accommodation with it. In pursuit of this end, language is an indispensable aid, but only an aid; it is not the end itself. Legal language accompanies and may even indicate intentions, and it records them, but it is not them and cannot be substituted for them.

Laws are agreements between the members of a society as to how they will allow themselves to act and how those individuals who depart

5 *How to Do Things with Words* (London 1962).
6 *Ibid.*
7 Karl Olivecrona, *Law as Fact* (London 1971, Stevens & Sons), ch. 8.

from the agreements shall be treated in order to preserve the society intact. It is an error of logomachy to assume that the language *is* the law of the society, when it is only an element employed in their facilitation. Language, in a word, is an instrument employed by the law, not itself the law. The law consists in those regulations which are expressed in oral or written language (or both), but it is a mistake to confuse what the language contains (its meaning) with what the language indicates (its reference). What the legal language means is given in the statutes, what these refer to are the social situations.

Legal relations are material relations, verbal tools are not the only kind. Laws are enacted by men in a language specifically designed for the purpose, their aim being to regulate conditions in order to prevent or if not then to settle conflicts. Laws do not initiate social relations but only recognize them and if possible bring some regularity to them. For it is the material conditions prevailing in a society that are the sources of its laws.

Laws are written expressions; they represent but never constitute the reality, which is substantive. They are verbal arrangements to elicit and establish order in a given culture, which consists in men and their artifacts, i.e. material altered through human agency to serve human uses. Societies, then, are composed not merely of human individuals, their beliefs and organizations, but also of cities, farmlands, mines and manufactures. Thus while the meaning of laws may be verbal, the references are not; they are ultimately to men and artifacts in the material world.

It is seldom recognized that almost all inter-personal relations are mediated by artifacts and so I must say a word about that here. One man may strangle another or rape a woman without the mediation of artifacts but these are rare exceptions for otherwise artifacts play a part in every transaction. Men never merely *behave*, they always behave *about* something, and that something is as likely to be a material tool as it is another human individual and usually both. Any morality which involves men with each other usually involves also chattels, tools, leases or titles. The material side of human culture has increased enormously with industrialism, and the laws have had to keep pace with this development.

Laws incorporate the existing morality, and that morality is made concrete and established in a society in one of three ways: through custom, through common law or precedent, and through statutory law. Of the three, statutory law is the best recognized because it constitutes a visible and referable basis for decision-making and behavior. Long-established laws are social, of course; and they are complex. For this reason mistakes are often made. Champerty, or promoting litigation by a person not a party in a suit in order to carry on its prosecution or defense in consideration of a share in its proceeds, was abolished in England by the Criminal Law Act of 1967.[8] It should have been adopted here, for there are now many cases to which it could be applied to good effect, but they would have to be analyzed before we could see plainly the elements of their composition. This is especially true of old laws so many of which differ markedly in character from new ones. Connotations as well as denotations have accrued to the old ones over the years, and their basic meanings may have been altered somewhat as the situations to which they were applied have shifted.

Many authorities agree that laws are norms; so for example Bentham,[9] Austin[10] and Kelsen.[11] In a certain limited sense they *are* norms, but that is not all they are. They are also imperatives. They not only *suggest* what ought to be done (or not done), they also *command* it; they not only *guide* behavior, they also *order* it. One need not obey if prepared to accept the penalty, but the law stands as a law just the same. Given a social situation in its cultural setting, only a single system of laws applies. The normative in such a case *is* the empirical. Normative laws are empirical laws adjusted for their suitability to local circumstance. Given a population with its inherited customs and institutions and the conditions prevailing in the environment, nothing else could have been considered.

The advocates of the normative interpretation may be confusing the law with its operation, the statute with the persons who are expected to obey it. *Of course* they should obey it, that is what the law means. But the law does not depend upon their obedience or its lack; it remains a law by its very nature and irrespective of the degree of its effectiveness, and only ceases to be a law when it is repealed. A law which becomes a "dead letter' is still a law.

Laws may be represented by statutes or by judicial decisions, but a law in the strict sense of the definition is not identical with the form by which it is given expression. A law *in esse* is the abstract universal proposition to which a statute refers. Laws as statutes are embodied in language, but the proposition to which it refers is extra-linguistic, as in-

8   Halsbury's *Statutes of England*, vol. 8, p. 574 (1969).
9   Jeremy Bentham, *An Introduction to the Principles of Morals and Legislation* (Oxford 1917, Clarendon Press), p. 17, note I to XIV; also ch. XVII, p. 330.
10   John Austin, *Lectures on Jurisprudence*, vol. I, pp. 86, 176.
11   Hans Kelsen, *Pure Theory of Law*, II, 7.

deed all abstract entities by their nature are. For the practical purposes of exposition we shall consider them equal in this treatise. Laws of course need not be written. Unwritten laws function just as effectively, and may be regarded as having been established, if not enacted, by custom and tradition. Unwritten laws generally represent an earlier state of affairs before the society was effectively established.

The negative aspect of my definition of law may be superficially misleading. Laws as such are positive. In order not to break a law one must follow it, but the law itself may be positive or negative. A law requiring all citizens to register for military draft is one calling for positive action, a law making homicide a crime is negative: it calls for avoidance. A law granting each citizen permission to cast one vote in every election is neutral; it cannot be broken by voting or not voting, only by voting more than once.

The definition of law I have proposed indicated that no law stands altogether alone. Laws in most instances are formulated to apply to specific cases and, as the definition indicates, laws are only laws within a given society. Laws cannot co-exist unless they can work together, and that implies the absence of contradiction. The laws of any given society, in other words, must form a system, however unformulated and unorganized that system may happen to be. I shall have much more to say about this in chapter X.

There have been many undertakings to discover laws that are valid within any and every society, perhaps even with some success; but to date they do not answer to my definition of law, for there is no one to prevent them from being broken. To achieve the full definition and yet have a law that is found in every society, there would have to be only one society and that society global in reach. We do not seem to be in sight of this goal yet despite the fact that an efficient technology seems to require it.

Two difficulties must be mentioned in connection with the system of laws at which all codification aims. The first difficulty is the result of the gap in time between the framing of different laws, the second is due to the diversity of human actions.

All legal systems suffer from the difficulty that the laws were framed at one period to meet one condition of society and applied in a different period when social conditions have changed. That is bound to result in maladjustments. Laws are in a certain sense obsolete the moment they are enacted.

The actions of men are infinitely diverse, and no attempts to frame laws to meet all possible cases have ever been altogether successful. No

legislators however astute have had the foresight to anticipate everything that might happen. It is simply imossible to arrange for the establishment of sufficient universals to take account of all particulars; some
of them are bound to fall between universals.

2. Origins

Most writers on the law have composed their works as though man were
an isolated phenomenon in nature and could be considered by himself
without relation to his material culture. Changing beliefs were reckoned
with well enough, but not changing material conditions, and especially
not the changing material conditions for which man himself has been
responsible. I think such an approach will not bear examination. In
order to support this contention it will be necessary to consider what
legal changes must have taken place when societies which had been
nomadic shifted over to a sedentary existence.

All theories of the origin of law work within the limits of the history
of civilizations, which occupies after all only the last ten thousand
years. Society, however, is older than civilization. What is now called
'pre-history' argues for some sort of society hundreds of thousands of
years before civilization, and should be able to do something to explain
man in his present state. Thus to credit the origins of law to custom and
tradition is not to trace it to its source but only to an earlier and less
formal social order.

To begin with, there must have been a number of small pre-nomadic
groups living by hunting animals, which included also killing each other
for food. Tribal living, which already represented a population increase,
required an in-group living in peace and holding down its killing to the
out-groups. Hence tribal customs. In thus setting restrictions on the
passionate and aggressive nature of man, a dichotomy was set up which
has never been successfully bridged, for we still have law-abiding citizens on the one hand and criminals on the other.

To say that the laws derive from custom and tradition is not to say
anything of an explanatory nature. Nothing so formalized as a social
contract was agreed upon, only an arrangement which came into existence casually. For custom and tradition imply orderly procedures
which are uncodified and thus in a sense unwritten laws. But as the
term themselves imply, society had a past, and so this only puts the
problem back a little and leaves it unsolved. One could well ask, what
are the origins of customs and traditions?

We have no factual answer to that question but it is not hard to imagine how they must have come about, for we can seen them all about us in little repeated ways. We may conjecture that the source of law consisted in the observance that men found necessary in order to live together. The first man to accomplish a practical task was an innovator, the second made it into a convention, the third regarded it from the point of view of a conservative. The next generation recognized the existence of a custom, and so started a tradition.

Civilization probably began when about ten thousand years ago the members of some nomadic tribe first fenced in its animals instead of following the herd, and planted crops to feed both the animals and themselves. This made necessary the establishment of settlements and provided for a continuous and inherited culture with its accumulation of unmovable artifacts. No doubt at first such settlements were exceptions and were raided by the remaining nomadic tribes which recognized no agreements and which lived by capture and kill. It was found in the settlements on the other hand that such proximity as its members experienced necessitated the making of social rules governing ordinary conduct. Thus arose the distinction between the peaceful pastoral, cattle-breeding peoples and the fierce nomadic tribes which had not adopted the new way of life and whose inroads were a constant threat.

For the understanding of man in a "state of nature", to use the traditinal phrase, we do not need to go back to a supposed primitive society of a sort which probably never existed. What Hobbes and Rousseau both meant to achieve by the phrase is man as a biological isolate, individual man with all of his organic needs and his drives to reduce them uninhibited by the external restraints imposed by societies. It is a fiction because man was never alone, or, if he was, then by definition he could have existed only for a single generation; yet it is a useful fiction because it tells us what society had to work with and suggests what had to be done if a collection of individuals was ever to be incorporated in a state.

Legal theory ever since the natural law doctrine prevailed in the Middle Ages has been dominated by the conception of the human will as the source of all sovereignty. Kant's philosophy is the ablest and finest expression of it. However, there are forces at work in human culture beyond those of the individual himself and his conscious will, beyond even a collection of such wills. Human behavior in search of the materials which can reduce human needs is not always deliberate, not always undertaken in the full understanding of conscious aims. The will is the recognition that under the conditions described particular actions are called for if the individual is to survive and prosper. The ever-present threat of disorder is the constant reminder of the demand for order.

It could be argued, then, that the origins of law can be explained without appealing either to the will of God or to the will of man. Every early civilization attributes its laws to the mandate of a god or gods, different for every one. The conflicts between religions in this respect, as in so many others, does cast doubt on the explanation. As to the will of man, we have stated that it is an internal response to internal needs or to those external stimuli which can be referred to the needs. Men do not "will" anything until they have been sitmulated to make responses. Hence the will is not an initiating force but only the way in which a response is activated.

The origins of law can be explained in two ways: by reference to individual needs and by reference to social exigencies. The two are of course related, but first let us look at them separately.

It is possible to find the origins of law in the organ-specific needs of the individual. In the pursuit of need-reductions individuals came into inevitable conflict. If they had been turned aside by this there would have been no need-reductions and so eventually no human species. To facilitate need-reductions individuals agree to cooperate, and this involved the voluntary surrender of some rights in order to form a social order in which conflicts could be avoided.

This leads us then to the second explanation of the origins of law: social exigency. Men had to deal with each other and with their properties and skills on the basis of some kind of social order or not at all. To reduce all of their needs they must live together, and they could not live together and manage their affairs without an agreement of some sort to which all subscribed and which was incorporated in established laws. The early social orders must have consisted in sets of rules which applied equally to all and were binding on all, and so recognized similarities. After these there are sets of rules which recognized differences between men with respect to their abilities to contribute to the total social facilitation. Together these two sets of rules constituted the law of the land.

We have no specific knowledge of the origin and development of these earlier societies, but we do know that from the earliest times the laws had a fixed character akin to the customs and institutions, the language and manners of a people. It must have been contained very much as we see it contained now in the unconscious common awareness, and must have been first expressed in lists of injuries and penalties and in the consequent regulations intended to be uniformly observed. The laws grew up with the culture as a matter of necessity to preserve order among all individuals and their institutions, and gradually assumed a character and gave rise to an institution of its own: the judges or courts with their laws, personnel and procedures. Habit probably accounts for the origins of all social structures, repeated performances which proved satisfactory finally crystallizing into a shape which all could recognize and acknowledge henceforth in their procedures. Once the process was sufficiently established it became deliberate, after which additional laws were made by men specially appointed to be lawgivers.

Thus social order and with it the laws can be traced back to the organ-specific needs of the individual and his efforts to reduce them. The community is a necessity if the individuals in it are to accomplish need-reductions, and the laws make the community possible.

A society, from the point of view of law, may be characterized as a homogeneous but partly disordered system; but it is not known how a horde became a society. Nomads had rules governing behavior, but whether these can be called laws in our sense is questionable. They may have contained the rudimentary origins of law. The transition from the customs of nomadic tribes to the laws of settlements probably came as a result of the increase in sheer numbers. With settlements came the ownership of land, and laws to deal with this relationship were the result. Many people living close together necessitated establishing observances, with penalties for their infractions.

Once there is a settlement there must be a community. The accumulation of artifacts and the apportioning of land within the confines of the settlement where it could be protected necessitated the making of laws respecting private property as well as the defining of the rights and duties of the individual with regard to his freedoms and his part in the mutual defense. Individual infractions had to be punished by proscribed penalties and procedures, and in general, deliberations began to play a large part in the lives of the members of the settlement, which in this way had perforce to become a community of law.

Reasoning among nomads had hitherto been entirely a matter of practical exigency. Current needs called for current actions only, and current actions called for no more than current communications. But this would not do for settled communities which could not be maintained without some planning for the future, and planning requires the use of abstractions. Thus abstract thought became necessary, and with it reasoning took more logical form in the cities; it was written down and recognized in "the sewn" as it had not been in "the desert."

Having altered his environment by the introduction of artifacts —
later in many instances even to the extent of replacing it by them —
man had perforce the task of adapting to it all over again, and this made
for considerable changes in his outlook. Man by himself is not a valid
isolate; he is what the materials he can call out in his environment and
the structures he can invent from them make of him when he adjusts
himself to their requirements. This will of course vary from culture to
culture; consequently, "finding nature" in the social field may be
enormously more complex a task than anyone has supposed.

Here then we see the birth of reason and with it of the need for law.
Beyond the settlements, which possessed some kind of social order,
there still lurked the nomadic tribes which posed a constant threat. Disorder always stood on the threshold of order, reinforcing its importance. As the settlements grew into cities and held off the nomads in a
more or less permanent way, justice arose from the reasonableness of
law. In the cities more people were living in proximity than had been
true in nomadic wanderings; more infants grew to maturity, and such
close living was impossible except under conditions of peaceful cooperation. If there was competition, then it had to be regulated by rules of
conduct and internecine violence had to be avoided.

A necessary precondition, then, for life in cities was the rule of law
and not of men. Social contacts among nomads were violent and rare,
and were concerned with the products of hunting. But suddenly such
contacts became quite common in the settlements where peaceful co-
existence was a precondition of success in the new ventures of animal
husbandry and agriculture. If men were not to fight over every possession, social relations would have to be regularized by established law.

Civilization means urbanization, the production and use of material
culture in cities, made possible by a legal system of some sort. Examples which support this thesis are not hard to find. A typical one is
to be found in the origins and doctrine of Zoroastrianism.[12] The con-
jectural dates place Zoroaster in the sixth century B.C. in what is now
Persian Khorasan and Western Afghanistan, a pastoral land which was
at the same time inhabited by nomadic peoples. In Eastern Persia
Zoroaster found a settled community busily engaged in animal husbandry and agriculture, and also a marauding tribal society which
menaced the more peacefully-inclined farmers. The former he termed

---

12 For my knowledge of Zoroastrianism I am indebted chiefly to R.C. Zaehner,
   The Dawn and Twilight of Zoroastrianism (London: Weidenfeld & Nicolson,
   1961), esp. ch. I.

52

"followers of Truth or Righteousness' and the latter "followers of the Lie," or those who defended the natural order and those who violated it.

Whenever nomads undertake a settled life they feel the need for an absolute order almost immediately. Perhaps the most vivid and detailed account is to be found in Exodus, where not only the Ten Commandments but also the laws which follow it were transmitted by Moses to his people as the first necessary step in ending their wanderings. The importance of the abstract truth is recognized in the concrete need to reduce social conflict.

Often there was a reversal of roles and the invading tribes brought with them laws which they augmented from those already in force among the conquered peoples. The result was a legal accommodation under which conquerors and conquered could be ruled. This is the story of the people of Hindu scripture who were contemporary with the ancient Hebrews. The Hindu Aryans were the raiding nomads but already somewhat civilized, evidently bringing their holy book, the *Vedas*, with them and encroaching upon the less advanced Dravidian peoples. The Dravidian elements in the Vedic Hymns have been sorted out; the non-Vedic gods had forest and hunting associations, and were worshipped in sacred groves: the Aryan gods by contrast called for ritual sacrifices performed in temples.[13]

In a life which is predominantly religious the laws take the form of prescriptions for ritual practices and purposes. A social order which is theologically authorized is an order no less because the rights and duties of the individual allegedly issue from God. The commonest form of social order in the past has been a religious order, one either ruled by priests or authorized by them. But a religious order is a social order, and the religious aspect includes the matter of sanctions. People are less inclined to disobey the laws if they think that a supernatural God has been responsible for them. This was true of both the ancient Hebrews and the ancient Hindus, and in more recent time it has been true of Christians in the Middle Ages.

Much of the havoc in human life has come from the fact that man has not been told why he is here but was given the wit to ask. This dilemma has resulted in the emotional pain of doubt, a deep sense of insecurity, and plain stark error. A few individuals have played on these

13 See C. Kunhan Raja, "Pre-Vedic Elements in Indian Thought" in *History of Philosophy Eastern and Western*, S. Radhakrishnan and others, eds. (London: George Allen & Unwin, 1952), 2 vols., vol. I, pp. 31-39.

feelings, each by insisting that he knew the answer, and endeavored to reinforce his version by claiming divine support for it. Unfortunately, the answers as well as the claims made for them have come into conflict, and as a result the followers generally have resorted to violence. Every challenge to an answer which has been accepted as absolute threatens a return of the doubt, the insecurity and the terror.

Religious law was probably the earliest form of law and still exists in many communities today, but it has largely been replaced by the laws of secular states. The improbabilities are apparent now even to the most pious; for, given the profusion of conflicting claims to the possession of the word of God, it seems only reasonable to suppose that He must at the very least be unaffiliated. The safest generalization nowadays with regard to individual conduct in a state is that the laws issue from the citizens of that state and remain answerable to them.

3. Development

The overall determinant in human affairs is *human culture*. (The generic term is *civilization*.) It is only in comparatively recent times that we have come to recognize the existence of organizations as large and pervasive as these; yet they are stronger and more inclusive than any of their elements. I define culture as man and his works, including the effects of those works on man himself. Thus the definition includes both the ideas he has discovered and the artifacts he has designed and made. The ideas may be abstract or concrete, universal or particular, and the artifacts are characterized by always having a material component. The discovery and use of materials by technology is as important in culture as ideas of law and philosophy. The highest forms of culture manage to encompass and incorporate both the ideas *and* the materials. Everything in a culture is affected by the culture as a whole.

The first thing to notice, then, in observing the development of law is that it reflects every facet and corner of culture. Every human relation and every artifact is represented by regulations of some sort. And of course the reverse is also true. For just as every branch of government no matter how separated its powers exercises a law-making capacity, so the legal system serves to slow down changes and in this way to stabilize the culture in which it operates.

The device of established law was developed to maintain cultures. It does not initiate them but it does serve to support them. The history of Greek culture did not begin with the tradition of Solon but his work occurred early in its history. The law, which is so necessary to culture, nevertheless follows culture. It does not guide but merely formalizes the moral choices which a society makes for itself through its most imaginative and aggressive individuals and groups.

Thus law is so to speak passive and subservient from the point of view of the whole society. It constitutes the stability and furnishes the continuity which a society needs if it is to function at all. When a society ceases to advance or progress, and when custom and tradition become guides to individual and social behavior, then the conservative force of the law gives it the dignity it requires but also an importance it hardly deserves. It can in this situation become such an end in itself that it stifles further progress and puts its stamp on thing-as-they-are as though they were in one-to-one correspondence with things-as-they-ought-to-be.

We can see something of these developments in the history of western civilization. There temporal succession did not always indicate progress. When Athens was conquered by Sparta, when both were made provinces of Macedonia, and when Rome took over, there were some gains and some losses in the level of culture, but the total effect was a loss. When the German tribes overran the Roman Empire in 499 and subsequently effected a collaboration with the Catholic Church to which they converted, there was a further loss.

The fallacy of *post, ergo melior* has prevailed many times in history as lesser civilizations followed greater. Communist China, for the moment at least (1972), has nullified all the glorious gains which the Chinese achieved in so many fields in the past in order to effect a uniformity of economic relations and a powerful central government. The truth of the statement that what comes later is not necessary better is often forgotten by the young who wish to sweep away the gains of the past along with some prominent wrong which glaringly faces them and which succeeds at least for them in obliterating everything that was right.

The law as such must stand helplessly by when large-scale and culture-wide events transpire. The police are given the task of preserving a semblance of order until stability can be restored on some basis or other. The legal system does not lead but merely follows the morality which prevails in a society always in excess of that society's establishment. The morality follows by bringing with it conditions of its own which it introduces informally in ways which are then formally expressed, and that is how the Greek conception of justice as the ideal of law and of law as the application of justice survived. As a consequence, the curve of the development of law did not follow the curve of the development of culture. No doubt Roman law marked an advance over Greek law even though it owed a lot to the Greeks. But the same cannot be said for canon law over Roman law. Again, the English common law marked another advance, this time over canon law. Thus the high points of culture are generally acknowledged to have occurred in Greece and modern Europe while the high points of law are equally acknowledged to have been reached in ancient Rome and modern England.

The device of employing established law to maintain cultures found its highest expression in the concept of natural law, a law which was supposed to exist before man and which he discovered rather than created. The theory of natural law is a form of the attempt to achieve a permanent stability in a society. It was so among the Greeks, it was so in the Middle Ages, it is so now. The theory itself changes in terms of the changes which occur in its justification: with the Greeks it was reason as a world condition, manifested in human reasoning and in the logic of events; with the Middle Ages it was divine authority: God; in modern times it has been the need for a reference point in reason and fact that would not be at the mercy of every practical exigency. In short, natural law is a requirement of a permanent social order, of a continuing culture, of a legal system which can function in an orderly manner. With codification came the conviction that what was required was a body of law which would be both internally consistent and complete and capable of covering all the material conditions it was designed to regulate, a logic elicited from those conditions and so to speak set over them.

But there was something more required of natural law besides stability, and that was freedom. In the distinction between established laws backed by governmental authority and force on the one hand and natural laws on the other there lay the restrictions upon state power and the preservation of the individual rights of a free people. We obey the laws because they have been established by our representatives but they can be changed as we or the duly constituted authorities find better. Natural law has taken turns, at one time reinforcing established laws and at another calling for their revision.

Kelsen's distinction between social fact and legal validity has a familiar ring about it.[14] Legal validity does depend upon conventions while the exigencies of survival dictate social fact, and yet the former issues from the latter. Legal systems are not arbitrary, they arise from the

14 Hans Kelsen, *The Pure Theory of Law*, I, 5 and 6.

needs of individuals in a given society at a given time, and subsequent generations of the same society can preserve them only by the appropriate alterations through suitable interpretations. Traditions are strong, and the desire to find justification in the principles and practices of the past is an understandable one. I insist only that man being part of nature, whatever changes he brings about in his environment and consequently in himself, whether through the adroit fashioning and use of material artifacts or through the establishment and appeal to abstract principles, are also natural. The legal system of a given society is as much a natural development as that society itself.

We are not now in a position to state the universal principles of human society in the same way we are able to state the universal principles of the physical or chemical world chiefly because we do not know that much about society. Physical laws may be the same everywhere, but we are learning for the first time that planets are not; the moon and Mars evidently resemble the earth in many respects, but in many respects they differ radically, and the same may be said of comparative human cultures: the basic needs of all human individuals are the same because their organs are the same and because they are genetically similar; and so in some respects the cultures they produce are the same; but in many other respects those cultures do differ. Among the similarities are the fact that they all have systems of laws of some kind; among the differences are the kinds of systems of laws they have.

An outstanding Greek contribution, in contrast with the oriental civilizations of the period, was the importance of law. It is well illustrated in Herodotus' account of the discussion Demaratus had with Xerxes in which the former praised the Spartans' respect for law. "For though they be freemen, they are not in all respects free. Law is the master whom they own; and the master they fear more than your subjects fear you".[15] The idea of law as a separate and distinct enterprise was developed by the Romans after its introduction in Greek culture. It certainly did exist there, but its full formalization to a set of principles beyond mere practice was the work of lawyers in Rome.

We owe to the Romans the introduction of law as an institution, separate from morality, to which nevertheless it is related, and associated with government, which is responsible for its workings. Laws, we have come to discover, issue not only from law-making bodies specifically so designated, such as legislatures, but also from the courts and

---

15 *The History of Herodotus*, G. Rawlinson trans. (New York 1928, The Dial Press), Book VII, p. 388.

also from the executive branches. Every institution is a source of law; the only distinction is whether the laws of an institution are for internal use only, as for instance they are with the military, or extend to the whole of the society.

In any case, the Romans were the first to consider the law as a separate and specific topic, and to institute law schools on a formal basis. The teaching of law was absolutely new, and the law professor who was familiar with the rules of procedure and with precedent produced an entirely new aspect of culture. The first teachers were practioners, but gradually a certain amount of theory came to be introduced. Cicero was responsible for the innovation, and Aulus Gellius in *Attic Nights* mentions a lost work *De juri civili in artem redigendo.*[16] Henceforth Roman law relying on Greek logic became a body of doctrine in its own right, with its own principles and its professional terminology.[17] Law was thus the only Roman addition to Greek education, but its effects were enormous. It turned the whole civilized world into a single country by means of justice, order and peace, that men might enjoy security, comfort and leisure.

That there was a whole society gave rise to the concomitant condition that there must be a whole legal system, one which is both consistent and complete. The state maintains itself by means of a body of laws which like itself constitutes an organized whole. In this total effort philosophy has continually made itself felt, and no less so in those periods, like the nineteenth century and so far in the twentieth, when philosophy was assumed to be of no practical import.[18]

---

16 I, 22, 7.
17 Cf. H.I. Marrou, *A History of Education in Antiquity*, G. Lamb trans. (New York 1956, Sheed & Ward), p. 290.
18 Roscoe Pound, *An Introduction to the Philosophy of Law* (New Haven: Yale University Press, 1968), p. 1.

CHAPTER VIII

THE LEGAL SYSTEM

1. Pandects and Peregrines

In an earlier chapter, chapter IV, I noted what a legal system is from the point of view of justice; here I must consider justice from the point of view of a legal system. We will encounter here, then, many of the same points, but this time in a quite different and more specific connection.

Laws are not usually loose collections, they are systems, even though, as we shall presently see, partially-ordered ones. Systems of laws are not equally advanced in every country. Some people seem to have a special genius for the making of laws, and when they have they are usually capable also in many other ways. Certainly this is true of the ancient Romans. Only a people capable of deriving abstractions from concrete situations could have a strong sense of social order. Such abstractions, moreover, are endless in their applications.

When I employ the expression, legal system, I do not mean to suggest that the law is a pandect; after all, Justinian's collection came only in the sixth century A.D., at the end of the long period of usefulness of Roman Law. The comprehensive digest of a coherent intellectual establishment is intended only to insure that the legal business of a society should be a more or less consistent set of procedures authorized by statutory law as indicated by the prevailing morality. The digest is a unity because it follows from a single morality, and because inconsistencies are eliminated as a practical matter of exigency whenever they arise.

Pandects are necessary to insure consistency, but peregrines are necessary also to provide completeness. Pandects are useful as the code word for efforts to organize the energies of men into lawful societies, and peregrines for the new or overlooked elements not yet incorporated in law.

Needless to add, the conception of pandects is very old but the companion conception of peregrines is not. Yet one is as necessary to the understanding of the legal system as the other. Peregrines — the term means aliens coming from abroad, from a Latin word for foreign — suggest that the world contains more than reason and must include elements which are not necessarily irrational but in which the order has not yet been seen and which therefore have been omitted from systems meeting the demand for order. Familiar only as Dionysiac elements, the wild and uncontrolled forces striving against all restraints, compel us to include in our legal system much more than has ever been counted on.

The conception of peregrines recognizes that the final challenge to the validity of any legal system is not only its consistency but also its completeness; that it must be sufficiently flexible and adaptive to be able to reach out and incorporate hitherto unrecognized disparate elements. In a world such as the present where more than one kind of legal system exists, each may stand in some respects for peregrines to the other.

Much of course depends upon how the laws were framed and who framed them. According to Plutarch, when Solon the Greek lawgiver was asked if he had left the Athenians the best laws that could be given, he replied, "The best they could receive".

In chapter IV I explained the three requirements of a system, consistency, completeness and categoricity. The laws must be for the most part consistent, they must cover all of the circumstances which might arise with sufficient formality to reach judicature, and they must be similar in kind so as to satisfy the requirement of categoriticty.

Everyone agrees that a body of coherent laws must have both completeness and consistency. Of the two properties, consistency is the better known and the easiest to check. It is found when any two laws conflict and its demand is met when the conflict is eliminated.

Completeness — this is where logic most often fails. Logic can operate only upon what it is given and then only in terms of consistency and deducibility. It is the task of those who are involved in the hurly-burly of exigency and contingency to see that the laws are complete. Only someone intent on validating the authority of language over what the language stands for would plead otherwise.

Men are forever making choices between things which do not exist on the same level of analysis and are therefore not legitimate alternatives. It is useless for example to debate the case of utility versus conflict — of the principle of utility of Bentham versus the social contract theory of Rousseau — when they fit so neatly together: the doctrine of utilitarianism to insure the completeness of the law, and that of contract to insure its consistency. Again, men are forever binding themselves in their search for pleasure and their avoidance of pain. One has only to substitute for pleasure the various organic need-reductions and for pain the usual threats to existence in order to bring this pair of alternatives together. Laws are social contracts intended to insure that the greatest number of individuals will achieve need-reduction.

If there is such a thing as a social order, however primitive, then there must be a corresponding system of laws. Speaking generally, the legal system is a species of ordering which has arisen and become established only through an act of recognition of some concrete and practical material order which already exists in the society.

Outside the special province of applied mathematics and engineering, formal standards are not imposed. Philosophical systems have been treated in this way; notably the philosophies of Descartes and Spinoza, both systematized by Spinoza, and that of Leibniz, systematized by Bertrand Russell; but legal systems seldom and social systems rarely. The most powerful and prevalent systems in social life were not precisely formulated until some time after they were introduced, and so their assumptions were not at the time correctly ascertained. Among these I count the legal systems which have been the guiding lines of so many societies in history. We have the records of Roman Law and of the English Common Law, the former codified after many years of employment but neither organized in accordance with the formal requirements of systems.

We have the records of the English laws as they were accumulated, and of American laws as they were codified. Laws at first are systematized only by the consistency imparted to them by a socially-accepted implicit morality. Later the presence of assumptions are disclosed by the establishment of principles in a charter, written or unwritten. It means in short that the systems had existed already in a tacit and unacknowledged fashion, silent yet none the less vigorous and forceful in their effects.

2. Legal Systems as Partial Orderings

Logical and mathematical systems are rigorous, vertical systems. Their principle elements are: undefined terms, unproved propositions (called axioms), proofs made in accordance with the rules of inference, and proved propositions (called theorems), occasionally interspersed with

62

definitions and lemmas (additional theorems proved for use in the proofs of other theorems).

Now consider the same type of system but this time not as rigorous, and as horizontal rather than vertical; which is to say, laid down along the time-line of successive events. The result will be what in logic is called a partial order, for it will satisfy the following postulates:

No individual precedes itself.
If a precedes b and b precedes c, then a precedes c.[1]

If we apply this to legal procedure, we get a partial ordering of the system. The ideal of the law is a concrete system of actual events constituting themselves axiomatic assumptions and theorematic consequences, a logical structure discovered and put in place in reverse: by starting with the kind of results desired, then abstracting from going practice, and finally employing the abstractions as guides to future practice. In this version the axioms may be represented by material things, or by positive actions involving persons and things. But the theorems come first, with the axioms taking the form of tacit assumptions. Concrete events function as theorems and lemmas. The proofs are the connecting events which make earlier events the cause of later. Litigations for example may be axiomatic events which start trains of consequences or proofs which may make earlier cases control those that come after. The stand-ins for the rules of inference are the encounters allowed for by certain forces, the proofs are given in legal statutes and connections, and the theorems are the effects which occur at the end of sequences of causes-and-effects.

It should be admitted at once that even this much logical rigor is a reading after the fact. There is some question after all of the extent to which a logical system can be made up of empirical elements. Yet one must be there for an order of any kind to exist. To the extent to which a legal system may be called a system at all, it is the result of growing up logically, with an accretion of theorems and their assumptions, and with definitions and lemmas but with no well-defined axioms ever explicitly stated. A system of law is always a partially-ordered, incomplete system, including among its parts a moral order, a constitution (written or unwritten), courts, police, lawyers, judges, all interacting chiefly in that one-way direction.

1 Alonzo Church, *Introduction to Mathematical Logic*, vol. I (Princeton 1956, University Press), p. 337. See also S.C. Kleene, *Introduction to Metamathematics* (New York 1952, D. Van Nostrand), Ch. II, 58, where "generated before" replaces "precedes".

A legal system as a built-in logical structure holds the society together. It has the additional feature of flexibility; it can be added to (as new laws are enacted) and substracted from (as old statutes are nullified). It is consistent if no two of its laws are in conflict, complete if the laws within the system cover all possible contingent eventualities, and categorical if its laws show a family resemblance. Laws must work together in a given society. The evidence of their systematic nature is the absence of conflict when they are applied, consistency demonstrated through non-contradiction.

Such are the requirements of logical systems, and empirical systems are logical systems disclosed in all their imperfections in the empirical social world. As it happens, the actual world of existence is more complex than the logical domain of essence, if only because of its dense and interactive nature, and so empirical systems have their own properties. All empirical systems must have the three properties of continuity, plenitude and gradation.[2] Continuity assumes that there are no missing laws; if between any two there can be a third, it must be in place. Plenitude implies that all the necessary laws must exist. And gradation suggests that there is a rank-order to the laws; they disclose a descending (or ascending) order of importance.

Systems of laws are devised to suit the types of societies they are intended to support. In medieval England for instance the laws did not apply to villeins but only to free men. Working rules cannot be set in opposition to a legal system when in fact they follow from it. There may be a long logical distance as well as a temporal disparity between the two, yet they are indissolubly connected. Working rules must be consistent and do not exist in a vacuum; however little a legal system may be recognized or referred to, it exists and stands necessarily in the background. Legal systems function in all sorts of political structures, in monarchies and communist states as well as in democratic societies. Those appropriate to an agricultural and aristocratic country would not work adequately in an industrial one. It is not particular laws, then, which constitute the invariants in the social situation but the fact that whatever they are they must constitute a system. The properties of any system whatever would also have to be the properties of a system of law.

We noted in chapter VI that the purpose of laws is to enable men to live together in a society and that the source of laws resides in organic and social needs. An ideal set of laws would be a consistent set which is

2 James K. Feibleman, *Ontology* (Baltimore 1951, Johns Hopkins Press), pp. 207-209.

the least number that would make the operation of the society possible. The aim of the law is facilitative and ancillary, however indispensable it proves to be. No society ever existed for the sake of its laws, but the laws do exist for the sake of society. The laws make it possible for society to do whatever it decides to do but the laws never decide what it should do. That kind of decision belongs to ethics, another domain altogether.

A system of laws is one which is stable enough to provide continuity, and flexible enough to change as much as necessary when new conditions arise. What is always at issue is the consistency of the system and its capacity to allow for orderly change. Thus there are tacit procedural rules whose axiomatic nature has never been sufficiently recognized. In an age of rapidly developing technology, such as ours, for instance, new conditions call for fresh legislation. Motors cars called for a different set of laws than horses. The advent of the commercial airplane posed fresh problems concernig common carriers. Then too labor relations, insurance policies, new types of investment securities, all had to be regulated. Hence the need for a fresh set of statutes to provide for the new uses and abuses.

Thus case law will always be needed to supplement statute law in order to give it that permanent condition of flexibility which constantly changing conditions require. But this is not to say that there are not principles silently assumed by both kinds of law to provide them with the consistency any working system must possess.

To sum up, the legal system is a built-in logical structure of internal relations which has as its aim the holding of the society together as a viable enterprise. It consists in axioms functioning as assumptions and of theorems carried out in actions, but has the additional feature of flexibility: it can be substracted from as laws are repealed and added to as they are enacted.

No actual system was ever precisely formulated, though this is the aim. For no actual system can be at best any more than a partially-ordered system, with its proportions altered to suit the task it is intended to help in performing.

CHAPTER IX

MORALITY

1. Morality and Legality

Ethics is the theory of the good. Morality is the concrete practice of some theory of the good. An implicit dominant morality is what determines the structure as well as the function of a society. It is implicit because it operates to some extent whether anyone is aware of its existence or not, and it is dominant because it stands behind the hierarchy of institutions, behind the selection of tools or artifacts, behind the preferred behavior of individuals.

What I have called the "implicit dominant morality" of a society is what Paton named its "positive morality". He described it as "made up of the actual standards which are adopted in the life of any particular community" and "imposed on the individual from without, for it has behind it the effective if unorganized sanction of public opinion."[1] I would argue that while what he says is true its nature lies deeper than that, being responsible for the ordering of the society as well as for the behavior of its citizens.

Now the laws of a society represent its attempt to codify its morality. Law differs from morality in two ways: first, it is deliberate and it is known; and secondly it changes at a different rate. The morality of a society is a constantly shifting affair and enters into all of its organizations and activities. It is to be found in the conscience of individual citizens, in the hierarchy of social institutions, and in the pervasive qualitative atmosphere of the ethos. Also, and more importantly for our purposes, it exists formally in the statutes. An implicit dominant morality lies behind the enacted laws and explains why they were

---

1 George Whitecross Paton, *A Text-Book of Jurisprudence* (Oxford 1946, Clarendon Press), p. 59.

enacted in the first place: it explains why those laws rather than others. When we say of an individual that he had a "moral right" to do what he did, we distinguish that from his legal right.

A positive morality is a system of obligations which respect to human behavior. It sets the guide-lines for how a people agree they ought to live. Though it may exist only at the level of feelings, it is none the less strong for that. A legal system on the other hand is the conscious and deliberate expression of a moral code. It is how a people have agreed that they must and will behave. Morality, then, is the unseen force which operates to back up and justify the law. As the morality provided a reinforcement when it is accepted, so it provides an easement when it is so no longer.

The law and morality are not the same, then. The law follows the socially-accepted morality at a respectful temporal distance; as the one changes, so also must the other eventually. Slavery in the United States was once sanctioned by law, as indeed all accepted and established practices usually are; but then as the practice was prohibited, the laws prohibiting it followed; after the end of slavery the same sequence occurred with respect to racial prejudice.

What elements go into the making of a positive morality? History, custom, tradition, religion, experience, each plays its part in modifying the whole social complex. Unseen and unstated, the morality still acts as a powerful force in day-to-day procedures, influencing the special pleadings and the decisions of judges. It is a living and moving thing and everyone must reckon with it.

The law is always a great leveller at the grade of the least common denominator. As one judge in England observed in 1879, "you have no right to expect men to be something more than ordinary men". Yet "something more than ordinary" is what some of them soon prove that they are. The courts are continually being reminded by events that if men were created equal they do not long remain so, for they very soon sort themselves out, a few becoming leaders in some kind of enterprise: captains of industry in one type of society, members of the politburo in another; while the great majority constitute themselves followers.

Laws are society-wide, and rarely extend beyond the land occupied by a social organization. They rest ultimately upon what the members of that society hold to be real. 'Real' here does not refer to the reality which is opposed to appearance — though that too perhaps; it refers more properly to what is believed to be the nature of things: reality as essence. This is never an arbitrary affair but a desperately serious one based upon supposedly incontrovertible evidence. In the Christian

Middle Ages, for example, reality resided in another world, not in this one, and the appropriate behavior followed accordingly. Men lived chiefly in terms of their hope for a better life after death.

Legality is but enforced morality. It is where the implicit dominant morality of a society finds its expression. It should be emphasized, however, that despite the close bond between morality and legality each has internal and external relations not possessed by the other. The law enforces the morality, which, in so far as it is enforced, is no longer a mere morality; and not because the will has nothing to do with it but only because morality initially is based on agreement, but the morality shifts faster than the law can be enacted, and so may have shifted by the time the law enforces it. This is a lag and unavoidable: men are compelled to obey the law until they can have the opportunity to change it. In a democracy this lies through the path of due process, in other political systems it works in other ways, not the least of which is revolution.

The law, then, is intended to see to it that people adhere to the established morality as laid down by the laws of the country. What they believe is what they practice, and what they practice is eventually made into law. Morality travels to codification via customs and traditions.

We saw in chapter V that the law has its foundations in what the un-consciously-held beliefs a people hold in common, not as a set of abstract rules but rather as a number of intuitions having connections in organic and social needs, there called the "public retention schema". When the corresponding laws are developed it is by an artificial process of making explicit relations out of the raw material of deeply-held convictions. Morality is always external but its basis is internal and subjective or rather inter-subjective; for the individual always entertains two kinds of beliefs: public and private. It is the public beliefs with which we are here concerned, for they are the basis of the moral order which prevails in a society. The private beliefs, the "private retention schema", are what the individual thinks or feels he should do in the world, and they are irrelevant to the morality so long as they are not inconsistent with the public beliefs.

So much for the subjective end of morality. Now for the objective end. Strangely enough, this is less familiar. Objectively the law exists in codification but also in the structure of the society, the institutions established in the society together with their artifacts. Men build according to their beliefs but they build out of materials. The material side of society has a shape, and it is this shape that contains the objective morality, for they build exactly in accordance with their beliefs

68

and the aims those beliefs engender. What a society as a whole intends is shown plainly enough for those who are able to read the meaning of tools and social organizations.

Of course nothing in the world is permanent. Laws change and so does the material culture in which the morality is imbedded.

The law changes with the morality, but to what extent is the consistency of the law — and legal systems depend chiefly upon this property — affected when one statute is replaced by another which is its contradictory? Is there that much room within the legal system to turn without damaging the system? The ideals expressed in the American Declaration of Independence and the Constitution of the United States can evidently be amended to make them justify the opposite of what they were established to defend. Shifting morality alters cases, as the XVIII Amendment of 1919 prohibiting the manufacture, sale, or transportation of intoxicating liquors and the XXI Amendment of 1933 repealing Amendment XVIII amply illustrated when what was held to be a serious obstacle to the good life as conceived by a majority was abolished and then reestablished some fourteen years later.

Even more common perhaps is the conflict between existing laws. Cardozo has cited a splendid example in Riggs v. Palmer, 115 N.Y. 506.[2] Should a man who murdered his testator enjoy the benefits of the will? In favor was the binding force of a will; against was the principle that civil courts may not add to the penalties of crimes. Over both, Cardozo maintained, was the principle that no man should benefit from his own wrong. Immense skill is required in order to decide when more than once law seems to apply. And if one adds to this difficulty the additional one of a changing morality and the consequent changes in laws and judicial decisions, the picture contains more confusion than consistency can master.

It is somewhat discouraging to note how much the Supreme Court of the United States has been influenced by the winds of fickle public opinion, how one version of the Court can overturn and even reverse decisions handed down by its predecessor. There ought to be more stability to it than that even allowing for a changing morality. For if stability is to some extent the bulwark of all institutions, how much more should it be in the highest institution of the American judicial process?

The law after all is a guide to human behavior. It carries the accepted

2 *The Nature of The Judicial Process* (New Haven 1967, Yale University Press), p. 40.

morality into practice. It has no other reason for existence. How it affects that behavior is a test of its validity as well as of its efficiency. Within a democracy the "will of the people" is, among other things, represented by the legal system: courts with their judges and lawyers engaging in a formal procedure which ends eventually in the hands of juries. Such a process cannot be dictated to permanently by idealists or intellectuals any more than it can by ministers or priests. It knows no master except the moral social evaluations of the day made in terms of accepted customs and traditions.

The United States has moved in the last few decades from an open democracy in which the principle of least government was the dominant consideration to one in which equal protection is extended in the economic sphere. From this addition the welfare state follows, and that is the direction in which the United States was tending in the second half of the twentieth century, a welfare state in which the guarantee of an economic minimum to all citizens was interpreted as giving the government through its various agencies the right to interfere in those transactions by citizens which affect them individually and even to legislate concerning them. Surely the actions taken or attempted by the Food and Drug Administration in the instances of the alleged cancer cure, Laetrile, and the artificial sweetner, saccharin, are of this nature.

What no one noticed sufficiently is that the shift from open democracy toward a welfare state meant an enormous change in morality. The two systems do not have the same moral code, however much the one may have come out of the other in an orderly transition. The welfare state represents a much tighter, more complete, organization, and this at a time in the nation's history when the immigration laws were the most relaxed and illegal entry the most active.

Despite the tentative steps which were taken in the direction of the welfare state, the dogma upon which the American democracy rests is in serious opposition to those the communists profess. It is a very long logical distance from Locke and Montesquieu to Marx and Engels, and one which could not be easily overcome. Those who have accepted the latter had no experience of living under the laws formulated in accordance with the former. Nothing is so hateful to men as a belief they do not share. We saw in chapter V that the legal system of a nation is installed to defend a particular set of beliefs as incorporating the morality standing behind that system (and behind that the theory of reality upon which it rests). The true enemy of the unity of mankind consists in differences in the character of the absolute truths which various groups of people accept. There is evidently always a tendency to be convinced that one's truth is the same as The Truth, and that in fact there can be no other. And men eagerly persecute and even destroy those who do not readily agree.

The principle which could be utilized to save the situation, which since the advent of the atomic bomb has become crucial for all, by eradicating the deep differences in beliefs between peoples is the distinction between positive law and natural law. The law of any particular society is always positive law, and it is not absolute because it cannot be equated with natural law and is never more than an approximation of it. Natural law and justice belong together and stand as ideals which cannot be completely attained. Such a conception must be accepted if we are not all to perish.

More and more, the boundaries between peoples are being broken down. Technologically improved transportation and communication have made this increasingly evident. But then events run straight into the fact that the democratic principle is not universal. Not all nations observe the same morality. An individual who goes to court to obtain justice thinks that his is a simple case of seeking to right a wrong. He does not know of the extensive involvement in which his action issues or of the social and political organization with which directly or indirectly it is connected. Certainly he does not recognize that the court to which he appeals is part of a legal system that is nation-wide, and that the nation in its turn has international relations and commitments which may be tangentially affected.

In terms of the Helsinki Accords of 1975, President Carter representing our government in 1977 protested the violation of individual rights by the Soviet Union. The East Germans in a feeble effort to reply sent photographers to a trial in Mississippi which the Russians thought they might use as counter-evidence that the abrogation of civil rights was not a monopoly of the Soviet Union. Evidently they did not recognize what they were admitting; but the fact is that, like it or not, and neither side likes it, all are involved with all.

This is a shocking discovery to every partisan, and is common to every field in which men elevate their own culture by regarding it as an ideal imbedded in the nature of things when it was only a local set of rules. John Austin was only applying Bentham's utilitarian principle but he thought he was creating a science of positive law that was based on a set of universal principles. It is not necessary to go as far as Richard Hooker did when in an effort to hold fast he proclaimed that

Of Law there can be no less acknowledged, than that her seat is the bosom of God, her voice the harmony of the world: all things in heaven and earth do her homage.[3]

in order to remind ourselves that the laws are no exception when the winds of change sweep up a hurricane which leave little standing.

If we look for a constant we may find one, however, not in law but in the moral issue which may center on the control and consequent use of power. The forms of power may change; it may lie at one time in the ownership of land, at another in the control of industry. This was the story of the later Middle Ages in England, in the first case, and in our own scientific-industrial democracy, in the second. Or it may lie in political advantage, as indeed it does in the Soviet Union and Communist China. When the state is the exclusive owner of all property, of all wealth, those who succeed in obtaining the most out of the use of it will be those who control the state.

Here perhaps we have the essence of politics: who has power over property? In our own day for instance morality has traditionally furnished many curbs on the abuses of wealth by recognizing the existence of other forms of power: artistic and scientific contributions to the culture for instance; but as that morality breaks down, wealth emerges more and more as the single criterion of prestige. We have seen enough how all criteria can become eroded except the single one of the possession of wealth. For we have given up everything else for it: good name, character, honesty, and integrity, and we pursue it without qualification. It is this way now regardless of the political form, whether western democracy or Soviet Russian imperialism. The moral decay lies deeper than the agreement as to who shall own what or how the government shall operate. A good illustration of a common failing is the current prevalence of crime at all levels and in all the principal countries.

The law exists to regulate whatever system of property has been chosen by a particular society. Morality is another matter and often stands aside from the particular situation. Behind it, and even more remote, perhaps, there is the question of ethics. The morality as represented by the legal system of a particular state may or may not be able to justify itself as ethical. That does not concern the law directly but does concern it indirectly through the demands of justice. And ultimately, if not immediately, justice is involved and has its own requirements.

---

3 *Ecclesiastical Polity*, Bk. I, § 16 8.

2. Rights and Duties

The whole involvement of morality is complex, and this is particularly true of its relations with legality. These will have to be broken down into their component parts. I propose to do this now, and afterwards to reach some conclusions. The picture which finally emerges will of necessity bring us back to the moral issues confronting a legal system.

Elsewhere I have tried to show that there are four grades of obligation. These were set forth as moral integrative levels.[4] They are individual morality, social morality, the morality of the human species, and the morality of the cosmos. Perhaps the distinctions can be made clearer by presenting them in a chart. The criterion in each case will be what the individual can expect in the way of rights, and what he owes in the way of duties. In addition to rights and duties there are also restrictions, but for the sake of brevity I will postpone the discussion of these until the next section.

		rights	*duties*
(A)	individual	from himself	to himself and family
(B)	social	from his society	to his society
	(moral		
	(legal		
(C)	species	from his species	to his species
	(human		
(D)	cosmic	from the cosmos	to the cosmos
	(natural		

Legal rights may be defined as those actions which are permitted by the state to individual, duties are those actions which are required by the state of him. A right is an interest by rules of the state. A duty is an obligation imposed on an individual by the state to perform a certain act, when the opposite would be a wrong for which penalties could be imposed. The individual stands in a number of moral relationships most though not all of which are limited to his society. But what we can say about the others will be helpful by way of contrast.

---

4 *Moral Strategy* (The Hague 1967, Martinus Nijhoff), p. 19 *et. seq.*

(A) *Individual Rights and Duties.* The difficulty with this conception is that the individual as such is not a valid isolate. If we begin at the beginning of human life, it is clear that no infant *per se* comes with rights or duties of any kind, only with a strong animal impulse to continue living and growing, though it is true that the state "endows" legal rights on an infant the day it is born, and some would argue now, the moment it is conceived. The rest is in the hands of parents or care-takers, in a world of others. Where in the infant organism would it be possible to locate any of the human rights? We will see that it is more accurate to think in social terms.

With the fully developed adult, individual rights take an internal turn. The adult individual has the right to strive for the development of his full potentialities; he has the duty to himself to do so. But since both immediately take him into relation with his fellows, these rights and duties cease to be exclusively individual. Ordinarily it is assumed that a man has a duty to himself to follow what his conscience dictates. The only trouble with this theory is that the contents of the conscience splits into what I have called the public retention schemata, the fundamental moral beliefs the individual holds in common with other citizens in the same state or other members of the same religion — both social by the way; and the private retention schema or those fundamental moral beliefs he holds by himself which differ from the public beliefs. The first kind would not make any problems, the second would.

Ronald Dworkin has argued recently that "a man has duties other than his duties to the State. A man must honor his duties to his God and to his conscience, and if these conflict with his duties to the State, then he is entitled, in the end, to do what he judges to be right".[5] If Dworkin means, as he seems to, that individual rights are absolute, and that therefore the individual must obey the law only when it does not violate his conscience, then no State would be possible, no orderly government could be conducted, and only anarchy would prevail.

5 "Taking Rights Seriously" in A.W.B. Simpson, *Oxford Essays in Jurisprudence* (Second Series), (Oxford 1973, Clarendon Press), ch. VIII, p. 205.

On the question of civil disobedience, Dworkin insists that there are only two groups, which he calls conservatives and liberals, and that, while they think themselves divided, they actually agree. Two errors here: there are four groups to reckon with, for to the right of the conservatives are the fascist reactionary types, and to the left of the liberals are the communist-inclined radicals. Each of them also holds a position with respect to the issue under discussion. *They* might agree, for both would be uncompromising in their condemnation of civil dis-obedience because both would like to see democracy eradicated in favor of some kind of dictatorship.

Of course "taking rights seriously" most emphatically does not mean taking them absolutely. Rights are always balanced by duties, and Dworkin does not mention duties. There is no doubt that there are occasions when the individual's duty to himself and his duty to the State conflict. What a good citizen of democracy follows in such a case is not his conscience but the path of due process: when he does not agree with the rightness of the law, he does not break it but follows it while undertaking to work through established legal channels to get the law changed. The Constitution provides for that. The whole point of Plato's *Apology* was that Socrates refused to disobey a legal judgment he thought wrong even though it involved the sacrifice of his life. I notice parenthetically that Dworkin confines his discussion to the situation in the United States. Any Russian who followed Dworkin's advice would find himself declared legally insane and treated with mind-destroying drugs in a mental hospital.

(B) *Social Rights and Duties*. What are ordinarily regarded as rights are those brought into existence by the fact that the individual is a member of a society: rights as such are social, and so are duties. The connection here is a moral one: the individual shares the morality which prevails in his society. This is what I have called earlier in this chapter the "implicit dominant morality", and it resides in the settled beliefs, and the customary standards of a particular community, always supported of course by "public opinion". Individual rights, then, are a gift of society; perhaps I should say of certain types of society. Western democracies are forms of societies which provide a maximum number of individual rights, in contrast with many other forms which do not.

The main subdivision of social rights is not moral but legal, and it is this one that will concern us the most. Legal rights are those rights which are reserved to the individual by the state. Legal duties are what is expected of the individual by the state. Strictly speaking a legal right is one recognized by a legal sytem, a moral right as such has no legal standing except as is accorded to it in a court of equity. Legal rights are better named civil rights; together they constitute an individual's relations with the state in which he holds citizenship. The greater the number of values recognized in the state the greater the number of rights it secures to the individual. Hence the more advanced the state the greater the number of dimensions it provides in individual lives. Dicey's famous definition of the rule of law with its three parts: the supremacy of law over arbitrary power, absolute equality before the law, and the constitution as the consequence rather than the source of individual rights, defines the rule of law in western democracies.[6]

(C) *Species Rights and Duties.* Species rights are what the individual can expect from all the members of his species, species duties are what he owes to them. Austin drew a distinction between positive law and ideal law.[7] The former is a matter for the moral code of a particular society, the latter a matter of ethics for all of mankind. Positive law is law within the confines of a legal system, ideal law the morality of the human species. At our present stage of evolutionary development, we are bound within the limits of a positive social morality but we are able to look out at the broader reaches of a morality which is humanity-wide, an ideal morality for the whole of the human species. This topic is usually treated under the heading of ethics. "Morality is the custom of one's country", Samuel Butler observed, and added "Cannibalism is moral in a cannibal country".[8] Yet everyone likes to remember that there is an ideal morality possible for all mankind even if it is only in the blueprint stage. For the law of the species has not yet been enacted into statutes. Ideal law, the law of the human species, has neither legal sanctions nor for that matter any legal standing. It is not to be construed as "law" in the full sense of the term, for it was never enacted.

What is currently being debated under the rubric of "human rights" is the one being considered here. What individuals owe to each other and what they may reasonably expect of each other regardless of group differences, differences of race or nationality or any other social, legal, or political affiliations of any kind, are what may be called human rights.

It often happens that states may seem to be taking these rights on, as when the Declaration of Independence talks about "life, liberty, and the pursuit of happiness", or when in the Constitution of the United States Amendment V tells us that "no person...shall be deprived of life, liberty, or property, without due process of law" but there are not the elements of a social morality, only of a legal one. The ideal of law is by itself too general to be used as a standard to measure the success of positive law. How for instance could "liberty" be interpreted? What actions may the individual legitimately engage in when he is in pursuit of happiness?

The individual may have been born with a certain potential but he

6 Albert Venn Dicey, *Law of the Constitution*, 9th ed. (ed. Wade), p. 202.
7 John Austin, *Lectures on Jurisprudence*, vol. I, p. 176.
8 *Notebooks*, p. 210.

cannot hope to develop it alone. In general it may be fair to ask of a state that it provide all human rights but there is no way to compel it to do so. There is in other words a gap between recognizing what human rights are and knowing how to secure them. The identification of human rights are and knowing how to secure them. The identification of human rights may vary from state to state, depending upon the form of the state. In Marxist states the interests of the state come before those of the individual, so that there are not preeminent human rights. Thus by themselves human rights remain as moral rights, rights of the human species, but empty of actualization.

(D) *Cosmic Rights and Duties*. These are rarely and imperfectly understood, but consist in the natural rights and duties of the human individual in consideration of all of his powers and of his being as a thing in the universe. His rights are what the universe owes to him, and his duties are what he owes to the universe. Let us consider them in that order.

Our ideas of natural rights come to us from Englishmen of the seventeenth and eighteenth centuries. They held to the beliefs that there are natural rights the state cannot remove. Rights, they thought, are inborn, not acquired, and there are no restrictions. One authority even said, "I define liberty as being the permission or power to do what one pleases without any external restraint".[9] Pound has pointed out that "they held even the criminal law as an infringement of natural rights, which were fundamental and universal qualities of human beings".[10]

What rights would an individual have to possess, what freedoms would he require, in order to make it possible for him to reduce all of his needs? This is the fundamental question of cosmic morality, certainly, and it involves the issue of natural rights so far as they concern the individual. Elsewhere I have tried to show that to reduce all of his needs an individual would have to control all of the universe.[11] For it is characteristic of him that his drives to reduce his needs do not stop when those needs are reduced. This is the case with the primary needs for nearby material benefits: for food, sex, etc. But he has other needs, the needs for unlimited aggression and for the kind of absolute security which would involve him ultimately in identification with the whole of

9   James C. Carter, *Law: Its Origin, Growth and Function* (1907) p. 133.
10 Roscoe Pound, "The Future of the Criminal Law", 21 Col. L. Rev. 1 (1921).
11 *Mankind Behaving* (Springfield, Ill. 1963, Charles C. Thomas); *Understanding Human Nature* (New York 1978, Horizon Press).

the universe or its cause. The drives of individuals, in other words, are unlimited and must lead to disaster if unchecked.

Social life, then, is possible only upon his surrender of the most ferocious and violent of his natural rights. The perfect social background for the unlimited pursuit of individual needs can only be provided by political anarchy. However attractive such a prospect may seem to those with a deep-seated resentment of the infringement of the state on the freedom of the individual, if anarchy were to be established it is the individual himself who would lose. For under the circumstances of Hobbes' "war of all against all" no needs would be reduced and individuals would all perish in a welter of unlimited aggression.

3. The Outcome in Social Morality

We have noted that the approach of the individual to his environment lies through aggression intended to effect organ-specific need-reduction, and this can in no way be altered. To reduce all of his needs the individual must be a member of a society; and for each member of the society to behave in the same way, his liberties must be curbed to the extent to which by exercising them he would threaten the liberty of others. Thus there come about types of aggressive behavior which are permitted by law ('right') and other types which are prohibited. In addition the law recognizes still other types of activity which are required and these are called 'duties'.

Rights, restrictions, and duties must be incorporated into a legal system in order to preserve the community and hold conflicts to a miniimum. All exist there as contracts between the state and its citizens and between citizens as provided by the state. All become effective in the application of laws to particular situations. The custodian of the legal system and its proprietor is the state. Neither rights, restrictions nor duties count unless the state stands ready to enforce them.

The systematic nature of rights, restrictions and duties is shown by the fact that they are society-wide. For instance if a citizen buys a house, henceforth he has a right to use it, but he may not burn it down in reckless disregard of his neighbors, and he must pay taxes on it. The transference of ownership is a contract which extends to the entire state, for everyone else in the state is prohibited from using it without his permission. In this sense every legal arrangement, such as a deed of private ownership, extends to the limits of the state and none are exclusively personal, for everyone is involved in the deed.

The state has two aims: to preserve to individuals the maximum amount of freedom of action, and to preserve itself in order that it may perform that service. To these ends it makes laws governing both the behavior of individuals and its own behavior. Laws governing the behavior of individuals are aimed at formalizing the three types of behavior: permitted, prohibited and obligatory actions. Thus in our society every citizen has the right to vote, none may own slaves, all must pay taxes. Rights, restrictions and duties are all expressed in the form of laws, which must be examined to disclose their types.

Rights are legitimate interests with their accompanying powers either preserved to a legal person or produced by the state; inviolability of reputation in the former instance, say, and the making of a will and the naming of an executor to sustain a succession, in the latter. A great variety of legal rights exist and are sustained by the state.

Restrictions are forbidden actions brought into existence by the state, as for example the one defined by the Eighteenth Amendment to the Constitution of the United States until it was repealed by the Twenty-First Amendment. The sale and use of heroin is prohibited to citizens of the United States.

Duties are actions required by the state of everyone, such as reporting crimes, stopping at red lights in automobile traffic, and disposing of the bodies of the dead.

All laws operate within the morality which is established formally or informally within a society. The limits of such a morality do not necessarily have to be spelled out to render it effective. The feeling of what is appropriate or inappropriate, acceptable or unacceptable, lies deep within most citizens, and aids the conformity to law from that coign of vantage. It is the force of felt approval or disapproval which makes of the rights, restrictions and duties as homogeneous a system as it roughly is, despite the many exceptions which no doubt exist and the changing circumstances which compel it to slow or sudden changes.

CHAPTER X

HUMAN NEEDS, MORALITY AND THE LAW

The difficulties arising in our democratic society when fundamental human needs encounter restrictive legislation cannot be explained simply. A prior comprehension of theory, including a study of the elements and forces involved, is necessary. Human practices in most matters follow from an appeal to principles which is modified by the exigencies of existing conditions. The usual situation is that the principles are inadequate, the practices incomplete, and the conditions largely unknown. It is difficult to ascertain exactly what the source of the trouble is. Success in this undertaking is rare, but there are reasons: the investigator is himself too involved, he is too close to the scene of action: then too the situation itself is highly intricate, for the most concrete is as it happens also the most complex. In this chapter therefore, I have sought an understanding rather than a solution. A problem adequately analyzed often amounts to a problem partly solved. But can it be wholly solved? There may be inherent limitations in any social context which renders its solution difficult and perhaps impossible.

I propose in this chapter to look at human needs as they encounter morality and the law, and I will draw my illustration chiefly from the sexual need because of its prevalence, power, and the social difficulties that are often involved. A human need, such as sex, is activated when the individual is confronted inadvertently or deliberately with a tropistic goal object, but he may in a democratic society such as our own be conditioned by morality in subjective terms as the sense of wrong (the conscience) or in objective terms as established norms of conduct (customs or law). Thus we have to account for the same phenomenon at three levels of analysis: the individual with his organic needs and his moral beliefs, the actual moral practices of his society, and the morality as legally codified and established, with penalties for infractions. Can these elements be rendered consistent? It will be our task to ascertain the prospects of personal and social harmony.

This is a highly simplified description. But we should be prepared to deal with it more than once. First let us look at the situation as it in actual practice. Secondly, let us observe the same situation as it ought to be according to established aims and ambitions. Thirdly, I will try to suggest strategies for getting from what-is to what-ought-to-be.

It should be noted that systems of preferences conceived as ideals bring with them their own immense problems. The very question of ideals, their composition and selection, is a separate speculative field. The ideal individual, the ideal society, the ideal morality, all presuppose established theories of ethics and politics, and behind these the metaphysics and epistemology with which they are consistent. The choice of a suitable philosophy is a complex question, involving the possible existence of meta-philosophies. But even if we do not wish to push the issue so far back, we have still the practical question of which ideal of individual behavior, social morality, or codified law, should have been chosen.

Ordinarily, everyone is more or less familiar with accepted preferences of conduct but less familiar with actual practices, and even less still with the techniques of strategy. For it is difficult enough to construct blueprints for desired conduct, yet few ever understand what is going on, and almost nobody has any idea that the social striving for the preferable from the actual can be done only in terms of plans, foresight and calculation. If we do not understand the complexity involved in designing the proper procedure or the conflicts within the forces with which we are dealing, how can we hope to control them or direct them sufficiently?

1. The Situation in Actual Practice

There is in the structure of the human individual a hierarchy of basic tissue needs and in his behavior a chronological order of drive activation and drive reduction. The equilibrium of the body depends on the structure and the harmony of operation of the body depends on the behavior. But there remains a complication. The hierarchy of needs is ordinarily determined by importunateness, yet there is coordinated with it another hierarchy constructed in terms of importance. One necessarily runs counter to the other. The needs in order of importunateness are: water, food, sex, knowledge, activity, ultimate survival. The order of importance reverses this: ultimate survival, activity, knowledge, sex, food, water. Thus one drive may interfere with the reduction of another and when the two orders shift the result can be a disturbance which is fatal both to the equilibrium of the organism and to its harmony of operation. For example, activity can interfere with sex, as when men go off to war; but sex can interfere with knowledge-seeking, as when married students are compelled to end their formal education in order to support a rapidly-growing family.

Among the individual's needs are to be counted the generic need for aggression and the need for novelty. The sexual drive is a species of the generic drive of aggression, defined as the drive to dominate the environment. Men need conquest and variety in their sexual relations. The sexual need in the average vigorous male is a continuing one, quickly renewing itself after reduction, stimulated by novelty and challenge. He needs to feel a struggle in his efforts to dominate the environment. Judged by his behavior, man is among the most active sexually of all animals. He needs readiness of access. Except for menstruation and childbearing the human female remains receptive more or less uninterruptedly from menarche to menopause and even after. But aggression is the need to be active in its most exaggerated form, and may take destructive as well as constructive form.

Variety is necessary for the alertness of the animal. Without some degree of novelty there is no consciousness. Monotony of input leads to unconsciousness, as every night driver knows who has fallen asleep at the wheel when the road lay straight ahead of him for miles. Men are naturally aggressive and wish through struggle to dominate the environment; they are inherently sadistic (though not pathologically so), just as women are inherently masochistic. Thus we see that to reduce the sexual need over any protracted period, some goal-object offering both resistance and renewal is required. There is a sense at least in which every woman who ever voluntarily went to bed with a man reduced his sexual needs, but if she did not resist, frustrated his need for aggression, and if she was the same woman, frustrated his need for novelty.

Can society and its morality and laws as presently constructed provide for these needs? The situation is actually more complex than any simply answer might indicate. Let us look at it a little more closely.

The individual endeavors to reduce his basic tissue needs by appropriate behavior. Also he has a set of beliefs. These can be divided into a subject which he holds in common with the other members of his society (the public retention schema), and a subset which are his own personal convictions (the private retention schema). These may overlap but they are never identical because the private retention schema arises as a result of unique individual experience. Conscience is the individual monitor which guards against infractions of the imperatives issued by the schemata. Not only does the individual hold before himself the ideal of moral conduct but also he feels it as desirable and understands it as preferable.

Belief carries with it a tendency to action. What he thinks is also what he feels ought to be done. Thus there are individual imperatives contained within the private retention schema, and social imperatives contained within the public retention schema. These do not always agree and thus can be a source of considerable conflict. Then, too, the power drives cut across the impulses to action proceeding from the schemata. What we privately believe we should do, what we publicly believe is expected of us, and what we want to do in order to reduce our organic needs, these are usually different things. Thus there are varieties of interference: social interference with individual and legal arrangements, legal sanctions against individual and social performances, and even individual and social revolts against law and order. Any of these conventions may coincide, but it is a rare day when they do. Which is only another way of saying that there are few occasions entirely lacking in conflict.

The power drives, specifically those of the generic drive of aggression and the sex drive, are not entirely amenable to cortical control. It does not follow that because society holds a man ought not to covet his neighbor's wife that he does not do so. The will is often alone in following the moral code, where it follows at all, for the human animal is more apt to respond to instincts than to conscience. Where the conscience seems strong enough to prevail, its success is often partly due to particular weaknesses in the individual's instinctive needs. Obviously, there is as much individual variation in sexual needs as there is in intelligence, length of femur, or astigmatism. Differences in individual needs and behavior are the natural results of the interactions between the uniqueness of the genotype and the diversity of the environment. It is the task of society legitimately to provide for these differences.

All of the education and training of the individual from the time of his birth has been intended to prepare him to receive as his own the external inheritance of material culture: the instruments and the language, and the skills stored and transmitted in both from the gains made in the past. And he is expected to incorporate his external inheritance as that part of himself from which he will thenceforth think, feel and act. And so he is as an individual an integral part of his culture. Whatever the public morality may be, for instance, it is in a certain sense his private morality. Culture with its ideals and values penetrated deeply into the individual, so that while he may recognize abstractly the degree of his dependence on it, this does not lessen the dependence. It is simply not possible within the physical confines of one culture to feel how it might have been to come of age in another, so deeply into the nature of the individual organism does the influence of his own culture penetrate.

So much for the individual; now let us turn to look at society. The actual social situation is complex; it is replete with contradictions and conflicts and far more difficult to see as an integrated affair. The purposes of society are twofold: those which arise as society faces inward toward the individuals who compose it, and those which arise as the society faces toward the species. We will discuss for the moment only the first. The inward purpose of society is also its democratic purpose, which is to provide for the maximum of need reductions for the individual consistent with the needs of other individuals in the society.

Actually, society facing inward has two systems of morality: the overt system of morality which it openly professes, and the covert system which it secretly and tacitly allows without penalty. The covert system is identical with the system practiced by many though not by all individuals.

What are the actual practices of society? First, it has established a morality which it considers ideal, usually as sanctioned by religious revelations. The adherence to this morality it considers imperative, and all of its moral suasion is in this direction. It says to the individual members in every case, you ought to do what we in this society have agreed is right and good.

That is part of the morality of the society. But there is another part, and this consists in the actual practices. These are only approximately in conformity with the established morality. Thus with respect to sexual practices, the established morality calls for monogamy. But monogamy is transgressed in two ways.

In the first way, a legitimate outlet has been provided by offering the possibilities of divorce and remarriage. The man or woman who takes advantage of this recourse too often incurs some derogation, but it is slight. Thus even what is required is somewhat relaxed. It could be better described as serial monogamy than as strict monogamy. Strict monogamy means one wife for every man and one husband for every woman. Serial monogamy means that, too – at any given time. It is now possible to have many wives or husbands, even though only one at a time.

In the second way, monogamy is transgressed surreptitiously by the practice of extra-martial relations. Everyone knows how wide-spread these are, though for obvious reasons statistics are difficult to come by. Fidelity certainly exists, but it is rarer than one might suppose. From the public point of view of a socially established morality, these practices are immoral, but the true immorality consists in getting caught. In our puritanical society, the individual who precedes with caution need have no fears of social opprobrium. It is not a matter of common knowledge but of airing. A community might know that a certain wife is unfaithful, and might think little of it beyond a slight delicious tingling of secret gossip. But if the husband finds out and sues his wife in court for divorce, that is another matter.

Women stand to gain more from monogamous society than men. What every man wants is an uninterrupted continuity of availability of sex relationships. In a monogamous arrangement this is impossible, due to menstruation and child-bearing. Women, on the other hand, need, in addition to sex, economic support for themselves and their children, which in monogamy is provided.

The masculine needs, then, are incompatible with monogamy altogether. The adjustments necessary to establish the system are required by the morality. Therefore deviations from the system are exigent. The law seeks to administer and enforce the morality by punishing deviations from it. But since these are needful, the game becomes one of a double morality: outward observance combined with secretly-conducted infractions.

I have talked about the actual individual and the social situation with respect to morality; now let us consider the law. The law is established to lend teeth to the generally accepted morality. The laws respecting morality are of course concerned primarily with its transgression. With certain exceptions, they are not laws commanding one to do something, but rather laws prohibiting one from doing something. Under American laws a man does not have to get married, but once married he does have to get a divorce before getting married again. And he is legally permitted to repeat both procedures any number of times. But now let us consider the two basic needs which we have found to exist in connection with sex, the needs for novelty and aggression. According to the laws, practices involving both novelty and aggression are forbidden. As for novelty, almost every state in the Union has laws against adultery and fornication as well as against bigamy and polygamy. As for aggression, the laws against seduction and rape are equally prevalent.

But what exactly is the morality which is guarded by the law? It is the one which was prevalent when the laws were written and enacted.

All statutes, like individual behavior, social customs and established moralities, are culturally conditioned. What is required in one culture is only too often forbidden in another. Suicide in Japan is an honor to the family, while in this country it is a dishonor. But it is not necessary to go so far afield for an example. In West Germany lesbianism is not forbidden, but in Minnesota, where the practice is oddly enough included under sodomy, it is punishable by twenty years in prison. Moreover, there is nothing that does not change in time. The morality moves on, it suffers revisions and alterations, following movements in customs, social and physical conditions, the incursion of new knowledge, or even slight shifts in convictions and beliefs.

Thus there is only a rough correlation at any given period between the law which purports to protect and guard the socially-established morality and the morality it is intended to protect and guard. We run counter many times to laws which have not been enforced, laws which no longer apply, or infractions of situations for which there is no legal provision. The attempt to keep the law abreast of the changes in morality is often made, but it is a difficult endeavor at best, and never more than partly successful.

The existence of laws rather than their use in the courts is a statistical measure of their violation, in the broad ethical sense intended here. The frequency of the enactment of laws is proportional to the expected and anticipated infractions. Customs which do not violate individual liberties or which are not usually violated are also not the subject of legislation. Thus a survey of the laws of a society would provide some kind of index of the behavior of its members. Laws which are dead letters are laws which society has abandoned not because of a change in its beliefs but only because of a change in its practices. How often does it happen that a law is invoked in a particular case if it is a law not habitually invoked?

The law recognizes morality but does not keep pace with it. The Kinsey report for all its faults is useful in reminding us of instances of state laws which are no longer enforced — and indeed no longer enforceable — because they were written during a period when the established sexual morality was far more stringent that it is now. Certain states make certain practices which are currently prevalent punishable, such as homosexuality or marital infidelity. The inherently conservative nature of the legislative process protects society against fashionable abuses which might result from enacting into law waves of sentiment or prejudice which sweep across society only to pass on and be forgotten. But the same conservatism assumes too much in this direction and does not provide sufficiently for change.

In connection with the discussion of the law as it exists, a word should be said about law-enforcement officers. The tragedy of America is its politicians, not all of them by any means, but too many, especially at state and local levels. The evils are not to be found in the political system itself but in those who use political offices for their personal advantage. Honesty is often neither fashionable nor expected. The system has for this reason little chance of functioning well. How many public officials today could stand the airing of their income tax returns, for instance? It would not be easy to estimate the unconscious and unintended but steady pressure on individual and social morality which the existence of corrupt administration exerts. As it affects all morality, so it must affect the sexual as well.

2. The Situation as It Ought-To-Be

The unacknowledged and unrecognized competition between ideals of conduct is a fierce one. Whose version of the ideal is to be accepted as the ideal, and why? Consider for instance the many alternative utopias which have been proposed; they are stiff and static plans, and would freeze society into some final mold of perfection; each seems to be pitifully relative to the date and place of its composition. No one has yet suggested an evolutionary utopia which would provide for the changes which are bound to occur in customs and institutions, in individual and social morality, and in the laws. The simple assumption has always been made that we know more about what ought to be than we do know.

Let us look abstractly at yet one more ideal as it concerns individual and social sexual morality and the law, having in mind that now thanks to modern biology and psychology we are obliged to begin with the more fundamental issues. The ideal of the individual is one which includes a perfectly coordinated set of basic organic needs, arranged in such a fashion taht they could take their proper turn at drive-activation and reduction. Where the needs were weak the degree of integration would drop down to make the proper allowances. The drives would not take precedence through force; they would be given it by other needs voluntarily rendered recessive so that the more urgent could also be the more dominant. Thus where necessary importunateness would give way temporarily to importance. Novelty would lead agression into less destructive channels.

One factor which must always be considered in any account of the ideal is the beliefs of the individual. At the deepest level of acceptance must be found an acquiescence in the arrangement decided upon in terms of what is considered appropriate to the natural society. Ideally speaking, there must be a one-to-one correspondence between the beliefs and the practices. Private retention schemata would as a result not conflict with but instead reinforce the public retention schema. Thus there would be no conflicts or interferences to render the drives self-defeating or to allow the environment to frustrate them as it were, needlessly.

Properly understood, there can be no conflict between individual needs and allowable social limits. Exact fitting requires a delicate adjustment of understanding of just what is involved in each instance, a perfect sense of obligation to the particular situation. Every fact is at once an arena for action and a set of limitations on action. The demands of the individual have to be recognized as preferential and those of society as imperative. Ideally, all kinds of sexual intercourse are permitted between consenting adults provided they do not violate agreements to which they have subscribed, and these acts should be as much in conformity with closed covenants privately arranged as with public covenants openly recorded.

The social ideal assumed in our version of democracy with respect to morality is not far to seek. The individual has a set of needs which left to his own devices he could hardly hope to reduce. In cooperation with his fellows, however, there is the possibility of need reduction for all. The cooperation must be by common consent and with the full approval of the majority, the morality established in accordance with the beliefs of the individuals respecting what is good and right. Individuals can petition for changes provided they do so through well-established channels (the "path of due process"), but in the meanwhile their practices must conform to those of the majority. If not, there are courts to decide and enforcement agencies to punish. The laws established by the society correspond exactly with the morality which that society accepts. The conscience serves to keep the individual in check so that he does not commit infractions of the morality and so run afoul of the law.

Both the individual conscience and the social norm of morality are assumed to be identical with those of the ideal society. The ideal of what-ought-to-be as conceived in democratic terms is identical with the ideal of what-ought-to-be as held by individual belief. Democracy is part of the nature of things as it concerns social organization. It is the natural society when achieved. Every society, like every individual, identifies its conception of what is ideal with the ideal, its aims and ambitions with perfection. Recognizing that its actual practices fall somewhat short of the ideal, it still insists that the ideal itself does not fall short, has no limitations and is not destined to be superceded.

The ideal I have been talking about is not the ideal that societies hold before themselves as desirable of attainment, but the ideal as it would be were everyone acquainted with the facts and capable of dealing with them. Every human society must adjust itself to the constraints of its own composition and to the possibilities of its environment. As to its own composition, there are periods of dynamism and periods of quiescence: the rhythm must be found and provided for. As to the possibilities of its environment, this sets allowable limits to the conduct of the society.

I revert to a suggestion made early in the introduction to this topic concerning the speculative field of preferences. What ought we to want for society?

In order to answer this question, it might be necessary to extend our consideration outside of society itself, to humanity as a whole, and so to the future as well as the present.

In the perfect society of the future, the individual will have complete liberty. He will use it to conform to the demands of society, obeying them before they ask it because that is what he will want to do. Thus his freedom is safeguarded and his dignity assured. The conscience he recognizes will not differ from the morality as socially-established, and the morality as socially-established will not differ from actual social practices. There will be no discrepancy between moral pretensions and moral practices. There will be no aberrant individual behavior to invoke the operation of the law with its penalties.

The ideal requires, then, that morality be identical with nothing less than the human level of nature. Natural morality is the perfect fitting of functional and ecological morality. The situation can be narrowed somewhat further. The morality of a society is the least common denominator of behavior under the channels established for reducing the basic needs given the local economic conditions and adopted political system.

The ideal is of course the natural society. And the natural society is determined both by the given stage of development of the human individuals composing it and by the peculiar type of physical environment in which they find themselves living. These two are the givens, and they are crucial. Neanderthal man would not have found a modern type of morality any more workable than Pithecanthropus before him, or the still earlier Australopithecus. The human being of the future might equally find it inadequate. Then again, what might be suitable in the frozen north might not be appropriate in a tropical zone. A society with a superfluity of women, such as existed in Berlin immediately after World War II, could not operate upon the same principles as another society in which there is a man for every woman.

By the natural society, then, is meant that social arrangement which is most suitable to a given set of individuals in their given environment. For this there are no known rules other than appropriateness. It is easier to predict what will not work under certain conditions than what will. In the ideal society, there would be a wide variation in individual aptitudes and preferences, and this variation would be required, expected and provided. Sexually, neuters are needed, and so are sexual athletes. There is a place for and hence considerable tolerance of the individual whose sexual needs are non-existent. There ought to be a similar place for and hence an equal tolerance of both the satyriac and the nymphomaniac. The world would be the poorer had Casanova and Madame de Staël not graced it. The conception of uniformity in sexual needs which monogamy presupposes does not fit the facts of biology which allow for considerable variation from individual to individual.

If individual variations exist within a society, it is not less true that similar variations exist in the societies themselves. Societies, like the individuals they contain, are dynamic affairs and highly susceptible to development and change. Uniformity of behavior is an ideal only in a static society, and a static society is not a human society. The cockroaches and horseshoe crabs do not develop, they have remained approximately the same for a million years. But man does develop and he has not remained the same; his changes over the same period are astounding. In all probability they will continue to show a similar rate of change in the future.

Parts are the agents of wholes. Just as the organs function as agents for the organism, thus enabling it to specialize in particular contexts, so individuals are the agents of society provided their specialization is adequate for providing new contexts. Mutations are not entirely composed of deficiencies. Exceptionally gifted or trained individuals form the leading edge of society, and enable it to move forward into new evolutionary developments.

Changes in individuals at the genetic level, are minute, and for the purposes of this discussion can be neglected. But at the level of society the situation is somewhat different. As we have noted earlier, society faces outward as well as inward, outward toward the species as well as inward toward the individual. In so far as it faces outward, evolution is an important factor which cannot safely be neglected in our considerations. The second purpose of society is an outward one. It is to enable the human species to surpass itself so that the next evolutionary development can be more quickly brought about. The human species is continually subjected to mutations. The appearance of stability is genuine but deceiving: nothing remains the same. Since all social planning for moral improvement must be in terms of long-range goals, it must reckon with the fact of incessant and continual change. Neither human individuals who change rapidly nor societies which change either slowly or cataclysmically have included in their plans the fact of change.

So much for the ideal society. Now let us glance quickly in the direction of the ideal law.

For social purposes at least, the individual is designed to live in harmony with his society, and the law is designed to see that he does. Society in this case is just as much more than the sum of individuals as is compatible with insuring that the liberty of no one individual shall interfere with the liberty of others. When liberty becomes license, the individual has exceeded the individual bounds which have been set by the society; he violates the law.

The ideal of law in a society, given the proper social structure and the proper individuals as members of it, is that of a body of codified instructions which when put in operation are permissive rather than restrictive. Not prohibitions with penalties, which forbid certain actions and prescribe punishment for infractions, but rules for regulation which enhance liberties. Not a law against the consumption of alcoholic beverages, which accomplishes little positive, for instance; but a system of traffic signals which make possible an acceleration of transportation, with a minimum of negative effect.

In sexual matters that marriage arrangement should prevail which is consistent with the proportions of population. For instance, in a society consisting of a predominance of females, polygamy would be the custom and the law. Whatever the laws ordaining marriage and fidelity, they will be obeyed, not because their infractions carry a penalty, but only because there will be no disposition to stray from them. Sexual needs will be reduced by partners whose arrangements — marriage or other — have been endorsed or at least allowed by society. No man will need to covet his neighbor's wife, and no wife her neighbor's husband. Temptation will not exist because of the ideal circumstances which are actual already.

The legal system will not be a rigid one. As human sexual needs are not simple, so the laws regulating them cannot be simple, either. Complexity must be provided to match complexity. Thus there could be prescribed periods for overhauling the existence statutes in order to determine which ones should remain in force, on the assumption that changes were periodically required. The slow but definite effects of social evolution would be continually expected. The ideal whereby society endeavors to surpass itself could be more legal than social, and more social than individual; considerations and laws would reach forward rather than backward in their effects. Society has been in the habit of obeying the laws corresponding to the morality before last; it would ideally be asked to cooperate in obeying the laws which might serve to bring about an improvement. For there is no genuine reason why the legal system has to be conservative rather than progressive. Why could a society not enact into legislation the first attempts to achieve things-as-they-ought-to-be rather than the last attempts to retain things-as-they-were?

3. From What-Is to What-Ought-To-Be

Morality is usually a matter of constructing an ideal from extended ethical speculations or of examining actual conditions in the light of an established morality handed down by religion, by custom or by some other authority or convention. If the former, then the discussion takes an abstract turn remote from all practical considerations: what-ought-to-be, just so, from the perspective of a revealed theology or a rational metaphysics. If the latter, what-is is discussed by comparison with the ideal in such a way that the gap between them appears enormous and the moral imperative negligible. The philosopher has charge of the first and the man of action — or more accurately his moral apologist — has charge of the second. Never the twain shall meet: they live in different world, and engage in endeavors so far apart that even a language of communication is wanting.

The results are not anything to justify such a procedure. They are exactly what such a distracting dualism would lead us to expect them to be. Each proceeds on its own basis, and people are torn apart through sympathies with one at one time and another at another. Serious discussions of the difficulties are without important issue simply because no one backs up to the minimum of presuppositions which a reconsideration would require. Men always look at the facts through theory-colored glasses; their vision is partly distorted by a reading taken from psychoanalysis, from Christianity, or from the traditional gospel of simple expediency. It seems more reliable somehow to judge from a solid ground of accepted theory or else just from the effort to patch up the present in order to get on with the work.

But there is another method possible, and it may be in order to say a few words about it here. I have already indicated that the effort to determine the ideal takes place in a speculative field and requires protracted consideration: whose ideal, what ideal? But let us assume at this stage of the argument that such a question has been adequately answered. We now know which ideal of individual and social behavior will be in conformity with the morality we have chosen for reasons which make it appear the best. Then what? We have also, confronting us, alas, the actual individual and social situation, which is from any point of view very far removed from the ideal. We must know exactly where we are, and, as we have seen, this is difficult to determine.

Let us suppose, however, that these problems and difficulties, too, have been successfully solved, and that we know exactly where we are and where we would like to be: we are — let us imagine — in possession of full information concerning the actual and the ideal. Then there will be still a third area which we have not discussed at all because it is rarely considered. This is the question of strategy.

The word itself has unfortunate historical connotations. It meant originally the technique of planning or directing military operations. We need now to add a broader meaning: the technique of planning or directing the achievement of the ideal from the actual. Strategy could be the theory of how to get from things-as-they-are to things-as-they-ought-to-be; in the particular case under discussion here, the study and design of the steps necessary to move from moral-immoral practices to other practices wholly in conformity with the ethical ideal. We do not ordinarily think of the moral life as a condition to be attained through strategy. Yet the logical distance between the actual and the ideal warrants such an approach. The discipline would of course have its own theoretical and practical components. The theory of strategy is a theory and not a practice; the practice would have to consist in the applications of the theory.

In terms of the life of the individual, the problem becomes one of how to increase the cortical control over the neurohumoral system without diminishing the power drives. Given the two known components of activation: direction and intensity, greater control is possible. With knowledge comes understanding, and with understanding the possibility of control. The role of reason among the emotions is so to guide motivation that within the allowable social, moral, and legal limits the drives will not occasion mutual interference and in this way add to the difficulties. Reason should not inhibit the needs but order the drives. The individual with his conscience rides above the drives, intent upon rendering assistance wherever he can in the matter of their reduction. But he has his own difficulties; obstacles exist in the private and public retention schemata: his conscience and the awareness that there are public penalties for infractions of certain rules which his needs may require him to abrogate. Surely sexual needs have reductions which are socially approved: but there is the need for aggression and the need for novelty.

Aggression as such, the need to dominate the environment, can find its reduction in other areas, the economic and the political, for instance, and novelty in the arts; but a residue of aggression and novelty remains over and pervades the sexual drive. Here strategy comes to the fore, and there is more to the devious path than meets the eye of the beholder. Against the background of Antony's military conquest of Egypt, there took place his affair with the Egyptian queen, who presumably was offered no choice. Thus aggression was satisfied, and the character of her response made up the second element. Not for nothing did Shakespeare recognize among her virtues that

> Age could not wither her nor custom stale
> Her infinite variety.

The fruits may be for the vulgar, but this does not apply to stolen fruits, which are sweet. How is one to reconcile such behavior with the approach to the ideal individual? Through repressions or violations? Society counsels repressions; honor does, too. Psychiatrists are not so sure, and neither is the Old Adam, who has suffered a sea-change but who is still with us.

The strategy of society is to persuade its individual members to behave morally in such a way that individual satisfaction is assured and ideal conditions attained. Offhand this sounds like a contraditory demand, but that may be merely because we have not learned to view the construction of ideals as a speculative field and have not thought of individual satisfaction as a means. In the case of sex, society has laid down a set of allowable customs by prescribing their limits; needs domestically activated and drives monogamously reduced. But what about continuity?

Every organ needs to function, that is what it means to be an organ; and when one is prevented from doing so, the equilibrium of the whole organism is upset. But moral development is involved in the recognition of the demands of the material environment. Obedience to those demands consists in natural morality. In seeking to sponsor a rational life, society has emphasized consistency over completeness. We may expend so much effort in keeping our actions consistent with our ideals that we have failed to make our ideals sufficiently wide. Whatever is inclusive but limited is also exclusive. Those forgotting elements which have failed to gain consideration in an inclusive system may in the end wreck it. Strategy requires that we bear always in mind the varied elements and functional variables of human needs and ecological behavior.

The human individual responds to whatever there is in his environment which can constitute a tropistic object and activate his needs into drives on cue. Thus where a certain standard of conduct is required of him by society in order to achieve or maintain a chosen morality, the strategy would be to provide the environment most conducive to its achievement or maintenance. It has been said bitterly that marriage is an institution which provides the maximum of accessibility with the minimum of temptation. But the same can be said of other institutions. There is no element in the human environment which can be left out of any account of the human ecosystem.

If environment determines behavior by providing its tropistic objects and cues, then the strategy would be to provide a rhythm of activation by properly arranging the environment with respect to whatever organ behavior we wished to produce. This would be a matter not of coercion but merely of providing the proper setting. Do we for instance truly want the continual low-toned sexual excitation which the environment of advertising mass media now produces? Is it possible to sell nothing without the suggestiveness of sex as an accompaniment and a stimulus? Here economic strategy has clearly run afoul of moral strategy. We plan for the former but not for the latter. Something is wrong here in the one instance or the other. The law is concerned with the limitations and penalties consequent upon infractions, and not with positive affirmations, realities or imperatives. The latter belong to morality, which in turn rests upon ethics. Ethics is the theory that a given metaphysics can issue in a morality. The law is nothing if not a codified recognition of morality which endeavors to keep pace with it.

The legal strategy for promoting the requirements of a democratic society while at the same time providing for its development into the next evolutionary stage of the human species would consist in the enactment not of specific statutes but of broad principles respecting those statutes. Judge-made law has the advantage of flexibility but it is advisable if and only if there are general guide-lines to insure that decisions will follow the spirit in creating the letter through precedent. The number of social variables being what they are, it is never possible to lay down the conditions which will have to be met in the future; and in a period of rapid change such as our own this is especially true. We can only hope to provide safeguards for liberty: equality of opportunity; sufficient law to protect the minority; these could and should apply to sexual morality as much as to politics and education. A codification is needed, in other words, more in keeping with the facts of flexibility with respect to individual variations in the need for aggression and novelty than the spectacle of a moving invocation shifting uneasily from dead letters to fresh formulations.

Law has the function of guaranteeing that the individual shall not by his behavior depart too far from the morality of society. It protects him individually in this, as in the laws against suicide, where it should protect only society. Cultural determinism is here emphasized when it ought to be minimized. Laws which facilitate are rarely felt as a legal force. When they exert force then the element of strategy is clearly missing. Laws at their most strategic should set about counter-balancing the society. In an over-administered society such as our own, laws ought to be under-enacted. To have great societies there must be great judges, men individually incorruptible who are yet practical philosophers and so competent to hold an immediate contingency in the same trembling consideration as an inflexible principle, able to bring these together with serious damage to neither and yet to see in organic human needs and drive-reductions the correspondingly directed means and intensity of ends which lie so obscurely in the indefinitive future.[1]

1 See generally: *The Psychology of Aggression* (1961): Dollard, et al.; *Frustration and Aggression* (1959): Duffy; *Activation and Behavior* (1962): Freud; *Civilization and Its Discontents* (1930): Hebb; *The Organization of Behavior* (1959): Magoun; *The Waking Brain* (1960): Spuhler, et al.; *The Evolution of Man's Capacity for Culture* (1959): Walter; *A Statistical Approach to the Theory of Conditioning*, in Jasper and Smirnov (eds.), The Moscow Colloquium on Electroencephalography of Higher Nervous Activity, *The EEG Journal*, pp. 377-391 (1960).

CHAPTER XI

INSTITUTIONS, LAW AND MORALS

The object of this chapter is to examine some of the problems involved in the relations which hold between law and morals on the one hand, and institutions on the other. It will be necessary to begin by defining and analyzing institutions. Then we shall be in a position to show how morality and legality are fitted into institutions and proceed from them.

An institution is that subdivision of society which consists in human beings established in groups, together with their customs, laws and material tools, and organized around a central aim or purpose. If this is the case, then, there are six necessary elements which can be counted parts of every institution. These are: the social group, establishment, customs, material tools, organization and central aim.

Anything that can be named is comprised under culture or its environment, and most of culture — though not all — is contained in social institutions. Thus it is that the description of the sweep of institutions will have to be painted with a very wide brush. We can in a short space do little more than examine the outline of institutions, show how they fit into the environment, and look at the chief among their various elements.

We shall begin by considering an institution as a system. It has a structure and a function; that is to say, its elements are operators or enabling invariants: they function or they facilitate functioning. Individuals, social groups, their artifacts and typical behavior, are sets of institutional variables; together they constitute the elements of a closed system. Now, the institution is an empirical system in a steady-state whose equilibrium is maintained by its super-imposition upon sets of lower empirical levels, from the physical to the psychological. Together with its environment it forms an absolute system. For it may be affected by anything in its total environment but can have effects only upon things in its available environment.

The organization of an institution consists in the way in which a group of persons together with their tools and prescribed rules of behavior are able to work toward a central purpose. The institution itself is a sort of corporate group from this point of view, a kind of limited society and a set of artifacts, with an organization consisting of reasons.

We may, if we wish, consider the institution as a sort of manufacturing plant, a structure of men and materials and procedures intended to turn out a certain product. And this is true to some extent regardless of whether the product is in turn a material object or another process. One institution may produce shoes in great quantity, another may produce good government — from the point of view here under discussion, namely, the organization *qua* organization of the institution, it makes no difference. An institution needs equipment, and we mean by this the machinery and the raw material it operates upon. An institution needs procedures, and this means processing. An institution needs personnel and this means employees. And we can add a descriptive word for the end product and its fate: distribution. The thing to remember is that the organization of an institution would not exist were there no reason to pull its elements together, and the reason is always the productive aim of the institution, and so always lies beyond the institution itself, for the institution in some way serves the society of which it is an integral part.

Organization depends upon formalization, and cannot exist, in fact, without it. The heart of the social institution can be expressed in a single word: establishment. Just what establishment is has yet to be explained, and this remains true despite the recognition which has sometimes been accorded to it as the essential factor in institutions.[1] Here we can only hope to make a beginning, and it is possible to distinguish two derivations. For establishment may be either customary or deliberate in origin.

Establishment may evolve from the codification of custom, the regularization of which was already being done. When statute supplements precedent, institutions add a new binding sense of obligation but with it also gain a new privilege: debts will be paid, property rights will be protected, wrongdoers will be punished.

Or establishment may be consciously and willfully arrived at, as in the case of incorporation under western systems of law. The business corporation, the charitable foundation, the church-run hospital — these are all instances of establishment in the deliberate sense.

1. See e.g., MacIver & Page, *Society: An Introductory Analysis* 15 *et seq.* (1954).

In both cases, however, in customary or deliberate establishment, we recognize an implicit moral code and render it to some extent explicitly effective. We recognize what it is that we believe and wish to continue putting into action; we externalize abstractly its principles by agreeing upon a set of rules which we intend to follow in a given pursuit of ends. The organization of an institution, then, means the establishment of definite procedures to be followed in the use of its equipment by its personnel.

Now that we know the elements of analysis of institutions in so far as these may be crudely discriminated, let us look at the organization of an institution as a going concern. How do the elements behave together when they are actually functioning? Organization within the institution consists in objectified systems of ideas, as conveyed by the procedures for dealing with the equipment by the personnel. But the systems of ideas do not come out quite as their planners had anticipated and so alter somewhat the variety in application of the ideas. Why? Because of the constituents of the internal environment of the institution and its atmospheric effects, effects which are hard to isolate chiefly because they simply do not exist in isolation; they are values stimulated into existence by the functioning of the elements. Just as in a physical body of some degree of complexity there is, say, hydrogen ion concentration, temperature and osmotic pressure, so in an institution there are properties of the internal environment. We may name a few of these: security, belonging, facilitation, prestige. The mechanism for the regulation of these variables is built firmly into the organization of the institution.

Let us revert to the question of organization as it applies to institutions. Institutions are anchored in individuals. But they can no more be reduced to mere collections of individuals than they can be treated successfully without individuals. Individuals are among the necessary elements of institutions, yet it must be remembered that they are nevertheless only elements; they are not the institutions, for an institution is not and never can be merely a name for a collection of individuals. In the case of individuals as elements of institutions, the same phenomenon occurs that is found in the case of single cells and organisms, that is to say, the whole is more than the sum of its parts in virtue both of an emergent quality which we do not name and of a structure which we do: "organization." The organization of the institution is one analytical level above the human individuals and their tools that constitute it. An extraordinary and judicious blending of human individuals into social groups and their use of equipment makes up an institution; and so the organization is a matter of structure, structure firm but invisible, consisting of many elements taken from divergent empirical levels: equipment from every level, physical buildings; chemical aids, as for instance in pharmacology and chemical industry; biological components, as in the institution of agriculture and farming; and also psychological ingredients, as when human individuals serve an institution. The structure in detail would have to be analyzed under the heading of separate and specific institutions. It will be enough to say here that we can group all the material tools of institutions under the general heading of artifacts. Such artifacts are as essential to the composition and functioning of institutions as are the individuals, and both require other elements, such as the charter.

We may well adopt here Malinowski's name for the collective purpose of the institution. He called it the "charter" of the institution.[2] It may be a code, containing normative rules, a formal institution, a set of laws or by-laws, regulations, standards or sanctions, compacts, a commission, a contract or covenant. It could also be an unspoken agreement, a prescription, an unwritten law, a formula. As the "specific doctrine" of the institution the charter stands for the abstract ideas on which it rests. The charter and its peculiar rules or norms are a definite feature of the symbolic material in terms of which the myth is expressed. The charter may be written or unwritten; more commonly it is unwritten, and even when it is written as the charter it may not correspond exactly to the charter in Malinowski's sense. For a charter may start out one thing and change or develop (or deteriorate) into something else, something in the end quite different. It must be remembered that institutions are fluid affairs, and so what they are or what they represent cannot be declared in any final manner.

The tendency in empirical science to get away from metaphysical speculation has proved, on the whole, a healthy one. In physics, chemistry and biology, the experimental inquiry into the conditions which prevail in an actual field has been amply justified. Sociology, quite properly, has wished to pursue the same method; only in this case there is a fresh difficulty. For metaphysics itself turns out to be one of the empirical elements in society. There is no choice, then, but to recognize it. In place of the term, metaphysics, we propose to employ another, one having less unfortunate connotations. Metaphysics is the theory of reality, and reality is the reliable because immutable aspect of what there is. We shall use the word, ontology, meaning by it systematic metaphysics. Another way to explain ontology would be to describe

2 Bronislaw Malinowski, *Freedom and Civilization* 157 (1944).

it as the contents of beliefs about reality, where reality in turn means reliability or quasi-permanence. Ontology is not a new term even in sociology; it has been used by others – by Mannheim, for instance.[3] It is however, given more prominence here, and sought in something of a different context. Among the many diverse elements to be found in society, there is a consistency; else the society itself would not hold together. Ontology here, then, shall be the consistency-rules between divergent sets of social data. Such rules are of course implicit rather than explicit; they exist imbedded in social structures and artifactual functions.

It is easy to see, then, how establishment requires metaphysics. The most fundamental of human beliefs are the beliefs about reality, and these are enshrined in institutions. Men dedicate themselves to what they hold most permanent, and in so far as there is a consistency to their efforts, they wish to hold onto the gains they have made in determining what will remain the most meaningful. Hence underlying every establishment there is a theory of reality, and behind every institution a metaphysics. This is no less so because the foundations are hidden from view and much effort is required for their exposure. It is of course not only easy but usual to link actions with presuppositions without being conscious of either in any deliberate sense. Those who by their actions either establish institutions or, more commonly, continue to support them by working in and through them, are rarely aware of how deep lies the source of their actions or what wide implications they indicate. Yet institutions could hardly exist without the elements of structures and functions which determine their mechanism.

What has been elsewhere called the implicit dominant ontology[4] or the concrete ontology[5] is contained in every institution. We must learn to consider ontology as a set of relations among materials (the concrete ontology) and as a crucial factor in the establishment of institutions and societies. The dominant ontology of a society belongs to the leading institution, but every institution has its own. It is, after all, in terms of a system of ideas held fundamental that men live their lives as well as sometimes give them up. The tenents of a religion, the laws of a nation,

3 See Karl Mannheim, *Ideology and Utopia* 14 (1952), and *passim*. The chapter containing this passage was a late edition written to introduce the work of English readers, and reflects the same shift in interest from epistemology to ontology as do his last books.
4 Feibleman, *The Theory of Human Culture* (1946).
5 Feibleman, Culture as Applied Ontology, *The Philosophical Quarterly* (Scotland) 416 (1951).

the rules of a court, the principles of a science — what are these if not varieties of systems of ideas? Such systems are objectively and materially determined and inter-subjectively held, as Max Scheler and Emile Durkheim maintained; not inter-subjectively determined, as Karl Marx and Karl Mannheim seem to have supposed. The primary question of culture is, how much of the external environment can be brought into society and incorporated? Whatever is done in this direction is the work of institutions, and whatever is acknowledged about this is summed up in a charter.

The charter of an institution is what lends it stability. "Every stable system has the property that if displaced from a resting state and released, the subsequent movement is so matched to the initial displacement that the system is brought back to the resting state.... An important feature of a system's stability is that it is a property of the whole system and can be assigned to no part of it."[6] Such stability is a product of goal-seeking. It is by reason of this stability that institutions are so enduring, that they offer such stubborn resistance and outlast everything human.[7]

We have noted that the formal adoption of a charter is called establishment. Now establishment is carried out by means of enacted law. The charter is generally a recognition, often dim enough, of a set of theorems formulated within the limits of the existing extenuating circumstances derived from the largely unrecognized concrete ontology. Every society has a concrete ontology, and some societies also have an explicitly established and derived version of it in a charter. Those who have the latter, survive; those who do not have it, perish. This is what is meant by stability. The stability contributed to society by established institutions is dramatic. When, for instance, the Moors overran Spain in the eighth century they came with established institutions — political unity and a new religion. It took them no time at all to erase the effects of the Visigoths who had come conquering three centuries earlier but without a tradition of established institutions.[8] Despite our nominalistic prejudices, the longer life of an institution gives it a greater semblance of reality, for reality in this sense means reliability and reliability can in some way be measured in terms of permanence or duration. It is, however, a set of preliminary procedures that lead to enacted laws, and these we may term natural laws in that such laws have to be sought

6 Eric Ashby, *Design for a Brain* 53-54 (1952).
7 Claude Renard, *La Theorie de l'Institution: Essay d'ontologie juridique* (1930), p. 31.
8 Americo Castro, *The Structure of Spanish History* 61 (1954).

through what experience reveals not to be workable, hence established on a *pro tem* basis on the road to enacted laws. When the truth is discovered, it will have religious authority, and men will enact it because they will recognize in it the proper guide to convention. In the meanwhile this is a goal rather than an achievement, and the process of codification proceeds by easy stages, beginning with one event standing for another (in the information-theory sense) and ending with laws written down and systematized (in the legal-theory sense).

Renard divided the juridical act into three parts: the contract, the law, and the foundation which creates the institution.[9] The drawing of the contract and its formal adoption puts an idea into action, thus implementing the goal-seeking function. A hospital, for instance, puts a charitable or a medical idea – or both – into action.[10] As for the law, every institution has its own legal system, and an individual is (partly) governed by as many legal systems as there are institutions of which he is a member. Foundation is no more than the stabilizing effect of the former two: the adoption of a contract and the enactment of law.

Charter is the over-all name we have given to the formal process of establishment, its rules and results. Before proceeding to examine the consequences of having the culture as a whole adopt the charter of the leading institution, perhaps it would be well to consider briefly the law itself when it functions as an institution.

The law is that institution which is concerned with the administration of justice. It has to do with the regulation and adjudication of crime and contract through regular channels of litigation and the use of police powers. It amounts to a separate institution, although frequently it owes its existence to government, and thus constitutes an additional regulative social organization. The law reinforces the similarities within the group (i.e., those upon which the group is based) and is itself a collection of rational similarities.[11] The establishment of norms is a distributed responsibility, when it concerns such diverse affairs as justice, boundaries, and scales, or public health. There are two notable features of the law as an institution which must be mentioned here, and these are its special ramifications and admissions.

The principle of equality stands for the generality of value. That thoroughly English derivation of common sense from the appeal to

9 Renard, *op. cit.*, supra note 7, p. 90.
10 Renard, La Theorie de l'Institution et de la Fondation, in La Cite Moderne et les Transformations du Droit (1925), p. 12.
11 Maurice Hauriou, *La Science Sociale Traditionelle* (1896), pp. 336-374.

decency betrays a belief in natural justice to which the name of equity
has been assigned. Standards of value are more powerful when assumed
than when expressed, at least so long as they remain in force. The virtue
of establishment is its lasting power, and the memory of a basis for
evaluation which lies back of the conscience is not as easily transmitted.
Equity is enabled to supplement common law in the English system by
the continuity of containment which underlies both. It is difficult to
see how there could be in law the principle of equity were there no
moral assumptions, and of course back of them in turn an implied
ethics.

The law is in some special sense a captive institution. That is to say,
it belongs in type to a separate category. Ordinarily associated with the
state as its arm of order, the law can also take dictation from a number
of institutions, and so we have also martial law and canon law, for
instance.

The laws which permit certain actions to happen point the way toward the goal of transparent facilitation better than those which forbid
certain others. Traffic laws are examples of the first type, laws against
homosexuality examples of the second. There are, however, ways in
which the laws can dominate and facilitate at the same time. Such is the
character of enabling legislature, as for instance the English Turnpike
Act of 1662, which authorized tolls on improved highways, to reward
the capital and labor expended on them. When the state features its
law, or when the law takes precedence over the state as an institution,
so that outsiders attracted by its principles come under its protection
voluntarily, often even after having fought the state, then we have a
law-dominated state, which is the best and far superior to a force-
dominated one. The political life of General Smuts in South Africa,
when he adopted the British after the Boer War, and the literary life of
Oliver St. John Gogarty who did the same thing after the Irish Rebel-
lion,[12] are good examples. The production of law whether half myth-
ical, as in the case of the Greek lawgiver, Solon, or conscious and
planned, as with Gaius and the compilation of Justinian's Code, is not
the starting point but rather the act of establishment. Distribution is
society-wide, and takes place whenever there is a departure from its
limits. The consumption of law may be said to be the order secured by
the adherence to it. Law-abiding citizens are approaching the ideal of
transparent facilitation.

The fundamental beliefs of the members of the leading institution

12   Oliver St. John Gogarty, *As I Was Going Down Sackville Street* 233 (1937).

are the philosophy of the culture. The power of the leading institution lies in a general social acceptance of its concrete ontology. It is important to remember the distinction we have employed between the implicit dominant ontology and the concrete ontology. The implicit dominant ontology is the name for the fundamental consistency of all the elements of a culture; the concrete ontology is the name for the same function, only as it holds within a single institution. When an institution is made into the leading institution of a society, its concrete ontology becomes the implicit dominant ontology of that culture, and thenceforth functions as the true center of power. It is what finally enables the leading institution to exercise control over the society. Whether made manifest as might, domination, authority, or as supervision, inspection, surveillance or comptrollership, the implicit dominant ontology is always to be found assumed in the background.

When a society adopts the concrete ontology of its leading institution as its implicit dominant ontology, it does so with the conviction that its implicit dominant ontology is the perfect ontology. For instance, it identifies its moral code with the truths of ethics. Its theorems become axiomatic in the culture; its members "know" what is right. No society, of course, ever established a code of ethics. But it does establish a code of law; and the law is the establishment by a leading institution of its moral code as the limits of procedures throughout a society. The law in this sense is a part of every institution and different for each one; but the leading institution has a law for the society: federal law or canon for instance. The apparent arbitrariness of the legal system selected for the society is no argument against its necessity; order is a necessity, some order is not some particular order. Behind the order which is in fact selected with a society, there is a silent and hidden implicit dominant ontology, which appears in the degree of conviction which the selection of a system of order is stamped. Law in this connection functions as the acceptance of the logic of rights and duties so far as these concern the social governance of persons, substances and actions. Such acceptance leads to absolutes in belief, the very root of tyranny; for who would regard the imposition of true beliefs as any sort of oppression? And who, having the truth, would give it up? The tribute which men pay willingly to the power of truth is always handed over to one of its alleged agents – this truth or that.

We have come to associate power with political power, the kind of power which is traditionally exercised by the state. But the power of the implicit dominant ontology lies in its free acceptance by those who are to be guided by it. It functions in direct relation to the degree of voluntary submission to its requirements in practice. The greatest freedom and efficiency, the most magnificent instance of transparent facilitation, is achieved by the institution which succeeds in becoming and remaining the leading institution with a minimum set of assumptions. The concrete ontology of the leading institution as it is adopted by the society must not be expanded but be kept to a minimum. The strength of an ontology is indicated by its fewness of demands, and this requires that it be a very limited axiom system. We have before us the splendid examples of religion in ancient Athens, and of government in the United States and in western Europe in the nineteenth century.

The political power of a religion is not necessarily synchronous with the greatest reach of belief, which may have been expended in establishing the institutuion. In the struggle between Pope and King, the Pope often triumphed, as was the case with Gregory VII and Henry IV; but we may ask whether the strength of belief at this late date in the Church's history was the same nature as that sort which called out martyrs. There may have been a change in its quality. For the kind of belief which will lead men to fight is not, after all, of the same high sort which will lead them to surrender. The priests who followed Cortez and accepted conversions in Mexico in all probability did not possess the same quality of conviction as did the martyrs in the Roman arena. Both had their convictions, this can hardly be doubted; yet we may be sure that something in its character had changed.

Starting with the matter-of-fact organization, we have been examining cultures with respect to their institutions, their legal systems and their moral codes. But we have been abstracting as we went, backing up finally to the concrete ontology of institutions and the implicit dominant ontologies, the hidden source of the beliefs about reality from which the other and more manifest elements derive their support. We have now to consider the last of these: a kind of over-all cultural value named the ethos.

What the cultural anthropologists have been calling the ethos of a culture is its peculiar atmospheric flavor, or, more precisely, its characteristic quality. It emanates in all probability from the myth of the master institution, yet can be distinguished from it. For the myth is a symbolic story, a narrative representing the nature of reality, while the ethos is a sort of axiological medium in which the entire culture is bathed, and no corner of any institution is exempt from its influence. The myth is known, the ethos is only felt. The ethos is a single pervasive value, but as such an object existing in the world and distinct from the faculties which may apprehend it. No one who has lived in a single cultural environment can understand what the force of the ethos is; its power is something of which we can become aware only when there is contrast. The ethos is what Renard tried to describe in the phrase "family atmosphere."[13] The social anthropologist learns as much as about his own culture as he does about the aborigine he has come to study, and the bull's eye view of the bird is no more the norm than the bird's eye view of the bull. It is a difficult if not often an impossible thing to become acquainted with the characteristics of the medium in which one is immersed; it is men and not fish who are the most aware that water is wet.

The ethos is derived from the master myth as its source, and envelops the culture slowly as it spreads from the leading institution. We should expect to get a different sort of atmosphere in a culture whose god, as Nietzsche said, knew how to laugh; and the high white light of reason which permeated classic Greece was a different sort of thing from that which diffused through the Middle Ages when interruptions in nature rather than the laws of nature were held to be the proofs of God. How close did Wagner come in his music dramas to catching the spirit of the primitive tribes inhabiting the thick dark forests which covered Germany during the first Christian centuries? We shall never know, but we shall know something of what he was trying to do, and this will tell us something too, about the ethos; for while the little artist usually tries to interest us in his solutions, the big one often succeeds in doing this for his problems; and the problems so presented tell us more about the field in which both problems are proposed and solutions tried than we could otherwise learn. For in the case of the ethos, as with any other quality, we can do no more than describe it indirectly by recalling the common kind of occasions on which it is experienced, and take the measure of some of its coordinates; for surely we can never hope to specify it any more for the benefit of those who have never themselves directly experienced these things than we could the taste of oranges or the visual impression of a certain shade of purple.

There is a characteristic 'feel' to every outlook, for instance the Catholic or the Hindu. To accept deeply a concrete ontology is to feel it, and, what is more forceful, to feel the world from it. This is why anything can be accepted if it can be made to seem ordinary, for "ordinary" actually means "consistent with a given atmosphere." Those of us who wonder how the Nazis could do the things that they did — how they could make lamp shades of human skin, and could perform

13 Renard, *op. cit.*, supra note 7, p. 155.

108

experiments upon human beings as though they were laboratory animals — have failed perhaps to understand that what seems acceptable to
the social group is quite commonplace to the individuals within it. The
most monstrous act, the wildest conceptions, seem mere matters of
common sense if they do not meet with surprise in others. In short,
what is acceptable to all individuals is obviously true for each individual. The ordinariness of the immediate is a sheer fact.

Here, too, and more importantly is the source of that good from
which right is derived, the point of origin of the moral code by which,
as we have seen, the law operates. Justice always incorporated an
earlier moral code as outdated feeling of what is good, but follows it all
the same. For it is here, so to speak, that the institutions furnish that
side of it, that agency, which is directed toward putting the culture together. "The necessity of the whole, felt behind the contingency of the
parts, is what we call moral obligation in general," Bergson wrote, and
he added, "it being understood the parts are contingent in the eyes of
society only; to the individual, into whom society inculcates its habits,
the part is as necessary as the whole."[14]

The social psychology of culture-makers involves a separation between the functions in which the conscious and unconscious minds are
engaged, for it is here that a deep wedge is driven between otherwise
graduated levels of awareness. Given a productive individual having the
power of origination, the more intense the degree of his concentration
the more free he is for the forces of which he is unaware to make inroads upon him. In other words, the more he attends to what is before
him the more his unconscious learns. Hence it is that the effects of the
ethos are felt more greatly by the artist, the scientist and philosopher,
than by the average individual.

We have been discussing institutions, their laws and their moral
codes, as these exist in contemporary and past cultures. We have
skipped from institutions to cultures, in order to make our points.
Intermediate between institutions and cultures, however, are societies.
The hierarchy of social structure runs: institutions, societies, cultures.
We have yet to say a few words about the application of our arguments
to societies, and we might take this opportunity to refer them to the
ideal organization of the natural society instead of to going societies.

In the natural society, one might imagine, there would be no imposition of style, and hence no authority as we have defined it. In a har-

14 Henri Bergson, *The Two Sources of Morality and Religion* 3 (Audra and Brere-
ton trans. 1935).

monic social situation there would be no need for reason, since nothing would be wrong. But when has there been such harmony? In a world society, in a single world culture, reason would be called out only with the police. The leading institution would dominate in virtue of its charm, while authority would become the triumph of style. Persuasion would win out over force, and the leading institution would be widely followed, much as now we surrender to an aesthetic object; we give ourselves to a work of art, a great painting, say, or a great piece of music, without asking anything from it, as a matter of superfluous caring. In this manner, individuals in the natural society come to care for the logic and the value – for the concrete ontology, the basic value system, the ethos – of the leading institution. The place of the leading institution would be held, then, not as a matter of superior strength but more because it was necessary to the structure which gave the greatest potentialities to the other institutions. In the natural society presumably, every individual and every institution is allowed to fulfill its maximum of potentiality not by organizing anything but merely because such allowance is inherent in the structure. In the sum total of the natural society, the leading institution would have the power to leave everything as it is, and everything would be left as it is only because everything would be as it should be.

Authority in the natural society, we have found, is a matter of inner necessity rather than of externally imposed compulsion. We have said that for the perfect individual what he wants to do is what he ought to do, and in the natural society what he ought to do is what the institutions toward which he is oriented want him to do. And what does individual freedom mean in this connection? Is he alone free who belongs to an institution whose organization is not rigid but operates instead on a basis of transparent facilitation? The natural society, from this point of view, is a way of referring to the balance between the individuals and the institution which is so complete that the culture as a whole seems to possess no lines of force.

Weber asserted that "'culture' appears as man's emancipation from the organically prescribed cycle of natural life,"[15] a sentence that no Greek could have written. For the Greek, ideals exist in nature; and this is true also of social ideals, humanity being so integral a part of the natural world. Thus the natural society would be in accordance with the fulfillment of the organically prescribed cycle. As Empedocles said in 450 B.C., "that which is lawful for all extends continuously through

15 *From Max Weber* 356 (Oxford ed. 1946).

110

the broad-ruling Air and throught the boundless Light."[16] Man and all his works are part of that environment which comprises the natural world, and they fit into it without any seams. Theology in this sense is cosmic sociology the identification of individual sympathy with the social group, the institution, the society, the culture, and finally with the whole cosmos.

16 Fr. 135, quoted in Kathleen Freeman, *Ancilla to the Pre-Socratic Philosophers* 67 (1948).

CHAPTER XII

THE STATE AS LEGAL CUSTODIAN

The human species is a plastic medium upon which all sorts of forces play. There are differences between peoples, as indeed there are between individuals, and even if these concern actualities rather than potentialities, they must be reckoned with. For instance, one people may be more concerned with religion while another is enthusiastic about science and technology. There may be large differences in the types of property developed, also in its ownership and control. Again, the same people may be peaceful in one century, warlike in the next. And all of these differences must be followed and served by legal frameworks which are rigid enough to maintain an established order and flexible enough to permit changes in it.

From Aristotle to Kant and Hegel it has been supposed that what separates man from the other animals is his power of reasoning. While some other animals are able to reason to some extent, only man, we believe, can reason abstractly. To do this, symbols are necessary, signs for abstract ideas which can be combined into abstract structures.

But there is another step which must be taken before men are able to live together in large numbers. The much-vaunted reasoning, which hitherto had been deemed sufficient when it was subjective and a power of the human mind and consciousness, had to be objectified. It was objectified in writing, and this added greatly to the power of reasoning; for many calculations could be made which were not possible before. But this was still not enough. Social laws had to be agreed upon, codified and promulgated. There were invariable infractions on the part of some, and so arrangements had to be set up for punishing wrongs and for settling disputes. Thus legal procedures were devised and these in turn were agreed upon, codified and promulgated. Law was devised as an established agreement made by the community respecting how its citizens are required to act under particular circumstances. Such procedures were in the hands of an institution constructed for the purpose by the authority of the state and so part of it, but consisting in law-makers, courts, magistrates, lawyers, police, together with the buildings and other physical appurtenances appropriate to the functions involved.

The processes of law, the "path of due process", consist in well-established lines of action permitted or ordered by the duly-constituted authorities. Laws not only measure infractions, they also serve as guidelines to law-abiding citizens. This is, so to speak, reason in action, rational procedures taking their place in society and in material culture which had formerly been confined to the human mind. Reasoning of course is still mental, but man is not alone, and his activities are shared with his fellows to a very large extent.

Communication between contemporaries can take place by means of speech, though not if the individuals are widely separated by space. But communication between the generations is possible only by means of writing. It is the written word of the ancient Greeks which still speaks to us today. Writing, like printing, books, and the rest, consists of course in artifacts, which are material objects altered through human agency for human uses. That is how the legal systems of the past are able to influence the societies of the present, how for example the Roman law has been passed down and how the Napoleonic Code and the English common law are currently made available. The law, like everything else in human culture, is artifact-oriented.

Abstract thought is a behavioral response to the signs which man has invented, and so a species of his continual and serial need to adapt to his own artifacts. Such innovative behavior of course always involves the alteration of materials: signs are meaningful signals. What corresponds to the reasoning powers of the mind are the rational procedures of the various institutions which together make up the culture. Institutions are the custodians of artifacts. Each institution has its own; and among those peculiar to the state are the legal procedures which make the state itself possible and which insure its orderly continuance.

Without legal procedures, human life would be irrational. It would consist in individuals acting on impulse to satisfy whatever needs were uppermost at the moment. This would lead to conflicts between them and to violence as a means of settling conflicts. It would lead to mob action as the only form of social control. Now, no state and hence no collection of peoples could survive for very long under these chaotic circumstances. Any nation operating on the basis of such conditions and with a total lack of rules would perish from inadequacies within or from the excesses consisting in the larger forces exerted by other states from without. Legal procedures, then, spell survival; they are not luxuries but necessities.

That such a framework of laws is established gives it a certain stability. Dissidents may argue against it but may not resort to force to effect changes. The current challenge to the authority of the state made in defence of individual rights argues the superior claims of religion and conscience. Those who make such claims have not offered suggestions as to how the state under those circumstances could maintain itself as a functioning organization. No state, then no laws; no laws, then anarchy, in which condition both the freedom of religion and of individual conscience must be wiped out altogether. For there is no alternative to law except anarchy or the short-lived order imposed by a rigid dictatorship of a single individual or group of individuals. Law of any sort almost is to be preferred to law of no sort. Only a legally-constituted society can survive by providing for its members anything like the security, if not the prosperity, they so much need. Only a legal order can insure the continuity of society and the orderly succession of rule and rulers.

And the legal order of a complex society is a product which represents many interests, some of them even conflicting, as the best compromise which could have been obtained; and so is a whole which is greater than the sum of its parts; its very universality requiring that it be a class not exhausted by its members nor by any collection of them. The true meaning of the rule of law lies in the recognition that the universal was to be elevated over the particular provided that it was a universal chosen by due process. The law so established provides for society its stability and continuity. No society could exist long without it and provide the kind of arrangement in which citizens can afford to forget it from time to time and go on about their business.

It is not essential to specify what kind of legal procedures are chosen. For just as every society must have a language of some sort, though no particular language is required, so a state must have laws and legal procedures, though just what laws and procedures it is not necessary to insist. We shall see much later in this book that all systems of laws and legal procedures are not equal; some are to be preferred to others, and the whole effort is pointed toward the discovery at some possible date and place in the future of the ideal legal system. But for the moment it is sufficient to repeat that a legal framework as the social surrogate of individual reasoning and rational behavior is a necessary element for the survival of a state.

The state and the legal framework are reciprocal. The stability of the legal framework *is* the state, and so the state protects it. Any attempt to change either by force is a challenge to the other. Both properly conceived provide for change by orderly process. To the extent to which the legal framework is subject to amendment, it is a creature of its social context in place and time; to the extent to which it is a system it aims at immutable representations akin to universal truths. Thus it always represents a compromise, and like most compromises tends to pull apart. It purports to be the immutable truth — as amended.

Despite Locke, Rousseau and Kant, men are not born free and equal. Freedom must be secured for them by the state, since it is a negative thing and largely a restriction upon their enslavement by others. Equality must also be politically secured, since it is only political equality which is meant. As citizens and before the law men ought to be equal; but in fact they are equal in no other respect: they are not all equally intelligent nor do they have equally strong characters, they are not all equally vigorous physically, and they are not all equally endowed with ability.

The state is the supreme coercive power. Its decisions in all matters respecting the life of its people is final. In a dictatorship it is the government which decides, and the same whether a king or a politburo. In a democracy such decisions reflect the choices of the people and remain sensitive to their wishes, but not always. Traditionally it may include some limitation on that power, the right of appeal, for instance. The state is not an abstraction after all; it is a community of rulers acting in the name of an established set of aims of a constitutional nature, as expressed in a charter written or unwritten. When we say 'the state' what we mean is the duly authorized ruling community.

The state has a monopoly of the supreme coercive power but it is by no means the only institution which has power. Every institution exercises coercive power to some extent; trade unions may do so to a dangerous degree, for instance, and so may the family. The state, however, has the ultimate power and may use it to reinforce or to nullify the power of all lesser institutions.

What I have called the ruling community must be distinguished from the state, to which however it remains very close. The state is a standing arrangement having some degree of permanence, while the ruling community changes from time to time. Institutions are not mortal in the same way that human individuals are. Hence there must be over a period of time a kind of succession of the ruling community. Now it often happens that there are provisions for such succession, as there are for instance in the United States, but it happens equally often perhaps that there are no such provisions. This is the case in the recent history of the Soviet Union, where in the struggle for succession men were as often killed as retired. In short, the ruling community may be authorized, as when it is provided for in a charter, or it may be the outcome of a successful struggle for power. In the former case the 'authorization' comes about legally, in the later case it comes about through the use of physical force. Both cases may be considered varieties of authorization. That reason is preferred to physical force follows from the nature of the aim at stability in the state.

It is very important to draw the distinction I have tried to make between the state and the ruling community. Confusing them by not recognizing the distinction has been the source of much damage to the legal framework. For it stems from the state and not from the ruling community, which is pledged to uphold it but does not always do so with the same unswerving loyalty when the results will not be the ones desired by the members of that community. In short, the ends of the duly authorized ruling community may or may not be identical with the ends of the state, and the status of the legal framework may become in such a case a pawn in the game.

In principle the state is a corporate entity with its own charter, its laws, its personnel, its artifacts and its aims. In practice, however, the situation is always somewhat different. The state in practice may be the determinations of an individual, or of a small group of individuals, acting with authority in the name of the state but interpreting its charter and its laws to some extent at least in terms of their own personal preferences; an individual or small group of individuals acting on their own to fulfill their own aims partly freed of the restrictions which the state usually imposes on individuals. In short, the principles of the state free their own leaders from acting within those principles provided only that the leaders can interpret the principles broadly in terms of their own aims and preferences, and they nearly always can. *"L'état, c'est moi"* said Louis XIV, but something of the same thought has either been expressed by Hitler and Mussolini, or acted upon though not expressed by Lenin, Stalin, Mao, de Gaulle, and Nixon. In such cases actions speak as loudly as words, and far more effectively. It is a difficult assignment not only for those who make the law and those who uphold it but for all concerned to cut themselves loose from established and traditional reference points; from Emperor or Chairman but also from charter or constitution, and throw themselves upon the hard but reliable authority of reason and fact.

It is a mistake to suppose that law-makers are free and answerable to no one. They are in fact answerable to the people through the pre-

116

vailing morality, and they are answerable to the Constitution written or unwritten if the country has one. Even the men who turn things upside down are not free, and if they are sensitive are aware of their bondage. 'The higher the more determined' is a rule which applies here. Those without connections and responsibilities may indeed be much more free. Napoleon declared himself "the most enslaved of men," entirely "dependent upon events and circumstances."[1] Statesmen are tightly tied into a system whch purports to lead but in a sense which they follow. "Which way did that mob go?" asked the running man of a by-stander. "I have to catch up with it because I am its leader."

The state derives its power not from the *will* of the people, as has so often been suggested, but from the *needs* of the people. The needs of individuals remain substantially the same but the needs of individuals in groups may change depending upon the size of the group. Thus large collections of individuals may have needs not readily evident to the separate individuals who compose the collections. Needs are not always consciously recognized.

That the state is not merely the individual writ large is attested by the new conditions brought about by the huge increases in populations. What applies to the individual no longer suffices for the state, and what is true of the state may no longer be true of the individual. For ex-ample, in most cases the individuals within a modern scientific-indus-trial state are no longer capable of understanding the artifacts which are now needed to operate it. The computer for instance has taken its place as a necessary instrument in handling large masses of transactions, such as exist in the post office and the bank. But most individuals are not capable of understanding the mechanism of the computer. Speaking generally, the situation is that man has not yet adapted to his new arti-facts, not certainly when side by side with them we find functional illiterates by the score.

The very compact organization brought about by the large increases in population, which have been paced by the corresponding increases in communication, transportation and transactions, makes of the state a monolith, and this seems inevitable in the very nature of the situation. The western democracies are drifting dangerously in that direction, while the eastern communist dictatorships strive earnestly and feverish-ly to catch up with western technology. Thus it often happens even against the will of the people that their needs determine the shape of the state and the strength of its system.

1 Quoted in Elie Faure, *Napoleon* (New York, Knopf, 1925), p. 51.

If anything were needed to demonstrate that a legal framework is a rudimentary political system, it is just this: that its end is so to speak its beginning, that nothing in it can be said to be independent of it. Laws do not operate in isolation but only as parts of a framework of laws. The justification of the framework is the intention of citizens to pursue such aims as they have in common while living together in a society. The typical politician in a democratic country has his ear to the ground and endeavors to lead people in the way he thinks they want to go, as a necessary precaution in the attempt to maintain his position. The lawmaker is no better off. He is no less a part of the framework within which he works than are the laws themselves, the morality which dictates the laws, or the people who hold to the morality.

Ideally speaking, in all well-ordered states the force of the legal framework is interposed between the duly authorized ruling community and the private citizens. The state is the custodian of the legal framework but is also to some extent limited by it, and the Rule of Law spells out under what conditions the exercise of state power shall be carried out and specifies that there must be orderly procedures which are appropriate for ensuring adherence to those conditions. The Rule of Law means that for the rights of individuals and their equality before the law it is necessary that the law itself be the supreme power.

The state is not the law looked at from another angle, as Kelsen maintained. For the state has many functions, the law being only one of them. The regulative function of the state is the law, but the state has also a number of facilitative functions, such as the operation of the postal system, the promotion of good roads, and the protection afforded by the military. The state and the law are necessary each to the other but this does not make them one and the same thing. Positive law is bound by the state but natural law binds the state.

The legal framework is itself an institution. This means that it operates to some extent at least within its own confines and is subject to its own restrictions and specifications. But it means also that it operates on its own and has its own aims. Institutions, like all other organizations may suffer from deformations, they may become too small or too large. Becoming too small, however, is a deformation that rarely happens to institutions; becoming too large is far more common. When an institution shifts its aims from the service of society to being served by society, then largeness becomes the typical kind of deformation. When you say that the law exists to serve society through regulation, you discover that 'society' is a vague term referring to something which no one can ever quite locate, and so the law often ceases to perform the service.

But people do not exist merely in order to obey the laws or even to be punished for their infraction. We see this error when too many laws are enacted and none are expunged from the records. Laws fail as laws when a majority of the citizens refuse to obey them. The laws that a majority does not approve are unenforceable. Legality, then, is not sufficient for a legal order; there must also be consent. The Eighteenth Amendment adopted in 1919 prohibiting the sale and transportation of intoxicating liquors created organized crime was repealed in 1933 by the Twenty-first Amendment because it could not be enforced, but thereafter organized crime continued to flourish. The trouble with the method of allowing laws simply to be forgotten when allegedly they no longer apply is that 'dead' laws may suddenly be revived or appealed to. A law is never completely dead so long as it remains on the books.

In periods of little or no cultural change conservatism acts to improve the practice of law. In periods of rapid cultural change evolution is impelled to improve the theory of law. Thus the concern of lawyers with the foundations of law is limited by the prominence of exigent considerations, while the concern of legal philosophers with practice is aroused only to the extent to which it can be made to test new and perhaps viable theories.

The utilitarian aims of law are accomplished through what is called positive law, the enactments and promulgations of the authorized legislators of the community or state. The transcendental element is provided by the ideal of natural law which stands behind positive law as that at which it aims. There is no need for the justification of a force beyond that of society, and none for surrender to the variable nature of society itself; all that is needed is for the society to establish the machinery to codify the morality which will make it into a state. For this there is needed the requirements of consistency and inclusiveness. It must not contain conflicting laws and it must contain all of the laws.

Positive law is said to be man-made, but within the meaning of this phrase there are alternative interpretations. It may be man-made, it is not man-decided. The decisions respecting law are made on the basis of individual and communal needs. Positive law, in other words, is dictated by practical exigencies; positive law is culture law, the laws generated by cultures with all of their biological and artifactual components.

Natural law by comparison is theoretical social law and it offers a justification from the other, or abstract, side for positive law. The codified law acts to stabilize relationships by contributing continuity and uniformity to customs. The law as such is a conservative force which must be balanced by the existence of evolutionary opportunities to amend or replace it. The laws of a society attempt to codify its morality; but law differs from morality: the law is overt, deliberate and known; the morality is covert, informal, and changes more slowly. And so the legal framework of necessity must lag somewhat behind the moral climate; when it lags just a little it acts as a preservative, when it lags too much it may precipitate a revolution. The question is one of goodness of fit, of niceties of adjustment, intended to allow for progress while not abandoning gains.

Socrates held that morality requires obedience to the laws even when these are immoral. If you thought the laws immoral, you should work to have them changed; but in the meanwhile you should obey them. This was Socrates' point. It was also the main point of the defence made by the Nazis at the Nurenberg trials. It was the defence of those stiff moralists who insisted that while you worked through legal channels for the repeal of the eighteenth Amendment you should not buy liquor. It is a matter of consensus. When nearly everyone thinks a law bad, then disobeying it is not immoral though it is illegal. A sense of proportion in such matters is important. Very few would agree that murder and armed robbery under any circumstances is acceptable, but nearly all would agree the laws in California making oral sex punishable by imprisonment need not be obeyed.

The maintenance of justice with its requirement of equality was made possible by restraints. Now restraints upon individuals come from the laws and the law-enforcing agencies of the states. Restraints upon states are non-existent so far as the use of force is concerned. It could come therefore only from a global agreement as to the nature of justice. That kind of agreement does not at the present time prevail, and so we live, as indeed we have always lived, in a condition of international anarchy tempered by temporary alignments and shifting agreements promoting brief periods of peace.

CHAPTER XIII

THE OPERATION OF LAW

1. How Laws Are Framed

To fully comprehend anything, it must be located in the two domains of history and logic: how it came to be what it is, and what it is in itself apart from its history. In chapter VI, I tried to show the historical origins of the law; in this and subsequent chapters I hope to develop a cogent legal theory.

Laws may be defined as rules respecting conduct. Customarily, laws are the regulations which hold equally throughout a society and which are enforced by the threats of penalties.

They establish procedures respecting specific situations involving persons and artifacts, to which the behavior of all citizens is expected to conform. 'Establishment' as the word is used here includes *recognition, codification*, and *promulgation*. The law as established usually includes penalties for infractions. Laws are not orders unless they apply, and they do not always apply. For example laws regulating interstate commerce do not apply to strictly local enterprises. There are few laws that have no exceptions: even murder is sometimes forgiven if it is committed in self-defense. Laws may be facilitative, as with traffic laws, or they may be merely prohibitive, as with the XVIII Amendment to the Constitution of The United States. In a monarchy of absolute dictatorship the law-makers are not bound by the laws unless they choose to bind themselves, but in a democracy the situation is somewhat different, for a democracy is a government of laws and not of men, and the law-makers, being men, are no exceptions. Whether the rulers of a communist state, for instance the Presidium of the Supreme Soviet in the U.S.S.R., are bound by the laws is open to question.

The law in operation is an enacted statute, a judicial decision, an administrative agency regulation or an executive order which is intended to serve as a guide for correct behavior and as a directive to the courts as to how they are to decide in the case of particular issues. The aim in such a case is the administration of justice. Thus the achievement of justice is the end of law. It must be remembered of course that the laws may exist and their operation may result only in injustice. Unjust laws and unjust decisions by the courts do exist, but these do nothing to abrogate the main intention of both laws and courts, and their continuance serves to insure that the aim will continue of approximating justice in most cases.

In my formulation, laws are framed as the result of practical exigencies to which sovereign as well as subject must be responsive. Custom is to some extent responsible but does not account for the effects of new customs. Changing material circumstances with their consequent changing beliefs alter customs and therefore eventually also laws. It is the implicit dominant morality of a people which calls for corresponding laws and which turns the authorities or the people's representatives into law-makers. The morality of a society connects the laws, which grew out of organ-specific needs and communal exigencies, with reality by means of an accepted theory of the good.

It is possible to trace the origins of laws further back than the sovereign who issues them as commands. Their point of origin lies much deeper in the society. Ordinarily laws are brought into existence when a need for them arises. The laws may be made by executive order, legislatures (statutes) administrative agencies (regulations), or by judges (case law). All, however, are responses to situations which had not been finally determined before and which called for incorporation in the order which the legal system in itself represents. The growth of the law is the result of the confrontation of the constituted authorities with novel kinds of exigencies. Legislative law, which is superior, is more theoretical; judge-made law, which is inferior, is more practical.

Culture is not merely a society of men, it is in fact a mixture of men and of what they have made out of the materials available to them, a mixture of men and of artifacts which in turn affect the men. Many human interests and even some human aims are if not determined by artifacts then at least heavily influenced by them. It would not do for instance to describe Western culture, the culture of Europe and America, in such a way as to leave out the airplane, the motor car, the computer or the wonder drugs. Every new artifact has necessitated a new set of laws respecting it. This is true of the Civil Aeronautics Authority, or traffic laws in the city streets, and of the Delaney Amendment prohibiting the use on humans of any drugs which produce cancer in animals. In this sense language is also a material tool and so are social laws: formulations in language which influence the behavior of men and their use of artifacts.

All social relations are material relations. No two human individuals can interact without the intermediation of some material element. It would not have to be a material tool as we ordinarily understand the word, it could be a spoken language. But such language is also a material tool, shaped sounds intended to convey a meaning, which itself involves reference direct or indirect to some material situation.

All legal relations, then, are material relations. They are enacted by men in a language designed for the purpose, and their aim is to regulate the material relations in society, preventing or settling those conflicts which could not be avoided. The material conditions prevailing in society are the source of the law. Laws are enacted in order to make the operation of society possible, not the reverse.

The law is not intended to initiate relations among men but merely to order those they have preferred. Law is the name for that ordering. Now relations among men take many forms, for men as a rule rarely come into immediate and direct contact with each other. Human relations are almost always mediated and the exceptions are rare. Sexual relations and hand-to-hand combat are among the few exceptions. The mediating factors may be those of language or those of artifacts. There are few occasions when men come into contact without the accompaniment of speech. Men may drink together, they may bargain for the exchange of property, they may play cards, or watch sports; they may work together in a factory or a farm or a business, but always by involving artifacts of some sort. Even sex relations and war can be and usually are bound by contract. The binding elements give the law a base from which to take hold. The law formalizes relations and gives them public recognition and recording.

2. Statutory Codification, Implementation and Interpretation

The attempts to meet the logical requirements of a system are represented in legal procedures by legislatures, which are responsible for codification, by executives (and their agencies), which are responsible for implementation, and by courts, which are responsible for interpretation. The legislature is the ultimate authority in the making of law.

Codification both clarifies and freezes the laws. It makes them clearer and more certain but at the same time more rigid. The professionalism inherent in meeting the criterion of categoricity, that the statutes be constituted as a class of similar structures, is intuitively met by those trained in the law to meet the specification, though of course not under the terms of this description. Code law is universal law in the sense that its statutes are stated as universals and intended to apply to all relevant cases. That it has to be supplemented by case law only shows the strain placed on it by the changing particulars which would render it without application in many instances if left uninterpreted.

It was envisaged by the French Civil Code of 1804 that nothing more would be needed by the courts than application. No freedom was provided for the judges who had merely to deduce from the Code to reach decisions. But that is not the story in common law countries. The judge is essentially a mediator, since he has both code law and case law to look back on when new situations confront him. The tendency is for the judge to add to his degrees of freedom by employing the code law and case law of the past merely as guide-lines and not as binding precedent.

The statutory interpretations of the decision-making judges, executive orders and administrative agency regulations join that of the law-making powers and propensities of the legislatures in adding to the number of laws. Few are even formally repealed, more are merely allowed to fall into the class of those which remain uninvoked. Leading cases succeed leading cases, too, in a similar pattern, few being specifically over-ruled, most being simply distinguished on the basis of dissimilar facts. Whichever way mass approval is obtained, whether by consent, as in the parliamentary democracies, or by coercion and propaganda, as in the communist countries, it constitutes a validating force. In the last analysis and at some interval of time, the executive, the legislative and the courts do what a majority of the citizens would approve. A functional approach, one more responsive to the needs as well as the wishes of the people, is gradually coming into vogue. However, it is merely a first step toward meeting the twin requirements of consistency and completeness, for only when the laws are plainly set forth and put into practice is it possible to see how they fit together and what they do and do not cover.

Invariably, since time never stands still, the laws enacted at one time are applied to situations which arise at another when the conditions have changed. This makes statutory interpretation necessary. The choice of deciding what is contained in a statute itself or of endeavoring to reconstruct what was in the mind of the legislators when the statute was first framed poses difficulties. Interpretation generally relies upon the wording of the law, its legislative history, and the collective meaning of previously decided cases. But there is a fourth alternative, akin to legislative history, which is to reach back to the spirit of the laws which prevailed when the statute was enacted. This is in effect to look for the laws behind the law, the understanding, prevalent at the time, of the natural law which would have governed the statute's innovation.

All those who are concerned with fundamental theory – and who in the legal profession is not – are perforce concerned with philosophy. Questions of what there is as well as of what constitutes reliable knowledge are always invoked. The background ideology influences the legal process more when that background is not recognized as existing than when it is. It is well known of course that the executive, the legislature and the courts are influenced by current trends in political and economic thought as well as by events in those fields, but what is not well known in our positivistic times is that they are influenced also though certainly in more subtle and ingenuous ways by ideas of what is real. In general the individuals who participate in this process are content to work inadvertently within the limits of the concrete philosophy which is theirs in virtue of their upbringing and not to question its conflict with others, of which for that matter they may be unaware. But when decisions with respect to enactment, orders, regulations or interpretation are called for it often happens that those limits are passed. Practice is the life of the law. It may consist not merely in what the legislators, executives or judges decide but in what influences them in making decisions.

It is equally the task of the legislator, the executive, and the judge to balance stability with change, to preserve the institution as it was constructed with the alterations required to meet new conditions and challenges, by mixing the guide-lines of statute, orders, regulations, and precedent with their own information concerning the social exigencies. New laws and their interpretations have to be made, however, in the light of codifications aimed at an attainable degree of consolidation. This is made easy and more flexible for judges than it appears because of the enormous number of precedents in most cases and for law-makers because of the recurring content and form of statutory provisions, orders and regulations. On the other hand, they are not entirely free; for over lower courts stand the appellate courts, the legislature and to some extent the executive power; over the legislature stand the courts and the veto power of the executive; and over the executive are the courts and the legislative. In the long run this process will be no better than the intelligence, the knowledge and experience, and the honesty of the people who carry out its separate functions.

Legislators, the executive and judges if they are capable and conscientious, arrive at their decisions by acting upon a feeling of fairness, counting upon the fact that the feelings of an experienced and rational man are apt to be rational. Reasoning alone is not the best guide to action, for by the time a decision is called for it is too late to reason correctly. But there is another and more important invariant involved. Reasoning always means making deductions from axioms. If the axioms are false the conclusions will be false, and the more consistent the reasoning the more this will be true. Action based upon reasoning alone therefore may be in effect irrational. Then, too, axioms may be false, or they may be true but incomplete and therefore inadequate. For axioms are laid down well before the reasoning which operates in terms of them goes into effect.

There is another way in which legislators, the executive, and judges may go wrong. If they act not upon reasoning but upon feeling without reasoning, the conclusions in action could be even more harmful. The ignorant are without a guide to action, and feelings of fairness are not enough to save them.

Those who are properly prepared will act upon feelings, but they are the feelings which only a rational man could have because they are based upon anterior reasonings. It amounts to this, that the feelings of a rational man are better guides to action than the feelings of an irrational man or those of a non-rational man. There is an order and a proportion between reasoning and feeling which cannot be ignored.

Over the years, however, the accumulation of new laws and judicial precedents makes necessary a kind of house cleaning. And so in some instances, though not in all, acts of consolidation are made. Paton has pointed out that in England in 1913 there were 132 statutes dealing with perjury.[1] The process of consolidation undertakes to combine those laws which bear on a single topic with all those which in a more general way apply throughout the society. Over the decades laws accumulate, and are enacted or promulgated often without reference to similar or overlapping laws which were already on the books. A consolidation is often attempted in such a situation with the aim of achieving consistency and of avoiding confusion.

1 G.W. Paton, *A Textbook of Jurisprudence* (Oxford: Clarendon Press, 1946), p. 186.

The ideal is a body of law which is both consistent and complete and therefore in no need of modification. This goal is an impossible one to reach because of the changing and developing nature of society itself. As new conditions arise new laws must be enacted to regulate them, and so the procedure must be an unending one. Consolidation, which works with existing laws to render them consistent, must perforce be a continuing process, one which is necessary to avoid confusion but which never constitutes much more than a temporary arrangement.

The assumption that a law can be found to fit every case either by direct appeal to a statute, order or regulation, or by arguing from precedent certainly implies that the laws taken together constitute an organic whole and not a mere random collection of rules. That such a body of laws is capable of growth and change is attested by a standing legislature whose duty it is to increase or amend them. Common law is not the outcome merely of *stare decisis et non quieta movere*. The command to stand by decisions is in general followed where it is appropriate but otherwise things at rest are moved where necessary by means of judicial interpretation, executive actions or by legislative act. The principle of plenitude, which is the condition of being absolutely full in quantity and degree,[2] is assumed though not stated in all developed legal systems.[3]

In the operation of a legal system not enough credit has been accorded theoretically to the binding force of the culture. Against constitutional law, statute and precedent there is opposed the influence of the interpretation placed on the law by the judges. The forces of the contemporary world brought to bear on that system and the people charged with the responsibility for its operation come from many quarters: from tradition and custom well enough, but also from innovations in individual life, from other social institutions, from new knowledge in the arts and sciences, and even more perhaps from everyday common experience as it changes and flows. All of these influences, seemingly disparate and original, still have a set of assumptions in common, no less powerful for being unrecognized, no less influential for being unacknowledged. Their effect lies in the direction if not of uniformity then at least of consistency. The culture itself thus proves a force for consolidation even though this still leaves room within legislation and executive actions for some new statutes, regulations and orders and some necessary reforms, and within constitutional and

2 James K. Feibleman, *Ontology* (Baltimore: Johns Hopkins, 1951), p. 207.
3 George Whitecross Paton, *op. cit.*, p. 150.

statutory interpretations for adjusting principles and practices to changing material conditions.

3. Belief in The Law

The law exists in two ways: in a society or state, as written and practiced by individuals and institutions; and in the minds of men, as part of their conscious or unconscious belief. I have talked about the written law, now I wish to add something about belief in the law.

A belief is a feeling that a proposition is true. Such feelings may be subliminal, indeed most of them are. Beliefs are for the most part unconscious — the older phrase is committed to memory. We are conscious of very little in the way of beliefs at any given instant but we may believe in a vast horde of propositions which at any time may be recalled. But it is simply impossible to be aware of more than at most a few of our beliefs at a time.

We must learn to distinguish between the holding of beliefs and the beliefs themselves, between, that is to say, the degree of tenacity with which we cling to beliefs and the contents of those beliefs. The holding of beliefs comes in various strengths, all the way from superficial acquaintance at one end to profound acceptance at the other. We shall be interested here of course only in those beliefs which concern the laws. What applies to belief in general applies equally to belief in the laws. We may know about a law but not give it much credence, for we may consider it either temporary or of slight importance. Or we may believe that a law is so fundamental to individual existence or to the existence of society that its abrogation threatens both of them. An example of the former might be a temporary ordinance indicating that the traffic on a street which was being repaired must travel one-way only. An example of the latter might be the law which made murder in the first degree a capital offense. Between these extremes lie all sorts of degrees of beliefs of various strengths.

The degree of beliefs may shift in a society, so that laws formerly held crucial are held so no longer even though they remain on the statute books. But in the last analysis what holds the society together is the profound belief of a majority of its citizens that its laws must exist and be obeyed and infractions be punished. Without this there is no society. Thus the stability of a state rests finally upon the contents of the unconscious beliefs of its citizens. When laws are used properly they operate as guide-lines within which human actions both individual and social remain at a safe distance. An individual who 'obeys' the law is simply one who never comes into contact with it. His behavior is not such as to invoke it.

This makes the whole thing sound tenuous and arbitrary, yet that is not the case. For beliefs are not themselves capricious or even subjective in their justification. C.S. Peirce[4] has argued that no one believes without reason to believe. The capacity for belief is not at the disposition of the will; beliefs are not arbitrary but always exist for reasons which appear to the believer to be sound. What is true of belief is true also of doubt; no one believes or doubts without reasons which appear to the believer sufficient. Belief itself is of course an emotional state, and as we have noted, it involves the feeling that a proposition is true (or false).

It is necessary to remember here, however, that what is believed is not merely emotional, it is also rational and factual. No one believes in a law simply because he has chosen to believe in it; there must be some external, material and logical reason why it appeals to him as a subject for belief. Beliefs admittedly are always subjective; that is to say, they have their existence subjectively but they do not have their justification subjectively. The reasons for beliefs are always objective, material, and hence stable, in a way that merely subjective beliefs could not be. Thus we see that there is a U-turn from the material world (including society and its artifacts) routed through the individual's belief and back to the world again.

4. Legal Procedures

Practical procedures are often conducted successfully on the basis of the alleged theoretical truth of false propositions. Such a radical statement calls for an explanation. It can be argued that every practical proposition is partly true and partly false. When its truth exceeds its falsity we use it as though it were true. If this were not the case there would be no successful applications, and everything would remain in the domain of pure theory. But lives have to be lived, institutions maintained and governments operated. From the viewpoint of strict logic, what is applied is false if it is partly false and true only if it is entirely true. Practicality requires, however, that applications be made continually and exigently. Thus strictly speaking it is on the basis of false propositions that societies are conducted.

4 *Collected Papers*, 5.370, 5.440, 6.516.

Let me see if I can show that this is the case. The operation of law is usually concerned with immediate and pressing problems and those involved have no time to notice the conditions by which it is surrounded and which make its operation possible. Those who act within a system are the beneficiaries of that system without ever noticing even that there is such a system. The police may arrest a man or serve him with a subpoena, the district attorney may charge him with a violation of law, and the court may try him, without anyone ever stopping to consider what is involved. Yet the proceedings may not have been like that in another country or in the same country at an earlier time. As things are, so they have always been and so they will always be — that is the erroneous assumption of the practical man. And yet there is no one on the scene to challenge that assumption, and no purpose in doing so, either; for it would not affect the viability of the proceedings as they are conducted.

Ideally, the legislature enacts the law, the executive sees to their execution, and the judiciary determines what the law is and how it is to be construed for a given case. However, a government can operate efficiently only if there is some degree of blending of these powers while at the same time providing for their separation.[5] The legislative power ought, for example, to be balanced by an executive veto power.

When the laws are infracted then there is indeed a reason for litigation. Going to court implies the following of a certain procedure. All happenings stand equally before the law, the same whether crime or tort; in any case a fact: an act or event. A juristic act is one which affects rights, restrictions or duties. It is legitimate only if the actor is authorized by law to do what he does. The object of the action must be such as is provided by law. All juristic acts are voluntary but may be formalized by a declaration of intent. The actor does not have to be the one intending the action but may act as an agent or though articles of assignment. Liability involves motive and intent, movement or forbearance as well as material effects, the circumstances as well as the consequences.

The administration of justice is not a random affair and by its very

---

5 Aristotle's *Politics* (Rackham's translation. Loeb Classical Library, 1932), IV, II, contains what is commonly taken to be the original statement of the doctrine of the separation of powers. The *Politics* describes governments as divided into three parts: deliberators, magistrates and judicial functionaries. Under our system the legal framework also exists to provide governmental services to the people, like highway construction, unemployment insurance. Hence the framework is not invoked only in cases of infractions.

nature cannot be. To the extent to which the procedure is orderly it emanates from a legal system. In every order there is some evidence of a system. The system is non-temporal and abstract, the order is its concrete, temporal expression. Legal procedures rely upon a fixed order, and this relation remains the same whatever the order and whatever the legal procedure.

A formal procedure is an objectively established set of relations among them. It is a standing protection against the abuse of power on the part of individuals, who must perforce follow the rules even when undertaking to right a wrong. Legal procedures exercise some control over coercion by submitting litigants to formalities which operate in the name of reason. The adversary system is a method of substituting an appeal to reason and fact for a resort to force. In this way constructive aggression is substituted to some extent for destructive aggression, and a maximum amount of freedom under the circumstances is obtained. The result of following legal procedures is facilitative rather than obstructive, its aim is to smooth the way for the eliciting of justice, and is not therefore merely regulatory. Regulations suitably selected and properly applied do facilitate justice.

Last but perhaps not least should be mentioned something which cannot be described, only named. I shall call it the peculiar quality of experience. Psychoanalysts are fond of pointing out that no one can fully understand the psychoanalytic method who has not been psychoanalyzed. This is true; only, it is equally true for any well-established procedure in any long-existing institution. The courtrooms of England are filled with the atmosphere which centuries of the common law have produced. No one who has not steeped himself in the close environment of the courtroom can entirely comprehend the effect of what is called the majesty of the law. Submission to the authority of fact and its logic is sublime in its simplicity yet supreme in its efficacy. It can be felt as well as understood, but the combination of the two is overpowering. That experience which Mr. Justice Holmes said that he considered "the life of the law" has been experience, as he affirmed, but it has been not merely brute experience, as one might have erroneously inferred from his words, but the experience of that very logic which he denied operates upon the facts to which he saw only the subjective reception. The atmosphere of a long established courtroom is unmistakable and yet qualities are always emergent properties requiring underlying structures, in this case of course the law itself.

The Anglo-American law recognizes the distinction between those rules which govern the mode of proceeding by which a legal right is enforced, from those which define the right, and which, by means of the proceeding, the court is to administer. Procedure in terms of the conduct of judicial proceeding is what we are concerned about here.

The procedure in trial court in the United States is well established, and from the beginning when the action commences with the plantiff bringing suit, if it is a civil case, or the state, if it is a criminal one, against the defendant. After selecting the appropriate tribunal, bringing the defendant before it, making the charges and asking for the proper remedies, both sides usually being represented by attorneys, the trial beings. The distinction between law and fact is well recognized in the procedure, which does not involve a jury unless the question is one of fact. Finally, there is the trial itself, involving the presenting of evidence the questioning and cross-questioning by attorneys, the judgment, perhaps an appellate review and finally the verdict, a remedy, followed by enforcement.

I have omitted for brevity a number of steps, such as for instance the pretrial conference with the judge or his charge to the jury. Both sides are given equal and fair opportunity to present their respective cases. The judge's role in a court trial is chiefly to confine himself to the supervision of procedure and not to take sides. He listens to the testimony, arguments and motions in open court and intervenes only when necessary. The jury, if there is one, is obligated to render a general verdict such as would be reached by a body of reasonable men. The jury must determines the facts in the case, the determination of just what law is relevant is left to the judge.

Trial in a court of first instance is a dialectical process. It ends with judgment and execution. But there may be a stay of execution to allow for an appeal. The possibility of error is of course always present and so the process of review is a valuable additional check. The appeals courts then constitutes a second dialectic designed to reconsider and so to confirm or overturn a verdict previously rendered. The system of appeal involves a hierarchy of courts with ascending importance and authority. The higher the farther removed from the experience of fact and the nearer to the familiarity with theory. The gain is intended to benefit from a more detached view which is bound to result from ease of movement among abstract ideas.

The procedure of the trial court as I have been outlining it is typically Anglo-American. There are sharp differences with French or West German procedures. The common law of England and the Roman law on the Continent account for most of the differences. In both systems there are two elements: a dialectical debate and an inquiry. Anglo-

American law stresses the former, French law the latter. But in both systems both elements are to be found.

The trial procedure is intended to be dialectical in essence, that is to say, it is primarily a dialogue engaged in by those who have the joint aim of discovering the truth. Either discussant could make the discovery for when he does so it was with the aid of the other. Ascertaining the facts is the task of the court, and it is a dialectical undertaking.

However, there is a form of corruption for every true endeavor. The corruption of the dialectic is called eristic. The two methods appear much the same yet there is a subtle and crucial difference. For where the aim of the dialectic was the discovery of truth, the aim of eristic is the winning of an argument. In dialectic the two discussants subordinate themselves to the truth. In eristic truth is not at issue, only victory, and so in the end one discussant triumphs over the other.

In the Platonic dialogues the method of the dialectic was that of Socrates, while the method of eristic was that of the sophists. In a properly conducted court case all hands are involved in a common effort to discover the facts. Yet how many court cases are properly conducted? Trial lawyers are not concerned with the truth but with success: district attorneys want to secure convictions, criminal lawyers want to have their clients declared not guilty as charged.

The adversary system which seems essential to any fair and impartial outcome is subject to abuses. Ambulance chasing, "kickbacks", and in many other ways, the spirit of the law is transgressed even when the letter is not. The larger the crime and the richer the criminal, the more he is able to pay for legal services. We often see the spectacle of organized crime defended by legal counsel more vigorously than the government is able to do as plaintiff, with the result that without involving anything illegal the criminal gets off and is free to repeat his crimes. The practice of law is never so profitable as when lawyers are engaged in defending criminals against conviction. At least one critic has observed that the law is in one sense "a parasitic profession ... with its unique ability to create a demand for its own unproductive services"[6]; the law, in short, invoked to prevent justice rather than obtain it.

The dialectical procedure is a logical one though not rigidly so. Logic provides only guide-lines, and these are furnished more in the negative conception of fallacies than in any rigid rules of procedure. The ability

6 R.U. Ayres, *Uncertain Futures: Challenges for Decision Makers* (New York 1979, Wiley-Interscience).

to detect logical fallacies in legal arguments must be one of the skills of a well-trained attorney or judge. But logic is more specific in ruling what not to do than in what to do. No legal system can have the accuracy and strict deducibility of a mathematical system if for no other reason than that there are too many variables in cultural relations for a fair assessment to be made of their interplay. If there is a limit to the number of facts involved in any episode it is not known, and the same is correspondingly true of universals. The trial court endeavors to ascertain the facts in the case and inductively to fit them under the appropriate laws or at least under those generalizations which can be reached through analogy to known laws.

The working lawyer sees the business of the law not as an attempt to see that justice is done in a particular case but rather as a way of settling disputes. Yet disputes cannot be settled except on the basis of established principles as these disclose themselves in a codified system of laws. There must be some reason to prefer one settlement over another. The primary function of all legal argument is to provide the confirmation of the justice which lies behind the laws, conceived as prescriptions.

The understanding of the law as coercive by nature is a negative understanding. There is a more positive interpretation when the law is understood as a set of guide-lines to safe actions in a society. Those who intend to obey the law as a matter of course use it as facilitative. Coercion only comes into play when the facilitation somehow fails. None of this would be possible were conflicts settled without regard to stipulated ideals. Communities simply could not exist for any length of time without them.

The part played by ideals in practice is usually understated if recognized at all. There is an ideal of justice implicit in the proceedings of the trial court as surely as there is an ideal gas, an ideal radiating black body and a perfect vacuum operating in physics, only the ideal of justice is perhaps more difficult to envisage. I had much more to say about justice in an earlier chapter; here it is necessary only to point out that there is no scientific method of legal procedure; instead there is natural law as a working universal.

There is a similarity between the scientific method of investigation in the physical sciences and the method of a trial court. Both employ the data disclosed to experience within a framework of principles, undertaking to fit them together as a matter of particulars and universals. But here the similarity ends. For the physical situation is isolable, and tests of accuracy of fit can be made in the laboratory; but there is no such isolation possible in a social situation. Natural law does not merely stand behind the enacting of positive law in statutes and codes, it enters into every juristic act and every judicial review. The judge, and, desirably, the attorneys and indeed everyone connected formally with a court, should have in mind not only what the situation is with which they must deal but also *what-it-ought-to-be* as a state which should be attained. The corrective procedures, the penalties and remedies, are intended to shorten the difference between the *is* and the *ought*. Justice as the goal of every legal procedure means precisely that and those who serve the courts are pledged to it.

There are no doubt many grave difficulties in the way of those who are enaged in the best intentioned trial. What are called facts are statements about particulars. There are two sets of obstacles in the way of accuracy of statement, and accuracy of statement is what juries are charged with finding when they are pledged to determine the truth about the facts in a trial. Elsewhere I have characterized facts as concrete individuals and claimed for them three properties: they are intolerant of opposition, they have a history and they are infinite both with respect to their endurance and to their divisibility, that is to say they are stubborn and they have depth.[7] In a word, they are complex, and to characterize them in language is difficult enough; but to make matters more difficult the language itself has its own difficulties and presents additional intractable aspects. Even with disinterested investigators the facts are hard to come by and even harder to express in unequivocal terms. Admissible evidence may be oral (as in the testimony of a witness), written (documentary) or material (a physical thing other than a document). The facts are always those of the past and are occupied with events, and hence relevant documents and witnesses may be somewhat beside the point. Memories are rarely accurate and descriptions rarely precise. Both the vagueness of sense experience and the vagaries of language conspire to prevent the kind of representation which both those who argue for an honest plaintiff and an honest defendant would wish.

Again, the law as usually stated is universal, while human life both individual and social is conducted in terms of material particulars; a universal is the absolute general which is referred to by an abstract term, and a fact is a statement about particulars characterizing an individual, and we know from philosophical studies that no number of universals can altogether specify an individual. For this reason inter-

---

7 *Foundations of Empiricism* (The Hague: Nijhoff, 1962), pp. 61-2.

136

pretations and applications of the law will always give difficulties and will continue to work hardships in some cases.

Of course all dilemmas with respect to actual situations are constructed arbitrarily. Consider the case discussed by Pound, in which one tailor takes another's cloth and thinking it his own makes a suit. The question is, who owns the suit?[8] Pound has found seven distinct solutions, none satisfactory; and he concludes that "no moral precept will decide it."

Of course not. For the question was wrong when it was assumed that there is one and only one rightful owner; but I fail to see the difficulty. There is no great issue of moral principle involved. Of course one with a sense of humor might solemnly have asked just who the suit was made to fit. ... King Solomon would have offered to cut the suit in half. ... A practical matter of this sort would have to be submitted to arbitration: either the owner of the cloth compensates the other for his tailoring, or the owner of the suit pays the other for his cloth.

In judicial decisions properly made, the principle of multiple causation applies. Many factors enter into every social situation, and legal cases often are no exception. Existing laws, previous decisions, shifts in morality, and the special extenuating circumstances connected with every particular case, must all be taken into consideration and each weighed separately. Even their collective weight does not govern, for to them must be added the judge's own feeling for the case on trial. Taking a case under advisement may be the reason for a delay if there is one.

Precedence assumes that the judge takes seriously the decisions of those who are his peers and who in making judgments before his were similarly circumstanced. If on a former occasion another judge ruled that a case was a particular under some general law, then the judge ruling now can argue that the case he is considering is sufficiently similar to apply the same law to it. Thus justification is sought through tradition and a principle of legitimacy erected upon what may be termed judicial custom.

Abiding by tradition in the settlement of particular cases, known as *stare decisis*, probably goes back to a passage in Aristotle's *Rhetoric* where the principle of utilizing previous judgments is first stated.[9] In all probability, however, the judge-made procedure of establishing law

8 Roscoe Pound, *Justice According to Law* (New Haven: Yale University Press, 1951), p. 7.
9 1422b20-24.

upon precedent has never had to go back at most more than a few centuries.[10] This limitation allows the system to be kept within cultural limits. Yet it is not unheard of, either, to construct a past which would reinforce the values, the customs, traditions and laws of the present. It is amazing really how easily we can convince ourselves that our customs are the only ones which belong to the nature of things and that as things are so they have always been. Sir Carleton Kemp Allen insisted that "the custom of monogamy goes back to the earliest known social origins of our race."[11] If he meant the human race, then nothing could be further from the truth, for there is no evidence to call on in defense of the statement.

Yet whether a judge is guided by precedents, by textbooks or by the use of analogy, by custom or by the ordinary practices of business, one thing is clear: what he seeks is consistency and continuity in the application of the law. The familiar landmarks may be filled out by others more remote, attained by reference to moral or political considerations, which also aid in remaining within what the criterion of consistency calls for. The courts are conservative because every resource is employed to continue the stability upon which the law depends; the necessity of meeting the demands of completeness are a challenge to it, while those of consistency are a reinforcement.

5. Crime and Punishment

Criminal law has a number of aims, all positive. It aims at the protection of the public, punishment and the rehabilitation of the criminal.
Its punitive aspect also has a positive aim: the prevention by example of the commission of similar crimes by others. In the United States reparation ought to be included as an aim, though currently it is not.

What the ideal of law, which stands above the laws and implements them, does as a goal to all those forces which strive toward it, is to make possible the continual reconsideration of practice. A good example is to be found in the society of the United States today (1981). The enormous and recent rise in crime is generally acknowledged, but what to do about it is not. There are some thin lines difficult to maintain which the Supreme Court often seems to have crossed. The legal

10 Sir Carleton Kemp Allen, *Law in The Making* (Oxford: Clarendon Press, 1958), p. 71.
11 Ibid., p. 72.

rights of the criminal may be protected in such a way as to nullify the discouragement of the commission of crime and to abrogate the safety of the law-abiding citizen. The Court sometimes seems anxious to protect and preserve the rights of criminals while being unmindful of the exposure of the fabric of society which it has thereby placed in jeopardy by ignoring the victims of crimes. There is a need for individual survival as well as for the survival of established social institutions other than those covered by legal rights, and these needs are threatened by the spreading crime wave. It may be that the rights of criminals have to be sacrificed to some extent to the rights of the society as a whole.

The increase in crime in the United States has been duly noted and its causes and cures suggested: crime is a product of poverty and inequality.[12] Reduce these and you will materially improve the social situation with respect to civil order, peace and security. But in the meanwhile what? The problem is greatly complicated by the fact that the increase in crime is world-wide. International terrorism, urban guerillas, are only extensions of the national problems into a larger domain where crime-fighting forces hardly exist and no international law offer any protection.

The answer therefore lies outside the jurisdiction of the law. It does not lie in the province of the apprehension and conviction of criminals any more than it does in the protection of their rights. That is too far down the line. It lies earlier in isolating and striking at those forces which account for the existence of crime in the first place. For crime as we have it now is not the exclusive nor even the predominant domain of the underprivileged. Well-to-do-people are as apt to be criminals these days as needy people. In every recent riot there has been looting by those of moderate means as well as by the poor. And if we can include organized crime in our catalogue, the criminal class also draws on the super-rich.

What all these people have in common is a decline in the respect for the law. Now when a majority is not law-abiding, when those who have the most to gain by upholding the law are the most vigorous in their efforts to circumvent it, not much stability can be expected of it in the immediate future. The prospect is one of anarchy, and anarchy is not a stable situation either, only a condition which occurs during the transition from one kind of stable government to another. Men who break the law by and large do not aim at injustice but only at self-advantage.

12 Charles E. Silberman, *Criminal Violence, Criminal Justice* (New York 1978, Random House).

Indeed they prefer where possible to work within the law, and it is only the anarchist who wishes to overturn it altogether. Injustice therefore is rarely system-wide. Most criminals prefer to work around the established order and indeed they rely on it; they are not engaged in the larger enterprise of upsetting it.

On all sides these days we hear protests against the pollution of the environment. No doubt such pollution constitutes a clear and present danger to human survival. We hear less in a general way, however, of human pollution, which consists in the moral corruption of society. It exists in an increasingly alarming fashion in almost every leading institution; in business, from the stealing of customers in retail stores to the political machinations of the largest corporations; in politics, from the policeman on the block to the members of the national Congress; and it exists also outside institutions in organized crime (the Mafia) and in crime in the streets. Lying, stealing, cheating, is no longer considered bad form; only getting caught is. We need to organize the same kind of passive drive against the pollution of society that we see now being organized to fight the pollution of the environment.

It becomes clearer and clearer, then, that the law is the state in so far as continuity and survival are concerned. No prevalence of law, then no state. It comes down to a matter of whether one wishes to maintain the American democracy in the form in which we have had it. Those whose only aim is the accumulation of wealth forget that their right to remain in possession can only be guaranteed and maintained by the state, and what they do to undermine the state when they contravene its laws threatens their possession.

The topic of sanctions has not been exhaustively explored. Law-abiding citizens by and large require no coercion, they obey the laws for the most part out of a combination of conviction and inertia; it is proper to do so and also easier. The stability of society and of the state rides on such considerations more than has been recognized and acknowledged.

Most laws internal to states are matters of voluntary agreement. That this agreement is never total is what accounts for the attachment of sanctions to laws. The chief function of the law is not to punish offenders but to insure compliance. No amount of law could maintain order were there no acceptance; order depends chiefly upon belief and the concurrence it prompts. There always are crimes committed by a minority and against these there must be sanctions.

Since sanctions must be imposed by force, a central authority with the proper jurisdiction is necessary. Thus the existence of sanctions im-

140

plies the existence not merely of laws but of a system of laws. Sanctions imply organized laws which are seldom encountered outside a state.

All of us some of the time and some of us most of the time are inclined toward the destructive variety of aggression. Under the circumstances the willingness to rechannel aggression into constructive or at the very least harmless activities is only grudgingly conceded. At the present time, observance of the laws, even in crucial and difficult instances, goes unnoticed, and yet it is no small thing. It is proper that there should be punishment for infraction of the laws intended to curb aggression, but there should be much more extensive rewards for positive and effective support of the laws. A man who not only obeys the laws of his country but persuades others to do the same thing ought to be rewarded in proportion. We have instituted the more or less new function of the ombudsman; we ought now to establish another office, that of the law-congener, for this purpose defined as one who is professionally adept at persuading others to a like feeling for law and order, to a sympathy for all other members of the human species. His office properly speaking might come under the positive side of sanctions, and he would be engaged in persuasion rather than in coercion.

CHAPTER XIV

HOW THE LAW IS CORRUPTED

1. The Miscarriage of Justice

Whenever there is an established procedure there is often a special kind of corruption, and this is as true of the practice of law as it is of anything else. For as soon as any intent is regularized and formalized there will be those it does not benefit (and even some it does benefit) who will immediately seek methods of evasion. All men are equal before the law but not all equally accept it, and those who do not present a problems to its maintenance and defence. Thus there have arisen procedures also for circumventing the law, which by their very nature could never be formally established but which have been no less effective.

Justice is an artificial arrangement, for no two societies employ exactly the same systems to bring it about. But injustice is built into the very nature of things as a necessary ingredient of their separateness and discreteness. According to Anaximander[1] things "give justice and make reparation to one another for their injustice, according to the arrangement of time". Plato defined injustice as "a mere hindrance of that which passes through",[2] though the hindrance is not always as slight as the term implies, and may in fact amount to a total blockage.

The law in practice starts with its enactment or promulgation, and it is there that corruption also begins. Harmonizing legal rules with the public opinion of the day is done procedurally and formally, otherwise the constitution with its implied or openly stated morality is in danger of being lost. Bringing inactive laws back into operation and allowing others to go without application, is one way of following the changing

1 Kathleen Freeman, *Ancilla to The Pre-Socratic Philosophers* (Oxford 1948, Basil Blackwell), p. 19.
2 *Cratylus*, 413 E.

morality of a society. The law, however, is not the whole of individual or social life but only its agency. It regulates life but does not undertake to live it. But the wording of legislation can make it seem as though it corrected a wrong when in fact it did not. A familiar example is the practice of attaching riders to bills as these go through the Congress. If enacted these become laws; and so it is correct to say that, in this instance, at least, the law is evaded by law. What must be recognized in legal practice is that a bad law is still a law; and however much we may wish to change it, such a procedure to be itself lawful must follow the path of due process.

Every culture has its peculiar legal system, which it equates as a matter of course with the standard way of doing things and regards as a perfect exemplar of justice. Every legal system suffers equally, however, when a necessary shift from the strict interpretation of the law to the equitable opens the door through which all sorts of loose interpretations can enter, as indeed they often do when equity gives way to fairness. How much failure in its legal system can a country stand and still remain a viable country with a stable government? Law is the fabric in a society on which everything is hung, and when functioning smoothly is hardly noticed. Transparent facilitation is the nature of that function. The law operates successfully so long as order exceeds disorder. No one has ever measures how much disorder a social system can stand and still remain a viable system.

The law in practice might be generally described as justice modified by expediency: anything along that line, in fact, from mercy to duplicity. Any system will work tolerably well so long as it is believed to have a basis in justice, that is to say, so long as it is thought to be right in principle. There is always some element of chance as well as of law. What can those who do not believe in chance say about the man who benefits from his errors and survives because of his mistakes?

Certainly it ought to be recognized that one of the true and almost fatal enemies of justice in the practice of law is ignorance: ignorance of the statutes, ignorance of past judicial decisions responsible for error in the determination of relevance, ignorance of the true facts in the case, and finally stupidity on the part of all those involved. Ignorance, error and stupidity are sufficient in themselves, but when we are compelled to add to them deliberate lying, cupidity and laziness, we have a combination which is very hard to defeat.

In addition to these there are ways in which the laws are circumvented which do not involve deliberate effort. Laws for example may be badly written, so that their meaning is obscured or they offer a choice of incompatible interpretations. It is difficult enough for anyone to say to his contemporaries precisely what he means, but when you add to this the fact that statutes and decisions were written long ago and that meanwhile the language has changed, it becomes practically impossible to be sure that you are following it precisely. Thus unintentional incapacity must be added to the ordinary catalogue. Good intentions do not always make up the loss, either, when men come to a formal judgment of each other. The mechanism of judgment may itself stand in the way.

2. Evasion

Evasion is a deliberate attempt to circumvent the law. There are as many kinds of evasion as there are procedures, probably more than anyone can think of. It will help to list a few of the more familiar — I name them more or less at random. Among them are: appealing decisions, seeking procedural delays, finding fault with trials, requesting changes of venue, pleading illness, corrupting judges, corrupting juries, lying under oath, helping the criminal to evade the law through the use of legal means, finding errors in the writing of contracts which enable the plaintiff legally to evade their clear intent, exercising legal powers in order to show the extent of federal control, collecting damages legally beyond the extent of injury. Sometimes it almost seems as though the law existed in order to be circumvented. Hardly a day goes by in any law court that one or the other of these evasions is not to be found.

There are other and more organized evasions, each directly attributable to some one aspect of regular court procedures.

First I suppose should be mentioned the trial itself. The cumbersome nature of legal machinery can do as much as anything to prevent the rendering of justice. Too many people are involved, too many steps have to be taken, too much time is required. In addition to ignorance, then, must be mentioned accident, the sheer fact that the procedure laid down for the law often gets in the way of its efficient operation. The path of due process is strewn with obstacles for which that process itself is responsible, there are rules and guide-lines to be observed, principles to be followed, penalties to be imposed.

When a matter is in dispute, it may be brought to a trial before a court. Two parties which are adverse will with the aid of lawyers develop before the court all the disputed points. The court, consisting in a judge and sometimes a jury will render a decision by handing down a verdict. The procedure wears something of the aspect of a game, played by two teams of lawyers with the judge acting as referee.

The ideal procedure under these circumstances is what Plato called dialectic: two sides to an argument engaged in the dispassionate joint pursuit of the truth. Its discovery is what both desire and work for in such a way that neither gets all of the credit for running it down.

However, there is a particular form of corruption corresponding to every true endeavor. The corruption of the dialectic was in the Platonic dialogues called "eristic". The two methods superficially appear much the same, yet there is a subtle and crucial difference between them. For where in ancient Athens the aim of the dialectic was the discovery of truth, the aim of eristic was the winning of an argument. In the process of dialectic the two discussants subordinate their own interests to the truth; in eristic truth was not at issue, only victory; and so in the end one side triumphed over the other. We see the conflict clearly in the writings of Plato. Unfortunately, in the Middle Ages the method of arriving at the truth in philosophy declined and the process became corrupted into the casuistry with which scholars of the period are familiar. Logomachy of this sort is only too often now the practice of the courts.

It is more often than not impossible to tell in practice just what is going on. The trial is a formal procedure designed to determine guilt or innocence, but more often turns out to be a legal contest to determine a winner. It ceases to be the cooperative effort it was designed to be, and becomes instead a struggle. Forensic eristic may be the result of the practicing attorney's desire to win at all costs, including even the sacrifice of the system. His scorn for legal theory means that he takes the framework of the system for granted as reliable enough for his requirements and asks no question either about its origins or its foundations. He is right of course in so far as his own private interests are concerned, but more is involved and he forgets that the system did not always exist and that it had to be forged for him by the experience and the abstract thought of countless others who went before him. He is unaware of or indifferent to the fact that it is now challenged by rival systems that prevail and the framework they provide.

The lawyers are of course chiefly to blame though it may be plaintiffs who corrupted the lawyers. Consider for example the "criminal lawyer" whose career is founded on defending those who confess their guilt to him in confidence. Legally his procedure may be correct for everyone is presumed innocent until proved guilty, even if morally it is not; for the protection of the criminal against society has the effect of defeating the intent of the law, which is to protect society against the criminal.

The lawyer needs clients. For just as the doctor cannot make a living unless people become ill, so the lawyer cannot if they are not litigious. It has been said that if you wish to break the law be sure first that you have a good lawyer.

It is part of a lawyer's task to plead a case. In doing so he may produce evidence. Now sworn testimony, written or oral, or anything material that is produced in court and can be shown to be relevant may be admissible as evidence. It goes without saying that men and women have on occasion lied under oath, so little do they think of the oath. The ideal society will never be achieved until that day when the word of a man can be taken from him to stand as a pledge, in the same way as in ancient times the weapon of a warrior, the wool of a woman or the plough of a peasant did. The subtlest form of deception is to argue that when something undeniable is produced it amounts to fitting a case under one class when in fact it supports another quite different.

There is no such thing as an absolute proof of innocence or guilt, only overwhelming strong evidence, which a jury or a judge may conclude is sufficient to justify conviction. But there is always room for an element of doubt in anything concerning human affairs, and this is precisely the opening wedge, however narrow, into which corruption may find its way to vitiate the results.

The deliberate employment of falsehood by practicing attorneys is the greatest possible betrayal of society. And the deliberate defence of the accused, who has privately confessed his guilt, in order to help him to avoid the legal consequences, though allowed by law, is in a sense a betrayal also. In these and other ways it becomes clear that the extremes of liberalism have served only to subvert the legal process. The Warren Court was in fact a legal disaster, for it markedly changed the face of justice.[3]

Lawyers, like criminals, are often the only beneficiaries of the system. As Anthony Nicholson remarked, no matter what happens they are paid.[4] For they are men of action when they stand before a court and plead a case, and men of action are always opposed to any legal principles which get in the way of policies they wish to pursue. And so they brush aside as out of date or of no moment laws which seem to

3 Cf. for example, *Miranda v. Arizona*. 384 U.S. 436 (1966), where a defendant's conviction of kidnapping and rape was reversed on procedural grounds by the Warren Court.
4 *Esprit de Laws* (London 1973, Wolfe Publishing Company), p. 22.

thwart their intent. And yet the very existence of society depends upon guide-lines which are never crossed.

At the lowest level it seems to some lawyers that people exist only for the sake of litigation. Nowadays a prospective lawyer will undertake to study only so much about the law as he might need to know in order to win cases and earn money. The profession under these circumstances can hardly boast of that ideal of perfection which made the great periods of law in western civilization the models they have been. Neither Roman law nor English law at its height could have been what they were with such aims. There is nothing wrong with earning money, and everyone must do so in some way or other. What makes of the law a sordid enterprise is when the criterion of success holds the field alone and does not have to be shared with the upholding of principles, with a counsel of perfection or with a model of excellence.

Everyone seeks to interpret the law to his own advantage. A defendant accused of a crime may be subject to illegal questioning and even torture, lawyers are in the habit of making irrelevant evidence seem relevant, and judges may be influenced by personal prejudice. There is in fact no end to the bending of the law by everyone, and the only wonder is why it does not break more often and so bring the system down with it. Too many unconsidered beliefs in the fluctuating mind of all men exist for the judge also and must influence his decisions without his knowledge no matter how much he may wish to confine the influences which play upon him to law and precedent, but in addition the corruption also exists. Judges and pardon boards for example should be held to some extent personally responsible for paroled prisoners who commit fresh crimes.

Whatever the structure of the legal system, whatever its constitutional base and its inherited laws, the judge's decision seems to go in the direction taken by society as a whole. A liberal society will mean a liberal court, with much condoning of criminals; a conservative society will mean a conservative court, with sentences as severe as the law will allow.

There is plenty of room for options within a judge's jurisdiction. Between precedent and statute he can find the room to maneuver in order to make whatever decision he reaches seem inevitable and impartial. After all, it has been possible for two honest and sincere judges applying the same laws and having the same knowledge of the facts in the case, to reach two diametrically opposed conclusions. How much easier then when the judges are corrupt?

Corrupt judges are no strangers to the legal system, and now that breaking the law is so widespread a practice among all classes, we must not be surprised to see the judicial process itself subverted. No matter what the political system there is always a ruling class, whether supplied by royalty, the church, the rich, or, as in the case of the Soviet, the Politburo, and judges are usually subservient to that class. Only too often they bend the law in favor of those who are in a position to reward or punish them, and they can do so surreptitiously because the law is always subject to interpretation.

The practicing judge has before him both statute law and case law, and so has the two-fold task of making deductions from accepted legal principles and inductions from empirically decided cases, a two-tiered set of references. He has to reconcile the results as best he may, but this leaves him a good deal of latitude. When every case that comes before him presents a problem of this sort, the results is a system which is too flexible; it allows for change whatever way the winds of fortune blow.

There is no simple remedy for this shortcoming. A more rigorous training of lawyers, a more specialized preparation for judges, might help; but in any case to some extent the problem will always remain. Perhaps the remedy will have to await a raising of the level of morality in the society as a whole; as for instance might be the case if the possession of wealth and power carried prestige with it only under the circumstance that they were legitimately obtained.

Impartiality is confronted with the circumstance that cases differ from judge to judge and often in our country laws differ from state to state. The next decision the judge hands down may be whatever he wants it to be, if without too much effort he can cite precedent. Evasions of the law therefore can exist at any level. The deliberate breaking of the law by criminals and the legal evasion by citizens can be aided and abetted by legal defense, and often they have now been joined by those in charge of the judicial process itself.

The very essence of democracy in the judicial system is represented by juries. The right of an individual to be tried by his peers is so important that it is written into Article III of the Constitution. Everyone knows that the system is defective, yet nobody has been able to offer a better. Juries are supposed to be without knowledge of the case being tried before them, and without prejudice; and no doubt the former is more common than the latter. People selected at random represent statistically the usual set of prejudices, and these are at all times many. The members of the jury may with the best will in the world be incapable of judging on merits alone the guilt or innocence of the accused.

148

Then, too, of course, juries are subject to the usual sorts of corruption. Members have often been bought and paid for, and only occasionally caught. Thus evasion may be a matter of deliberate corruption as well as an inevitable result of ignorance and prejudice; jurors may be simply incapable of understanding many subtle involvements or highly technical complexities yet held responsible for a verdict. Numbers of individuals randomly selected form natural groupings, for there are natural leaders. Thus since it often happens that a single member of a jury can sway its verdict, only that one needs to be influenced unduly to determine the direction of the verdict.

What I have been maintaining here about lawyers and judges is true about courts in general. The courtroom drama remains very much today as Dickens described it, "a pleasant, profitable little affair of private theatricals, presented to an uncommonly select audience".[5] It is difficult to keep in mind the undeniable fact that any social order is in the best of times and circumstances no more than an uneasy fit, and however long established its support by a system of laws, their infraction is as inevitable as their enactment was definite, and remedies must be provided as essential parts of their establishment.

Thus courts with their judges and lawyers are as necessary to the social order as that order itself is to the society. That is why any serious challenge to its existence threatens the society. Ordinary corruption is dangerous enough, but when it is joined by the infiltration of elements of organized crime, and even by influences from outside the country, the situation becomes more serious. Organized crime is a subordinate system of law designed to subvert the larger system without destroying it. The criminal regards the reduction of his own needs as taking precedence over those of society. He must incorporate his own aggressions into the existing social order without upsetting it. For instance there has to be a sufficient flow of members' dues into the pension funds of a labor union if the Mafia is to tap it.

The success of any system of laws is the law-abidingness of the body of its citizens, and no number of enactments will produce that. What makes the citizens of one country possess that virtue while those of another do not? At the moment we do not know, but everything in the future of mankind depends upon finding this out. No legal system will work in the end unless its citizens sincerely want it to, and if they want it to then any system will work. Does this make all systems equal? I think not; for the final test is what that workability produces. If it

5 *David Copperfield*, chapter xxiii.

produces the unusual combination of personal happiness and cultural achievement, then it will have been worthwhile. Until then we have no choice but to struggle toward it as toward a desirable idea.

CHAPTER XV

THE SPECIFIC LAWS

The specific laws are concerned ordinarily with contract, persons and property. It is a thesis of this work that contract takes precedence, and that legal personality and property relations are derived from it. First, then, under this theory it will be necessary to examine contract.

1. Contract

A contract is an agreement which recognizes the origination of rights and duties between two or more persons and is enforceable at civil law. It may also recognize the assignment or cancellation of rights or duties already in existence. Care should be taken to remember that while a contract is a verbal instrument, what it refers to is not merely a matter of language. Language does not originate anything in the law but merely records relations. Language has a reference outside language, to which its meanings correspond. Just what those relations are is acknowledged in the contract. The agreement is not merely a common state of mind, a *consensus ad idem* in common law, but one committed to speech or writing. It formalizes an arrangement and this makes it public. It thus gives substantive force to an agreement. Contracts once made may extend beyond the agreement, for instance when one of the parties to it no longer wants it. In this sense the contract has an objectivity which an agreement may not have. In this sense also a contract may have an application that one or more of the parties to it did not intend. It is important to note that contracts have the force of law; an agreement between the state and an individual (including of course any legal person, such as a corporation), for example, or one between two or more individuals backed by the state.

A corporation is of course a contract, or a series of contracts; the act of incorporation makes it so. Individuals rarely deal with each other directly but usually under the umbrella of written agreements. This applies to everything from marriage to partnerships. The nature of contractual relations in general is not yet fully understood. It came in with civilization, which is too new a thing in the world to have been examined properly. Yet everyone is constrained to deal with it in many of its varied forms, of which the relations to the state are the most general.

A juristic act is never unilateral. It always involves the state as a party. The validity of a will made by an individual is not to be viewed as established until it has been probated by a court having competent jurisdiction. Until then it does not have the force of a contract but is made in anticipation of possible enforcement. A bilateral contract as a juristic act also involves the state as a third party. Again, it is this third party which makes of it a contract. Without that it is merely an agreement. Of course for some agreements no contract is necessary. Not all associations need to be bound in this way because there can be no occasion for enforcement. This applies even to some strong associations. There is no contract of friendship though there is of marriage, a strange distinction when it is remembered that agreement is involved in both and that friendships sometimes prove stronger than marriages and indeed sometimes last longer.

The system of order within the state rests on the establishment and enforcement of contracts. This applies to all formal arrangements, including the state itself. There are cogent reasons why in pure logic self-reference is inadmissible. Remember, however, that the logicians are not dealing with material relations but only with formal systems. Remember also that the state is a legal person, and is represented by the ruling community. By becoming a citizen the individual surrenders certain rights to the state which henceforth will act for him. The contract after all is revocable by either party. Upon leaving the state to become the citizen of another country the citizen may voluntarily surrender his citizenship. On the other hand, a government may revoke the citizenship of any citizen, as the Soviet Union sometimes does with its dissidents. Citizenship is a contract, and the "social contract" also is a contract.

Maine made a true judgment when he wrote that "the movement of the progressive societies has been from status to contract".[1] In contemporary societies in Europe and in those which are products of European civilizations the tendency has been to move the governing relation. By

---

1 *Ancient Law* (ed. Pollock, 1924), p. 174.

status is meant a fixed and often irrevocable position in society, such as membership in a class or caste, but meaning also any situation involving claims and powers determined by law, marriage, for instance. It might be possible nowadays to claim that contract creates status. It does so in the case of formal appointments, such as the one to a judgeship.

Status is characteristic of the older societies, the landed aristocracy, titles of nobility, serfdom, and so on. Contemporary societies tend to be more fluid, and it is possible to move both upward and downward in the social hierarchy. Wealth can be suddenly gained and as suddenly lost, and such movements are followed necessarily by the contractual arrangements that match them. In other words, status is typical of early societies, contract is typical of more complex societies in a later stage of development.

Kant's "will" theory of contract is inadequate because the will does not make any mark, only the act does. When will becomes translated into action there is something external to be judged. No one knows for certain what is in a man's mind, and it often happens that the man himself does not. Actions follow from beliefs of which the will is only the instrument, so we must look deeper than the will even for motivation. A contract is tangible evidence that an agreement was reached, and it holds sometimes when the agreement no longer exists.

Contract is in fact the essence of established order. No contract, then no government. Laws, constitutional and otherwise, rest on contracts. Back of the contracts are of course the belief in their efficacy, but that belief is not arbitrary; it is based on an accepted theory which is no less real for not being always openly expressed. Contracts are verbal agreements, and in words that have reference as well as sense. Only the sense shows, because reality is the reference, or at least some selected theory of reality. Nevertheless, without a reason to honor such agreements the very fabric of society falls apart. Hence its importance to law.

2. Persons

A person may be defined as a free-standing human individual. Nothing more nor less is meant by it than a member of the species, *Homo sapiens*, who is not limited in any way except by his (or her) capacities. A legal personality is a person recognized as having a place in the law. The legal personality of the human individual is that human individual so far as the law is concerned with him. The legal person is a bearer of rights and duties under the law, a *persona* in the ancient Roman sense.

We have noted already that the individual becomes a legal person when he enters into a contractual arrangement with the state. This is done for minors by parent or guardian when births are registered. An infant has no obligations or duties but it does have rights. In Louisiana where the Napoleonic Code was retained a man must provide in his will that his children inherit a part of his estate. The legal person is a product of the contract between the person and the state. The legal person is usually a citizen, but in English common law it extends to resident aliens and in some instances even to visiting aliens.

The legal person is only one side of the human individual, who has many other sides. He may be a friend, an unpublished poet, a private religious believer, in none of which connections does he enter into a contract of any sort. On the other hand, the individual is only one kind of legal person.

The human individual is a complex organization and has many sides. On one of these sides he is confronted with other individuals and with material objects or artifacts, and enters into material relations with them. In so doing he encounters the laws of his society, when a legal person is constructed to represent him. It is an abstraction though not a fiction because it truly represents him. Above all it is important to note that it is contractual in nature. For by according an individual a legal personality the state recognizes that individual's rights and duties and agrees in advance to allow him full recognition under the law, as for instance when he wishes to assert his legal rights or is compelled to meet his legal duties. The legal person, in other words, represents a contract whereby the state agrees to recognize the rights and duties of the individual. Not all contracts are with human individuals and not all human individuals are contracted to be legal personalities. But all legal personalities are so in virtue of a contractual arrangement. In this sense, even if in this sense only, legal personality is a subclass of contract.

The legal person, then, is not a whole person but that side of a person which is turned toward his formal connections with society. In any such formal connection the law is involved. Not all human individuals are granted legal personalities, which are within the province of the law to bestow or withhold. Infants are human individuals but they are not legal persons in all senses, and in some societies born idiots and condemned felons are not legal persons, either.

Legal personality begins when a birth is registered with the state, but it does not end at death. The contractual arrangements of the individual continue to be recognized and honored after his death through the execution of his will after it is admitted to probate. This remains true even though the dead have no other rights and for instance under English law cannot be libelled.

As noted previously, individuals are not the only legal persons. Any entity recognized by the law and established may have a legal personality. Thus corporations are legal personalities; they may sue or be sued.

From a legal point of view, the personality is a contractual arrangement. This follows from much current thought in jurisprudence, though it has not often been brought out in exactly this way. Under the laws of the state, every sane human adult individual living within the state is accorded a legal personality, as much of a contractual arrangement as the legal personality of a corporation. But to say that legal personality stems from contract is not to make it less real. It is a real material relation, and as much of one as an individual's relation to the house that he "owns".

Social groups are not new things in the world. No doubt associations based on one kind of interest or another are as old as the human species. The use of corporate personality however is not. Corporate personality enables an interest-group to function as a person, for instance to sue or be sued apart from its individual members. Social groups still exist even in a formal sense, as for example families and partnerships. But the corporate personality has added new dimensions based on specific contractual arrangements. The articles of incorporation constitute such an arrangement, thus reinforcing the functioning of contract, a dramatic illustration of the subordination of legal personality to contract. The corporation was granted a legal personality not only to limit liability but also to secure some measure of permanence. Without it there would be no large undertakings engaged in by heavy industry without public support.

To say that legal personality is an artificial arrangement brought about by the law is not to say that it is not natural. I do not recognize the distinction between *physics* and *nomos*, between what is natural and what is artificial, except in a very limited sense. What we call artificial is what is natural under the circumstances, and circumstances differ according to date and place. A naked Bushman in South Africa would not be though to be exposing himself, a naked American in New York might. Such changes are themselves natural too, and we recognize them in law.

The theory that a single human individual is real but that a group of individuals organized around a central undertaking and engaged in a succession of common enterprises is not real stems from a metaphysical theory which came in the Middle Ages to be named nominalism. It is not to be confused with materialism, for some materialists are nominalists but not all. There are levels of organization within the purview of the human species as with all other material entities, and any one is as real as any other. That corporations may be dissolved is no argument against their reality while they exist any more than that a man may be killed is an argument that he was never alive. We recognize this in fact in law, where the legal personality of a corporation receives the same recognition as the legal personality of a single human individual. Both obtain their legal existence from the state through its laws, and both legal personalities have come into existence as recognitions of necessities.

Group life was not created by the state but such associations come into existence because they satisfy individual needs in a way no other organizations can. Individuals do exist and they do agree to engage in joint enterprises which may and often do extend beyond their lifetimes into a period when they will be taken up by other individuals who will suffer the same fate. It is impossible not to recognize in both kinds of legal persons exigencies which must have legal recognition if the social order is to be preserved by means of a legal system. What is real about the human individual so far as the law is concerned is his indubitable existence as expressed through his rights and his duties. The corporation exists in the same way. It has rights, it can sue for instance, and it has duties, such as the paying of taxes.

If someone wishes to argue with Kelsen, that it all comes down to the living human individual in the end, this is to ignore the very real facts of human culture. Human individuals both singly and in concert alter materials in their immediate environment in ways intended to influence themselves and others, as they do through works of art, and often even extending beyond their intentions, as the pollution of the environment does. Culture is as real, as stubborn and as undeniable as the people who make it and who in a sense are powerless to unmake it. The institution is more than the sum of its parts even though living human individuals are among those parts. Bombing a society into submission does not unmake the culture, it merely brings about a cultural desert with the consequent effects upon those who were not destroyed in the process. A desert of this sort is emphatically not a non-human natural object.

3. Property

Hegel thought of contract in terms of property.[2] I think of property in terms of contract. Property rests on contract. There is no such thing as inalienable ownership as an arrangement between an owner and that which he owns. Ownership means that an arrangement is made with the state and takes the form of a contract respecting the relations with a thing. That relation may depend on use, but not necessarily. Thus the state may determine the criterion of ownership, which may be use or function, or may leave it to the person and his heirs and assigns to determine.

For the purpose of legal theory the understanding of matter must be widened. We shall be primarily concerned with two kinds of matter: artifacts, which are material objects altered through human agency for human uses, and the human individuals themselves. Property exists at various integrative levels: the physical (hills, for example); the chemical (salt mines, oil wells); the biological (cattle, pets); the phychological (other minds or brains); and the cultural (musical compositions, copyrights). The reader will perhaps boggle at the notion that other minds can be considered property. They are not, in any legal sense. And yet to the extent to which one man adopts profoundly another's ideas, the latter has made of the former's mind an artifact, in the definition of artifact I have been employing throughout this work, for it is a material object which has been altered through human agency for human uses.

In so far as the human individual has a material body, including a material brain and nervous system, and in so far as he communicates his thoughts and feelings by means of material signs: modulations of sound waves and marks on surfaces which together we roundly call languages, we are still dealing with matter. It is not a dead and inert stuff as was formerly believed; since modern physics we have known it to be volatile and a form of energy, in this case complex and rare.

Legal relations therefore will have to be regarded as a species of material relations, for they are arrangements between individuals and social groups respecting both each other and those objects which in law have been known as property. Matter has a larger range of kinds of materials, and the materials offer a greater complexity of potentialities than anyone had supposed or perhaps even yet supposes. How rich we can make human life we are yet to discover, though we are beginning to glimpse a little of its vast possibilities.

2 *Philosophy of Right*, § 40.

With all of these enormous discoveries in range and depth of complexity in both the sciences and the arts, the development of the law must keep pace. And not merely by means of proliferation of new laws to regulate new situations, but also by means of a new system of laws designed to provide the requisite completeness as well as the requisite consistency.

The direction of the development of economic exchange, it has been noted, runs from barter to money to credit. We are at the stage now of shifting from the second to the third. Increasing abstraction is the constant function and it discloses the essentially contractual nature of the relation involved. Money is of course a form of property, whether it exists in coins of precious metal, in tokens merely or in the form of credit. Money, and these days that means usually paper certificates, is a contract with the state to guarantee the holder a given amount of purchasing power of material goods or services. But property of whatever form is the individual's only hope of being able to obtain those materials which can reduce his organic needs and so to survive and flourish.

The contract is the lawful part of the culture, using the term in its broadest as well as its narrowest sense. For a constitution is a contract entered into by all of the citizens, and laws are extensions of the constitution: agreements by which all shall abide. By and large, contracts spell out both rights and duties, and this is true both of civil law and of "the law of the land". In the language of real estate, most property is "improved", houses are built on lots but also metals are mined and made into cutlery, motor cars or computers. Men enter into contracts concerning their relations to each other and to various pieces of property.

There is no such thing as the absolute private ownership of land even in the most capitalist of countries. Where private ownership is allowed it is dependent upon government, and remains only such as the government endorses. There is a definite territory over which the government exercises control, and it has a monopoly of force over that territory. The ownership of land is an enclave within that jurisdiction and remains subject to it. Thus ownership is ultimately vested in the government, as much *de facto* in a modern democracy as it was *de jure* in feudal England, say, when all subjects held their land from the king, or in a modern communist state where there simply is no private ownership on any large scale.

With the rise of very large populations, which is a comparatively recent happening, and with the increase in complexity that science and technology have made possible for industrialism, the fundamental nature of property has shifted, and the shift is a significant one for all human relations. As we have seen above, it is from substance to function; from a static substance to a dynamic function. Property now plays an active part in the society, where formerly it had been, like the legendary passive maiden, merely fought over.

I am not suggesting anything anthropomorphic, only that there are continual shifts and changes and that the function is an ever-present consideration in human relations. In human relations, therefore in legal relations. Without material owned by someone or some institution, then no human relations in need of regulation. Degree of individual freedom, economic security, personal ambition, all involve the use and even the ownership of property of some sort. In addition, property plays a much larger role in industrial society than it does in primitive societies because the production of some artifacts is so much more complex, difficult and rare. Not everyone can make a cobalt generator, an office typewriter, a motor car, a computer, not everyone can construct synthetic penicillin or an office skyscraper.

The material component of human society, the component which indeed makes of a society a culture, has been much neglected in European and American thought since Marx. Marx and Engels have of course based their social and political theory on materialism, but one would not have to accept their analysis of their solution to consider matter important. One may be a materialist without being a Marxist. The new conception of matter does not even seem to make this necessary, for if theory, like everything else according to Marxism, is derived from the mode of material production, then Marxism itself is out of date, for the mode of material production has been changed considerably since Marx's day. Now we have a greatly altered and much more sophisticated mode of production, so much so that the old canons no longer apply. The belt line and automation, for instance, have come into common use. There are other considerations which negate Marxism. For instance competition has sharpened rather than destroyed capitalism. The means of production while still under the control of a small group is no longer exclusively owned but is the possession of millions of shareholders. Government has constrained business to an important degree, and controls have been put in that were not thought possible before. In addition, the rise of the labor unions has changed the power balance and given to labor a larger percentage of profits from the operations of industry.

There is of course such a thing as property which is in the possession of the state. In the United States there are for instance federal and state owned lands, federal schools and state universities. It would be interesting to ask whether property in such an instance is a contractual arrangement. On the basis of the meaning of ownership it would seem so. It is necessary to take the position that ownership of property by the state is legal shorthand to cover its ownership by *all* of the citizens collectively. I revert again to the fallacious claims of the subjectivist. It is my property, said Kant, if I have exerted my will upon it. Unfortunately, we have exerted our will upon many properties without that activity necessarily having made it our own. This is rather the claim of the thief. Moreover, everything does not have an owner. The center of the earth has no owner and yet all of us need it, and this is true of the sunlight as well. A man can be deprived of sunlight by another who puts him in a sunless jail cell, yet nobody owns sunlight just the same. Possession means physical control, and such control can be secure only to the extent to which it is guaranteed by the laws and enforced by the state.

The ownership of property is formalized and hence established by contract. No contract, then no ownership. And a contract is nothing if it is not backed up by the enforcement powers of the state. If the state were either unable or unwilling to enforce a contract then ownership could not be sustained. Landowners and shareholders tend to forget their utter dependence upon the law-enforcement agencies without which their right of possession would not be supported.

Ownership has always led a contractual existence even when it was of a vicarious nature. It is often surrounded with so many restrictions that it becomes of dubious benefit and can even be a liability. In medieval Europe the landowner was entitled to the benefits of the land but could not sell it. Under the Church of England the parson had a freehold which secured to him its revenues but did not entitle him to transfer it to another, only to resign it. In some instances the member of a golf club may not sell his membership without the consent of a board of governors and the owner of a cooperative apartment is often bound in much the same way.

There is no such thing as property as such. Material things exist as property in virtue of contract. If in the case of private property in a state in which it plays the chief role a fortune is handed down from parent to child for generations, it is only because there is a long-lasting continuity in the form of the state which provides for it.

The success of the Marxists in overthrowing existing governments and in establishing their own has occurred only where there have been flagrant abuses of property rights. There is a middle ground between absolute private property and the ownership by the state of all of the means of production. In Russia and China prior to the communist take-over, feudal conditions prevailed. The Soviet citizen has not only more freedom but also more property rights than his ancestor who was a serf. Marxism has scored no successes in those advanced democratic and industrial countries which were the very ones in which Marx himself expected the earliest revolutions to occur. Marxism, in a word, succeeded only where it was able to present its actions as a redress of wrongs incurred in the conduct of material relations.

Property as possession means the limited rights to the exclusive use of a material or of an artifact. What is called "unimproved" land, land to which nothing has been added and from which nothing has been subtracted, may be a property, but so may a motor car, a bank account, a pencil or an airplane.

I said 'limited right' because ownership is never absolute. The question arises whether the owner of a crucial property has a right *not* to use it. Ownership, then, is not merely negative, not merely the right to keep others off; it is an obligation to proper use. Any use which endangers society in any way is not part of ownership.

Ownership has not been altered in its essentials with the modifications which have come about recently in politics and economics, but it has been greatly modified. It is absolute now only in a restricted sense. The power to do what one likes with one's own is limited now to consumable products. It rarely applied to the members of a family and now applies only in some instances to the means of material production. The owner of a small drug store can close it and go out of business, but there is at least some question whether if a single individual were found to be the controlling owner of General Motors he would be allowed to do the same thing. Ownership has become reduced to the legal privileges and obligations the owner incurs in virtue of his contract.

When the same conditions prevail for long periods of time, they begin to be enlarged as irrefrangible. In a society such as our own where private property has existed for many generations, men of substance regard their ownership of land and improvement, of stocks and bonds and other securities, as irrevocable. In communist countries, however, the institution of private property was abrogated, at least so far as the means of production, and land as well as industries were included in the broad sweep of that phrase. The communists have proved at least that property is a contractual arrangement guaranteed by the state. No doubt if communism remains in effect for a few generations, the state as the sole owner of the means of production will be regarded as irrefrangible and irrevocable in much the same way. The philosophers come to our aid at this point. They are fond of reminding us that nothing formed of material is eternal. In time everything gets swept away, though this is a hard thing to acknowledge when institutions have had such a long life.

CHAPTER XVI

THE METAPHYSICS OF LAW

1. The Two-Story World

Our problem now is to work out the metaphysics of law. What are the presuppositions of the legal system? I take it that they are to be found in the prevailing morality, for every morality is anchored half-way between an abstract metaphysics, on the up side, and an actually existing society with all of its conflicts and confusions as well as its partial ordering, on the down side. It must be consistent with a highly remote theory and yet compatible with the brute immediacy of events.

But the prevailing morality is the system of order of the culture as a whole, since it is usually put forward by the leading institutions and adopted by the others. I am not interested here in learning just what that morality is in any particular culture but rather in understanding how it permeates the legal system in all cultures. If the legal system follows from the prevailing morality and the prevailing morality follows from a covert metaphysics — what I have elsewhere called *the implicit dominant ontology* — then we should expect to find that the metaphysics permeates the legal system even if it got there only at second hand. Thus while it must always seem to practical-minded men that it is a long way from the theory of metaphysics to the practice of the courts, the enactments of statutes, the decisions of judges, the pleadings of lawyers and the action of police, still there is, I would argue, a necessary reference which accounts for the differences found in such practices in different countries and in different countries at different times.

The hierarchy from which law derives its authority runs somewhat as follows.

Reality	(metaphysics)
Morality	(ethics)
Legality	(laws)

This is not a chronological arrangement but a logical one. Back of every morality there stands a theory of what is ultimately real, and back of every system of laws there stands a morality. This derivation does not have to be conscious or deliberate for it to be true. A man may appeal to the laws to justify his beliefs or his actions, but he may appeal equally to his religion, his conscience or the social or cultural tradition of the society in which he lives. Yet these are carriers, they are not doctrine; and he has not said why they are justifications. For the fact is that he is appealing *through* them, not *to* them, and the hierarchy in some pervasive way lies in their direction.

What are we faced with exactly in our search for presuppositions? If we work backward from existing situations to the metaphysical domain, it must be in terms of the assumptions or presuppositions of those existing situations. The situations are concrete, the metaphysics abstract, and so we should expect the metaphysics to be a set of generalizations of the situations. Let us see if we can frame a metaphysical theory which will take care of the existing situation within a particular system of ideas.

For this purpose I propose to employ definitions already constructed. The ontological domain of *existence*, then, is the condition in which material things affect or are affected by other material things. Matter, I remind my readers, is now the static form of substance, and is capable of being transformed into energy, which is the dynamic form of substance. Thus when we talk about material relations we mean them to represent both the logic and the values (qualities, forces) of substance.

A sharp demurrer must be entered at this point against confusing this doctrine with Marxism. Not all materialism is dialectical materialism and this is particularly true of what I have called the new materialism, a materialism based on the new conception of matter which is to be found in modern physics and chemistry.[1] The new materialism is neither atheistic nor authoritarian.

The material world is the scene of all happenings, all things and events. These contain not only many regularities such as qualities and values but also negative properties, such as privation, discontinuity and inequality. As a result, existence is the arena in which forces are exerted, in which things happen by chance and from cause, and from the mixture of chance and cause, a domain of facts and events. Existence contains both order and disorder, conflict as well as harmony. By

1 *The New Materialism* (The Hague: Martinus Nijhoff, 1970).

an 'order' is meant an abstract structure whose elements can be put into one-one relation with the positive integers, and by 'disorder' is meant the elements of order out of their proper order. Now there is a segment of existence occupied by members of the human species and their material artifacts, organized into social units. The material relations with which we shall be concerned are confined to this subset of all the material relations in existence.

All of the material relations which exist at any given time are themselves only a subset of all those which could exist. The totality of material relations, then, is a larger group than the group of those which *do* exist, and includes not only those which *did* exist, but also those which *will* exist, all subgroups of that larger group of relations which could exist. This last group includes all the others as special cases, and is called the domain of logical possibility, or *essence*.

Material relations have two sides always. They are logical but they are also axiological, that is to say, they are affective as passive qualities and values and active as qualities (forces). As logical they are inclusive and non-contradictory; as axiological they exhibit continuity (they are without a break), plenitude (they are everywhere full), and gradation (they are arranged in levels).

The domain of *essence* is an empty domain in the sense that it is not substantive, it does not contain anything except possibilities, and these can be actualized, when they are, only in existence. But possibilities are not quite nothing. They provide the status which anything must have when it is not actual, and there is always more that is possible than is actual at any one time.

The domain of essence, then, is ideal by nature and is governed by logic. By 'ideal' I should quickly add I do not mean mental, although its understanding must of course occur in minds. That is why Plato referred to it as the domain of "Ideas" and in another place as "intelligible things" in contrast to "sensible things."

Before elaborating the details of either of the domains I have sketched out above, let me add the third and last of them. This is the subdomain of the domain of existence, that part of existence in which efforts are made to establish and maintain a semblance of order. For want of a better term we may call it the domain of *destiny*. *Destiny*, in a word, is a movement operating in part of the domain of existence and aimed at the conditions which prevail in the domain of essence, a drive in existence toward essence.

Like the domains of existence and essence, destiny has its characteristics. Events in existence which have the destiny properties are those which can be described as functions; in the mathematical sense, they have generality and they are full of potentialities. Ordinary things and events not destiny-bound have the same properties though not to the same degrees. The urge toward extension and expansion, the undertaking to operate with a greater number of elements and to render actual what had hitherto been only a set of possibilities, is typical of organizations in this domain. It is a man and not a dog who wishes to extend his operations to more of his environment, to include great numbers of his own ˙species, and to do all of that of which he feels himself capable. Above all, there is a strong tendency in the human individual to wish to increase order, an order governed by himself no doubt but still an order, and if possible a wider and wider order.

We now have our three metaphysical domains, and it is hoped that together they are capable of doing what all metaphysical schemes are intended to do, which is to provide a framework into which everything there is, whether of a concrete or an abstract nature, can be fitted. The collective name for the three domains is an anciently endorsed one: reality. Philosophy may be defined as the study of reality, and every original philosophy must be constructed in terms of its own definition of reality. I define reality as *equality of being*, which means that any of the three domains has as much being as any other element.

In order to show the philosophy of law it will be necessary to explain the legal system in terms of the metaphysics. Given the metaphysical scheme, our next task will be to show where justice and law belong in this framework.

2. The Three Theses

In the course of this work I have tried to demonstrate the three theses. These were: *the importance of material relations, the interpretation of justice as the demand for a system of laws,* and *the centrality of contract*. I now propose to show how these fit into the metaphysical scheme which I have just suggested.

Existence is represented in connection with the laws as those material relations which exist in the state between human individuals, social groups and institutions, and those material objects which have been altered through human agency and which are owned (artifacts). There is an area where conditions hold and events occur. Propositions about facts are attempts to describe them. Due to the nature of language as composed chiefly of universals, such propositions are only approximations of the truth. 'John struck Mary'; 'Tom broke his agreement to sell his house'; 'A fire seems to have been set deliberately'. Such facts are material particulars, actionable under the laws. Decisions determining which situations are legal and which illegal depends upon certified regulations. These regulations are governed by laws establishing and continuing the elements of a social order, but they exist also as elements of disorder. Society is never more than a partial order, but until the elements of disorder outweigh the elements of order, the state continues to exist and to function.

All legal relations are undertakings to deal socially with material situations which stubbornly exist. The need to deal with them is a result of their existence and not the reverse. Things and events are not the consequences of the language we use in order to cope with them, but in order to cope with them we use language. The legal language is no different from others in this respect. Legal relations exist to the extent to which certain of the elements in existing situations are to be rendered permanent.

It is not true that because contracts are verbal they are merely matters of language. The positivists would have to contend that when a man has been appointed a judge, the appointment is a matter merely of words and that nothing has been added to him. But surely this is not the case, something has been added. A new position has been extended him, one which carries with it a new substantive function; henceforward his orders will be obeyed and his judgments executed provided only that they lie within the legitimate sphere outlined by the office.

Words, language, consists in symbols materially conveyed, either by means of conventionally-shaped sounds or by conventionally-shaped marks on a flat surface, and these are the tools which are employed in legal transactions. What is thus conveyed is a set of intentions to behave in a specific manner with respect to persons or property or both. Thus language is employed but only to refer beyond language to specific particulars in the materially world. Rights and duties are originated, transferred or extinguished through legal transactions effected by contract.

Legal relations are everywhere found in the most commonplace transactions. The English pound sterling is a promissory note to pay the bearer one pound on demand. The American dollar indicates that it is legal tender for all debts, public and private. In both cases legal relations are involved and *nothing else*. Neither is any longer redeemable. All that is left is the contract by means of which monetary transactions are made possible. And they are possible because someone to whom money is owed can be paid off in the same promise by which he was paid. Money is a kind of generalized contract, for it holds between any two individuals in a state without their having to be named. The promises it constitutes are upheld by the state in all cases, and so may be relied upon for an undefinitely extended time. Money is, in other words, a ready market in promises.

Since money has a certain exchange-value in commodities, if such promises are not themselves substantive they can be readily made so. The important point to remember in all this is the substantive nature of the reference in every case. It is appropriate bundles of matter and energy which are the objects of the references. Money, contracts, every material relation which is part of the social matrix, refers eventually to something substantive on which rely the hard facts of property and even the social contacts of persons.

Essence is represented in connection with the law by the centrality of contract. Here however there is an intermediate set of qualities and relations prevailing. Although a contract, remember, is an agreement which originates rights and duties, these are not random. They are selected in the light of the demands of some anteriorly accepted standard of conduct. While contracts are commonly classified according to the element in them which is brought into prominence, they are specific or general. A specific contract is one which holds between two or more individuals but only between them, an agreement to buy a certain house for a specific price, for instance. A general contract is one which spells out penalties for infractions.

Here Essence appears as an accepted morality which is consistent with the implicit dominant ontology and from which the laws of the society are deduced also exists. The ontology is described as 'implicit' because it is covert rather than overt, it is described as 'dominant' because it provides the consistency-rules between divergent sets of empirical data and in this way accounts for the cohesive properties of the culture: at any given time there may be no other. If the implicit dominant ontology shifts, so does the prevailing morality, and as the morality shifts so does the notion of contract. The inviolability of contracts may be overturned. Contracts which had been in effect between citizens in Czarist Russia were not upheld by the new masters of the Soviet Union. When the British government transferred its power in India to the Congress Party by means of the Indian Independence Act which set up the Dominion of India on August 15, 1947, the principle of paramountcy which had been guaranteed to the Native States by the British was thought to be protected by Article 7 but in fact was never honored by the Congress Party.

A pervasive social morality exists in *every* society. It exists in the beliefs which the members of that society hold in common; it exists in the institutions which they have established and in the rank order of those institutions; it exists in the preferences which the society expresses through its customs and through matters of taste and choice; it exists in the direction which it takes, and in the aims which it has. Such a morality is concrete in the sense of its acceptance, yet its existence takes the form of that peculiar vagueness of generality which all universal values possess. Every formal legal arrangement is a contract of some sort, and if we have in mind the principle of direction it follows that contracts are eventual reflections of the conceptions of what the corresponding logical conditions in the domain of essence are like.

Destiny is represented in connection with the law by the interpretation of justice as the demand for a system of laws, and that demand takes the form of law-making, implementation, and enforcement activities. I have pointed out already that in the existence of a society there is to be found a large amount of order and a smaller amount of disorder. The disorder is a threat to the continuance of order and so it must be eliminated by legal force. That force is represented by the police and the courts, which were designed to deal with those activities which run counter to the permitted activities within the society under the established order. In this way so far as social order is concerned the preservation of the law is the chief activity of the importunate aspect of destiny in so far as it concerns the drive of existence toward essence.

Deliberate aims, then, do not begin with the morality but with the attempt to implement that morality. The codified laws of a society, its statutes, orders and regulations, its law-making and implementing bodies, its courts and police, are concerted efforts to capture and apply the consequences of that morality through regulation and enforcement. There is also an important aspect of destiny, which consists in the universal of justice upon which all particular codifications and administrations of justice depend. Justice in the universal sense becomes contracted by local conditions to particular legal actions.

Since the domain of destiny is that segment of existence in which energies operate deliberately and efforts are willfully exerted, there are conflicts. Within a civil society such conflicts take the form of disputes. From the point of view of the practicing professional, the machinery of the law — the law themselves, courts, lawyers, enforcement officers — exists in order to settle disputes.

However, from the point of view of the higher destiny, implicit in the possibilities of society and envisaged in the minds of men as the ideals to be aimed at by the improvement of society, it is something closer to justice that is sought. Destiny from the legal point of view is justice, and justice can be attained only in the perfect society. As everyone must know, that society exists as a possibility only in the future. There could be a perfect society even if there is not one now and may never be one. Perfection is the ideal and it serves a purpose in the present as the measure of the extent to which a given actual society falls short of its aims.

APPENDIX

RIVAL THEORIES OF JUSTICE

I wish now to investigate by a method of sampling the extent to which an apodixis based on some previous theories of justice can be demonstrated. It should be possible to confirm my definition by means of generally accepted principles, in this way grounding upon the experience of others what without it could be a mere opinion.

CHAPTER XVII

SOME ANCIENT THEORIES OF JUSTICE

1. Plato

The formidable shadow of the form of justice, in which all those stand who, through Aristotle and his followers, reflect the ideals of Plato, can be defined by assumptions as surely as can the rights of individuals, also unstated but accepted by means of the assumptions of the English common law. Justice is an universal principle which while remaining essentially unknown is assumed as applied behind every particular theory of justice and every legal system which has ever continued in effect. In other words, behind every relative theory of justice there stands the ideal of an absolute justice at which the relative theory aims.

This is nowhere more clearly borne out than by Plato. In a number of places but chiefly in the *Republic* Plato outlined his theory of justice. The inquiry is in the first Book[1] and the exposition in the fourth.[2] Justice was for him one of the four virtues, the others being wisdom, temperance and courage. Justice is the practice of virtue; and since everything in the universe has its own station and task, virtue is the right condition which enables each man to do his own task best, an end attained when the three parts of the soul, the reason, the emotions and the appetites, are in their proper order, with reason dominant over the other two, for then the whole man is a free citizen to follow that activity for which he is best qualified by his nature. The individual can attain harmony only in an ordered state. It is the same in the state with respect to the three classes of citizens: the rulers, the guardians and the artisans; they, too, must be in their proper order. Each class has its own virtue: wisdom for the rulers, courage for the guardians and temperance for the artisans.

1   351 ff.
2   441 C ff.

No one has noticed particularly the systematic nature of Plato's theory of justice chiefly perhaps because they could not see the whole for the parts. The *Republic*, which is by common consent of his commentators an essay on justice, calls for a system of order: an ordering of the individual through the proper arrangement of his three faculties and an ordering of the state through the proper arrangement of its three social classes.

More particularly, Plato insisted that justice is the same for the individual and for the state[3] a harmony that brings "oneness of mind and love".[4] What is a harmony if not a system qualitatively presented? It is "the bond of justice which binds all political elements into one,"[5] a justice which belongs to the highest class of goods which are desirable for their own sake.[6]

We emerge from these considerations with an emphasis on consistency. Since everything in the state has its proper rank and station, there is no possibility of conflict. Justice for Plato is harmony, the performance by each thing of what is proper to it, while injustice is what follows from the denial of this principle.

2. Aristotle

Aristotle does not differ from his master but carried out the same conception of justice in more empirical terms. He saw the ideal in the actual, the justice which exists both in the laws and in their violation, the principle of justice which underlies the administration of justice and stands implicit in the meaning of acts of injustice. Although the laws with regard to the virtues are to be understood as "commanding some acts and forbidding others" and justice in this sense is "complete virtue," "not part of virtue but virtue entire."[7] Aristotle's analysis of justice produces a more fragmented account which discloses a system more complex. However, note well "complete" and "entire."

Artistotle defined justice as "the unwritten custom of all or the majority of men which draws a distinction between what is honorable and what is base."[8] But "justice is of two kinds, one unwritten, the

3 *Rep.*, 4.435 ff.
4 *Ibid.*, 351D. Cf. 951D.
5 *Laws*, 945D.
6 *Rep.*, 357D-358A; 367D.
7 *Ethica Nichomachea*, 1129b24-1130a10.
8 *Rhetorica ad Alexandrum*, 1421b37.

other legal."⁹ In other words, there stands behind the code of laws an unwritten justice from which the code was derived. For Aristotle law is either special or general. By special law he meant "that written law which regulates the life of a particular community; by general law, all those unwritten principles which are supposed to be acknowledged everywhere";¹⁰ the general law follows from universal justice. Thus universal justice is distinguished from justice as its exists in the community of men.

It is this universal justice which stands behind Aristotle's distinction between natural and positive law. Since man is part of nature there are laws not subject to his fiat or will as well as laws which he together with his fellows promulgate. A distinction between ideal law and actual law is clearly indicated. Ideal law is a consequence of universal justice, actual law is embodied in a code.

Aristotle defined the just as "the lawful and the fair, the unjust and the unlawful and the unfair."¹¹ There are two principles here: one is the just as the lawful, theother is the just as the fair. The "rightly framed law" commands some acts and forbids others. "All lawful acts are in a sense just acts; for the acts laid down by the legislative art are lawful, and each of these, we say is just."¹² So much for the lawful; as for the fair, fairness has a definite reference other than what can be sensed or judged on its own. For in positive law "the just is the proportional; the unjust what violates the proportion."¹³ There is in other words a standard by which to judge fairness, which is not for Aristotle a psychological category but has a definite objective reference to the principle of proportionality.

Aristotle had two principles of justice. Justice itself he defined as equality. The two principles were as follows: the first principle stated that all men are equal. The second one stated that they are unequal. To the extent to which they are equal they should be treated equally under the law. To the extent to which they are unequal the differences call for extenuating circumstances and this is the principle of proportionate equality.

According to Aristotle's idea of universal justice, men are equal; according to his idea of distributive justice,¹⁴ they are not. Actually men

9 *Nicomachean Ethics*, 1162b21.
10 *Rhetoric*, 1368b7-10.
11 *Ethica Nichomachea*, 1129a37.
12 *Eth. Nic.*, 1129b12-24.
13 *Ibid.*, 1131b17. Cf. also *Magnalia Moralia* 1194a20.
14 *Eth. Nic.*, 31a10-24; 32b24-30.

are equal in some respects, unequal in others, so both conceptions are correct. The concept of distributive justice does imply completeness, since its proportional rewards and punishments are intended to each to every member of the community.

The instrument for applying the principle of universal justice by means of proportionality is called by Aristotle "equity."[15] "The equitable is not the legally just but a correction of legal justice."[16] True, "sympathetic judgment" is involved, but judgment is the right discrimination of the equitable,"[17] and "sympathetic judgment is judgment which discriminates what is equitable and does so correctly,"[18] for the wise man does not act on the basis of his own feeling for what is fair; he "must not only know what follows from the first principles, but must also possess truth about the first principles."[19]

In summary it would seem proper to point out that both Plato and Aristotle thought of justice as concerned with social order understood as stemming from a legal system, although Plato was inclined to emphasize the feature of consistency and Aristotle that of completeness. We must turn now to sample some more recent theories of justice where something less than such coverage prevails.

15 *Eth. Nic.*, Book V, chapter 10. See also *Magna Moralia*, Books I and II.
16 *Eth. Nic.*, 1137b11.
17 *Ibid.*, 1143a20.
18 *Ibid.*, 1143a20-24.
19 *Ibid.*, 1141a17.

CHAPTER XVIII

SOME TRADITIONAL THEORIES OF JUSTICE

1. Kant

For Kant morality is not social but internal to the individual. Only the legal system is external and involves enforced conformity to the provisions set by the laws.[1] The consent of the whole population is a condition and it must be represented as the united will. The political power is that of the collective universal will made absolute and obligatory. Societies exist in virtue of the social contract as embodied in the legislative power which must at the same time provide for maximum individual freedom.

Kant was most occupied with the idea of consistency, the "highest obligation of a philosopher,"[2] but also with the idea of system.[3] But he sought the unification of the civil law in the process of abstraction: "instead of the multiplicity of civil laws we should be able to fall back on their general principles."[4]

The social contract theory of Hobbes and of Kant's contemporary, Rousseau, was just what Kant needed to objectify the collective universal will. But at least we can see here how the requirements of consistency and completeness were to be met. That such a will is a fiction and that the social contract itself was never an actual contract between consenting citizens no one noticed. Collective will and contract together got Kant over the difficult transition from a subjective volition,

---

1 Kant struggled mightily in an attempt to bring law in line with his inherent subjectivity, even to the extent of conceiving of "private laws". Cf. his *The Metaphysical Elements of Justice*, John Ladd trans. (Indianapolis, Indiana 1965), pp. 51-72. Kant was forced to understand it in terms of possession.
2 *Critique of Practical Reason*, I, I, § 3.
3 *Ibid.*, I, I, I.
4 *Critique of Pure Reason*, B 358.

which was after all only an impulse, to an objective legal system, which was a positive fact.

The same awkward transition had to be effected in the case of property. Property for Kant is an expression of personality. Like all German philosophers Kant was too much influenced by idealism, and unable to see the importance of artifacts, a word which I have been employing throughout this work to describe material objects which have been altered through human agency for human uses. For societies in which work is largely manual, such as primitive societies and the Chinese, this might do very well; but it will not do for the scientific-industrial culture, in which the design, manufacture and ownership of the products of technology have to be included. For while it is men who make tools, it is also true that tools remake men.

There are advantages to Kant's theory of law in his having seen it from the subjective perspective. This perforce highly individualistic view was a matter of consciousness, to which Kant appended the matter of the conscience. It is a valid perspective for the consideration of anything to ask how it affects the human individual, for that is of course just what each of us is. Unfortunately, it will not do as an over-riding theory, for each of us is not only a member of a community and possessed of a common humanity but also a participant in the cosmos. Kant's theory of law is inadequate to cover these aspects.

Kant's other mistake is that he thought that because man is endowed with reason he is distinct from nature. There is every evidence that he acquired both his existence and his properties from nature, including the property of reason. All animals are able to reason to some extent, and if man is able to do so to a much greater extent that does not make him any the less natural. The existence of laws in non-human nature: in the physical, astronomical, and chemical worlds, is evidence that something akin to reason is ingredient in all of nature.

As for the freedom with which individual man is endowed, this just does not seem to be equally the case. No examination of individual man no matter how detailed will disclose the existence in him of anything that could be called freedom. Biological man is as capable of slavery as he is of freedom, as the entire lives of millions of people in the past have mutely attested. Both freedom and slavery are conditions of the individual provided by the society in which he happens to live. It is chance that brings him there and the state which operates to produce freedom or slavery for him, whichever happens at the moment to be the effects of the law of the land.

2. Hegel

Kant thought of the state as a law-state, Hegel thought of it as a culture-state. Hegel was perhaps closer to the truth. Both the individual and the state, like all things, could be considered parts of the whole, and indeed all are, like Reason and Spirit even, stepping-stones in reality toward the Absolute Idea. Hegel's language is the language of dualism and relativity, but its message also includes a message of monism and absolutism.

Yet although the State somehow transcends the individual, it is in its details not itself transcended. It is a curious fact that while Hegel's philosophy of law begins with the ideas of freedom and the individual personality, it ends with the most rigid of state controls over the individual and the consequent loss of freedom.

Perhaps the way in which freedom got lost in Hegel's system is the way in which it became objectively embodied (which it had to be as a subject, since the subject is only a subject and because everything in Hegel's philosophy eventually turns into its opposite).

The will, we are told, by means of the intermediary stage of abstract right, becomes embodied in three kinds of objects: property, contract and wrong (tort and crime). "Property" represents the exercise of a person's will, "contract" the common will formed by the union of one person's will with that of another, and "wrong" the extent to which one person's will is not in accord with the universal will.

Hegel does not deal with the concept of justice. Without ever saying what justice is, Hegel thought that to maintain it is the right and the duty of the public authority. Justice for Hegel was a matter for the courts, which had the task of interpreting and applying the law. He envisaged no higher conception of justice. And since he thought international law must remain forever in the domain of the "ought," the state once again is supreme. It was not really answerable to any lesser authority and it would never be called to task by any higher. The state is absolute, a view which later found actual expression in the Marxist state: Marx was not influenced by Hegel for nothing.

In Hegel's philosophy all things are parts of the one whole and as unreal as the whole is real. This gave him a guarantee of completeness if not of consistency. There is trouble about the consistency, although he strives for it, because of the contained contradictions and conflicts. Hegel was perhaps the first philosopher to see that without containing contradictions no system could be complete when it was a system of the whole without remainder, but that with the contained contradictions it could not be consistent.

He did not apply this aspect of his philosophy to the state and its laws in quite the way his system itself would have allowed. In a democracy contradictions and oppositions are contained and allowed everywhere; allowed in the opposition of political parties, indeed required by them if they are to function properly; and allowed in industry in the form of business competition. Democracy comes closer therefore to the application of Hegel's ideal in politics than his own politics does.

He had to abrogate his metaphysics somewhat when he applied it to politics in order to make it absolute, and he had to abrogate it again when he declared that there is no power beyond the state, thus ending the dialectical ascension at the state level and forever making international law an impossibility. And just as international law must be without sanctions, so national law can have no justification in any conception of a justice which extends beyond the state. Justice is a universal conception, but Hegel's philosophy, idealistic though it is claimed to be, does not in the last analysis admit of such universals.

In place of justice, we have noted, Hegel substituted the right, which is for him the form not only of all morality but of all social organization, and even of law in civil society. The law, he admitted, is something on its own account and the business of the administration of justice in the courts. The law in this sense was for him positive law. Justice is mentioned only in connection with administration, with judges and courts. Neither justice nor law (nor anything else, for that matter) has any independent existence or meaning: all is woven together in a single fabric of being. This makes for the kind of closed world for which there can be no detached evidence, no objective view; for from where could it have been made? Hegel surely was not exempt from the system of philosophy he posited.

But let us pursue his idea of development of law in the state a little further. Like so many academicians, Hegel's encounter with facts was theoretical only, he knew little or nothing of their particularistic, insistent and irrational nature, and so the solution of practical problems seemed overly simple. For example, crime proves to be "the subjective willing of evil"[5] and the colliding interests of producers and consumers can be brought to a fair balance "automatically."[6]

Hegel is usually regarded as a subjective idealist, and it must be admitted that a strong case can be made for this interpretation because of his characteristically subjective language. But while the language is the

5 *Philosophy of Right*, Paragraph 232.
6 *Ibid.*, Paragraph 236.

language of subjects, the philosophy is the philosophy of objects; subjects turn into objects but not objects into subjects. The passages on property illustrate this point quite graphically. The relation of property and contract to persons very soon becomes the relation of persons to property and contract.[7] Property is private, unless the state makes its rare exceptions. Contract is opposed to property because it involves the relinquishing of rights.

---

7 *Ibid.*, Paragraphs 41-81.

CHAPTER XIX

SOME RECENT THEORIES OF JUSTICE

1. Radbruch

Of the fifteen legal theorists whose work was surveyed by Arnold Brecht, only one considered justice to be of the highest value: Gustav Radbruch.[1]

Radbruch's definition of justice: "Justice means equality,"[2] suggests that all men are equal. The inflexible conception of equality as usual makes allowance for those extenuating circumstances for which the principle of equity was designed to provide. His excellent brief definition of equity restores the balance. "Equity is the justice of the individual case."[3] These contain in essence the two principles which Aristotle discovered and which everyone had adopted in one form or another ever since.[4] Few have recognized, however, that while in practice they offer both the impartiality of the law and its modification by extenuating circumstances they are in a sense in conflict: either the law operates impartially or it does not.

"Commutative justice is the justice of private law; distributive justice is the justice of public law".[5] ... "Distributive justice is the prototype of justice."[6] and, in another place, "... we determined the essence of justice, of distributive justice, as equality: equal treatment of equal, and

1 *Political Theory* (New Haven: Princeton University Press, 1967), pp. 303-04.
2 Gustav Radbruch, *Legal Philosophy*, third edition, translated by Kurt Wilk, reprinted in *The Legal Philosophies of Lask, Radbruch, and Dabin* (Cambridge, Mass.: Harvard University Press, 1950), p. 74. All references to Radbruch are to this edition.
3 *Ibid.*, p. 75.
4 *Ibid.*, p. 87.
5 *Ibid.*, p. 74.
6 *Ibid.*, p. 74.

184

correspondingly unequal treatment of different men and relationships."[7]

Radbruch saw clearly that justice is not a subjective but an objective affair, and despite the legitimacy of individual morality it has a different direction and therefore requires a different judgment.[8] Radbruch was correct, it seems to me, in assuming that justice is an objective affair in that it is a relation between human beings[9] and that the meaning of law is to serve justice.[10] Justice stands above the law and is carried out in society.

The objectivity of justice is contained in Radbruch's conception of law. Justice is the idea of law.[11] Law is justice in the social order, objectified justice. Thus Radbruch did distinguish between justice and the law when both are ideally conceived. Law is the cultural side of justice, "a reality the meaning of which is to serve a value," but also "the application or the observance of a law," or that law itself.[12]

Radbruch combined a belief in the equality of individuals with a relativism of legal systems, indeed he has come to stand as the leading exponent of value relativism in legal theory. This did not prevent him from seeing that the balance between justice for the individual and justice for the state had somehow to be reconciled and that such reconciliation could be affected only in local terms which could meet the peculiar exigencies of a given situation. I differ with Radbruch, however, in that I hold some political views to be demonstrable and some refutable. They can be defended on grounds of consistency and completeness and attacked on grounds of inconsistency and incompleteness. Their axioms can be defended by the very fact that they lead to the former and attacked by the fact that they lead to the latter.

Despite the universality of his concept of Justice Radbruch, like all nineteenth century Germans, seemed incapable of thinking even of absolutes except in human terms. For him absolute values "reached the empirical world" by way of individual or collective personalities and human works. That any values lay beyond the human of which the human might constitute a subclass never occurred to him. But he did see the necessity of devising a legal system which would be a system of systems and a kind of relativistic standard. He might have suspected

7 *Ibid.*, p. 107.
8 *Ibid.*, p. 73.
9 *Ibid.*, p. 73.
10 *Ibid.*, p. 75.
11 *Ibid.*, p. 73.
12 *Ibid.*, p. 74.

that his third kind of value the value of human works, of artifacts, was a material value in as much as the artifacts themselves are material, and he might have seen some of the vast implications of the "transpersonal" values they entail.

Those who like the later Radbruch were repelled by the relativism of values because it would seem to admit the values which Hitler had elicited from the German people overlooked the fact that the existence of value relativism does not preclude a ranking of various systems of values in terms of an over-arching absolute. Such an absolute might well consist in an idea of justice which encompasses the whole of the human species, just as lesser definitions of justice apply to limited societies. Whichever lesser definition of justice best approached the ideal would be preferred to the others. On this argument the democratic ideal, with its unlimited application to all peoples, achieves a much higher ranking in the hierarchy than the German national socialism which was designed to benefit only "pure" Germans. Value relativism is acceptable, then, not with legal systems equal in value but with systems ranked in terms of their proximity to the absolute value of justice.

Justice can be considered absolute not as the decree of God nor of any sovereign but rather as the parameter of truth standing behind all lesser and necessarily relativistic formulations. It is not possible to separate truth and value in the way Radbruch undertook to do when he declared that justice has to do only with the good and not with truth.[13] In the administration of justice the issue hangs on the truth of a factual statement as often as it does on the interpretation of a statute, as indeed it did in the famous Dreyfus Case of 1894.[14]

But justice as a parameter is a function of a system of order, and a system of order must include in its applications the principles of due proportionality. In this sense justice is wider than truth, as when for instance the truth is withheld from the dying in order to avoid adding to the agonies which already have to be borne. The truth must prevail, except where it gives rise to injustice, and it does so when lies are told to gain a political advantage. Due proportionality enters in the one case and not in the other, and justice still stands as the parameter of truth which moves to endorse the first instance and condemn the second.[15]

Radbruch took care of the requirements of consistency and completeness in his legal philosophy through the idea of a legal science and the idea of legal system. "The work of legal science ... is done at three

13 *Rechtsphilosophie*, (Wilk trans., p. 91).
14 Guy Chapman, *The Dreyfus Case* (New York 1956).
15 Plato, *Rep.*, 335b, 591 d.

186

stages: interpretation, construction and system."[16] "The task of legal science ... relates not only to a single legal institution but to the *totality* of the legal order, "*system*"".[17] The idea of totality is that of completeness, the idea of consistency that of system. Culture, it develops, is a systematic construction.

2. Del Vecchio

Del Vecchio, like Kant, made the mistake of endeavoring to bring the logical and the empirical together inside the human individual, subjectively in the human mind, where they have a residence but not a determinative focus, as they have on the outside. Man's nature which is both positive and transcendental will not support the further distinctions which are required. Hence the confusion in Del Vecchio's writings between the form of justice and the sentiment of justice, so that the form of justice proves to be the concept of law.[18] To objectify the essence of justice after a Kantian start like that, Del Vecchio had to fall back on that lame object, inter-subjectivity. Del Vecchio tried to save the objectivity of his conceptions of justice by resorting to a kind of Hegel-like interpretation of Vico's reliance on social history.[19]

Del Vecchio's Kantism was considerably modified as his philosophy of law developed. The influence of Plato crept in through the formulations of Vico, Del Vecchio saw that behind the positive law as embodied in statutes and codes there stood the pure theory of law, needing no theological justification or foundation, but standing as the ideal toward which positive law strives.

That Del Vecchio recognized the consistency which is inherent in the idea of justice is clear at the outset of his treatise. Justice, he declared, "in the most general sense, connotes a conformity, a congruence, a proportion of some kind."[20] That he recognized its completeness is implicit in his further provision that it represents "a principle of co-ordination between subjective beings."[21] He failed, however, to recognize that subjective beings, i.e. human beings, could not be coor-

16 *Ibid.*, p. 141.
17 *Ibid.*, p. 147. Italics mine.
18 Cf. the position of W. Freidmann, *Legal Theory* (London, Stevens & Sons, 1949), p. 101.
19 *Ibid.*, p. 102.
20 *Justice*, trans. A.H. Campbell (Edinburgh: University Press, 1951), p. 1.
21 *Ibid.*, p. 2.

dinated by anything less than some material object which would of course be not subjective but objective.

That is to say, he failed to recognize justice as being material in its effects but he did know it as established law, as law "incorporated in the prevailing system" of justice.[22] He detected the objectivity of justice in the existence of positive law and he recognized it in the presence of a "trans-subjective standard."[23] Del Vecchio did understand that justice belongs with the acknowledgement that the other may also be a subject, and that "recognizing subjectivity in others is in fact equivalent to recognizing objectivity in oneself."[24] The notion of "alteritas," or "the objective positing of the self,"[25] is very Hegel-like but gave Del Vecchio a firm purchase for the objective content of consciousness.[26] But this whole conception never quite led him to consider the legal aspects of material objects which are non-human except as human beings have altered them. Del Vecchio's entire legal conception floats in an ambience provided by the inter-subjective exchanges of the human consciousness, unassisted by relations from the world of property.

There is a tendency discernible in theories of justice toward the abstract ideal of justice which stands behind and informs all less general theories and even guides applications of justice. Something of this can be seen in the size of positive legal systems. National law is positive law, but there are many positive legal systems, as many as there are nations. Philosophers of law take various positions toward international law; some hold it to be undesirable and impossible (Hegel), some hold it to be desirable (Del Vecchio), while some hold it to be desirable and possible (Kant). I hold it to be desirable and possible but improbable given the ambivalent nature of man and his need for destructive as well as for constructive aggression.[27]

The defense of international law as something desirable runs definitely counter to Del Vecchio's support of fascism, and it is necessary to draw a veil over this part of his work if the earlier work is to be applauded. Fascism allows neither the autonomy of the individual nor the unity of mankind that international law implies, and so must be held to have been an aberration on Del Vecchio's part.

22 *Ibid.*, p. 157.
23 *Ibid.*, p. 158.
24 *Ibid.*, p. 78.
25 *Ibid.*, p. 80.
26 *Ibid., loc. cit.*
27 James K. Feibleman, "The Ambivalence of Aggression and the Moralization of Man" in *Perspectives in Biology and Medicine*, IX, 4:537-548.

CHAPTER XIX

SOME CONTEMPORARY THEORIES OF JUSTICE

1. Rawls

The analytic school of legal theorists, whose members are committed to the analysis of ordinary language in the wake of Wittgenstein, have had a prominent representative in the philosophy of law in John Rawls. Rawls' ideas have been known hitherto chiefly through the medium of journal articles. Chief among these is "Justice as Fairness" which appeared in the *Philosophical Review* in 1958 and has been reprinted.[1] Now he has emerged at last with a comprehensive treatise on justice, in which there is no doubt he makes a major claim.[2] How important is it? Judged by the enthusiastic response he has had from serious critics, very important. In the present chapter I have set out to see for myself just what the nature and extent of that importance is.

Rawl's new treatise on justice is in the main an elaboration of the ideas presented in his previously published articles. He wishes to endorse the social contract theory, refurbish it, and employ it to demolish utilitarianism. In order to do this he prepares the ground by proposing a definition of justice and extending it by means of two principles.

Accordingly, he defines justice as "fairness."[3] The two principles he states as follows. "First, each person is to have an equal right to the most extensive basic liberty compatible with a similar liberty for others. Second, social and economic inequalities are to be arranged so that they are both (a) reasonably expected to be to everyone's advantage, and (b) attached to positions and offices open to all."[4] This in the main is

1 In *Philosophy, Politics and Society*, P. Laslett and W.G. Runciman (eds.) Second Series (Oxford: Blackwell, 1967), pp. 132-157.
2 John Rawls, *A Theory of Justice* (Cambridge, Mass.: The Belknap Press of Harvard University Press, 1971).
3 p. 12. All the references unless otherwise stated are to Rawls' book.
4 p. 60. Cf. also p. 302.

his position, and he uses it to support the social contract theory of Locke, Rousseau and Kant, and to reject the utilitarianism of Mill. "The theory that results is highly Kantian in nature."[5]

This is the barest outline of Rawl's theory, but the book is a long one and he has many elaborations of it. It will be my contention that the conception is confused, that its part do not fit together, and that it does not accomplish what he sought to accomplish by it, that is to say, that it does not support the social contract theory nor demolish utilitarianism. Most of all, therefore, it does not provide us with an acceptable theory of justice.

Perhaps my criticism should begin as Rawls' does with a discussion of the definition of justice as fairness. It is one we will find referred to in many places through the argument.

Rawls' treatise is devoted to the theory of justice. Justice he defines as fairness, no doubt following Aristotle.[6] But he nowhere defines fairness, as one might suppose he would have done considering its importance to his theory. If justice is fairness and whatever is *considered* fair is fair, then whatever *is* considered fair is just. This would seem to reduce justice to a matter of opinion. Presumably he means something like the Oxford Dictionary's third definition, "free from bias, fraud or injustice," especially of course the latter. But that clearly does not help much, for if added to Rawls' definition of justice it becomes circular. We still need a conception of fairness in order to know what is just, and we are not provided with one.

According to Rawls something is right if it appeals to an ideal observer as right.[7] He reminds us of the source of his definition in Hume and Adam Smith. Rawls finds "no conflict so far between this definition and justice as fairness." Like all psychological definitions of ideas which are not in themselves psychological this one is tautological and tells us nothing. Who is the ideal observer? And did he become one by making the correct evaluation of something which is right? Is right, then, merely mental or is it a mental recognition of something non-mental? If the former the tautology holds, if the latter then we can ask, what is it that is non-mental in the idea of right? Is the same analysis to be made of the wrong? We are not told; but it would be fair to assume that the same kind of definition would have to be made on grounds of consistency. Then how could one tell right from wrong? Only through the authority of the ideal observer.

5 p. viii.
6 *Eth. Nic.*, 1129a34.
7 *A Theory of Justice*, p. 184.

It is my contention that "fairness" means whatever Rawls wishes it to mean, and he means different things in different places. For instance, the term "fairness" is certainly a psychological category, for it applies to whatever appeals to the individual as fair. As such it is highly personal. Under Rawls' conception there is an appeal to an anterior moral position which he does not recognize, for it would mean beginning with something other than fairness in the understanding of justice. Rawls' account presupposes the conditions prevailing within an existing society with its established morality. But the criterion he adopts is still a psychological one, and under this dispensation no change in the morality could ever be effected. Rawls tries to help by informing us that "a theory of justice ... is a theory of the moral sentiments."[8] If Rawls' theory of justice requires the moral sentiments, that is certainly not the way he sees it, for he derives morality, or at least a theory of the good on which a morality is ordinarily understood to rest, from justice. We had been warned that the conception of the good to be adopted committed it to a "moral neutrality" because "to construct the conception of moral goodness, the principle of right and justice must be introduced."[9] The cat is out of the bag: justice does not depend upon morality, morality depends upon justice; and so also for the right. I would have thought that the right exists only within legal systems since it involves the freedom of the individual, whereas morality extends beyond them. But clearly not for Rawls.

According to Rawls, justice is sandwiched in between two theories of the good. It requires a "thin theory" and itself is required for a full theory.[10] For the thin theory only "self-respect and a sure sense of one's worth" is enough.[11] The full theory includes both a descriptive sense and its use in giving advice and counsel, the latter presumably in accordance with the account of speech acts by J.L. Austin.[12]

Here Rawls' allegiance to the philosophy of ordinary language as advanced by Wittgenstein's followers comes visibly to the fore. He adopts the descriptive theory of the good and considers it sufficiently explained by that theory together with a general theory of meaning, despite a disclaimer early on that "the notions of meaning and analyticity play no essential role in moral theory as I conceive of it."[13]

8 pp. 50-1.
9 p. 404.
10 p. 396.
11 *Ibid.*
12 p. 405.
13 p. xi.

192

Somehow goodness emerges from this treatment defined by rationality.[14]

One devastating point before moving on. If justice is fairness and the
definition of justice requires the thin theory of the good,[15] then justice
requires only "self-respect and a sure sense of one's worth." Fairness
seems on this argument to rest on selfishness: whatever is selfish is fair.
I don't suppose that this is what Rawls means but it is what his words
say and I can only follow the lines of the argument. And the argument
here is inconsistent with the argument elsewhere.

Back of the notion of fairness lies the acceptance of a particular
morality on which is based a particular system of laws. Both Rawls'
definition of justice as fairness and his two principles leave open the
question of whether the laws which implement them are themselves
just. A legal system could be devised which would meet these requirements inside the system but which would in the larger sense of justice
be unjust, for instance a slave state where everyone is equally a slave;
and yet even if no impartiality is shown, justice in the broad sense
would hardly be served.

Justice does not rest upon fairness either as a feeling or as a judgment. It does not rest upon anything nearly so subjective. Personal and
material relations have to be regulated if men are to live together in
social proximity. Individuals must not be murdered nor property stolen
not merely because men might regard these actions as unfair, but because society must be protected in order to survive.

Fairness is not justice but the judgment that justice has been done,
the recognition that it has been successfully applied in a particular case.
It is therefore subjective and not the ground for any invariantive conception of justice. The entire legal machinery turns on the idea of justice, which cannot be allowed to rest on what strikes one as fair. But we
soon learn that this is not what Rawls means by the term. In his treatment it becomes a cover for an amazing number of propositions concerning laws, institutions and society.

"Justice is the first virtue of social institutions."[16] It "generalizes
and carries to a higher level of abstraction the traditional conception of
the social contract." "Justice as fairness is an example of what I have
called a contract theory."[17] "Society is well-ordered when ... it is effec-

14 p. 405. Cf. also ch. VII.
15 p. 396.
16 p. 3.
17 p. 16.

tively regulated by a public conception of justice."[18] We have been led by these passages to believe that justice as fairness is a social conception.

But is it? I would have thought that justice for Rawls is a psychological category and so applies to the individual only. There are times when Rawls seems to support this view. "Each person," we are told, "possesses an inviolability founded on justice."[19] Again, "The theory of justice is a part, perhaps the most significant part, of the theory of rational choice."[20] The position is reinforced on the succeeding page. We are told later also that "a theory of justice" describes "our sense of justice."[21] That "justice as fairness is the hypothesis that the principles which would be chosen in the original position are those that match our considered judgments and so these principles describe our sense of justice."[22]

We now heve two different theories of justice as fairness. On the one hand it is a virtue of social institutions, indeed an example of contract theory, and on the other hand it is part of the theory of rational choice. But that is not all, for there is also some confusion concerning the relations which do or do not exist between the objective, or institutional, and the subjective, or individual conceptions of justice as fairness. Although Rawls warns us against confusing the principles which apply to institutions with those which apply to individuals,[23] he confuses them himself. For instance there is a principle of fairness distinct from the definition of justice as fairness, a principle moreover which makes individual fairness dependent upon institutional fairness. "This principle holds that a person is required to do his part as defined by the rules of an institution."[24]

Elsewhere we learn that "the principle of fairness has two parts, one which states how we acquire obligations, namely, by doing various things voluntarily, and another which lays down the condition that the institution in question be just, if not perfectly just, at least as just as it is reasonable to expect under the circumstances."[25] What is the relation of this principle, especially in its two parts, to the two principles which

18 pp. 4-5.
19 p. 3.
20 p. 16.
21 p. 46.
22 p. 48.
23 p. 54.
24 p. 111. See the whole of § 18.
25 p. 343. See the whole of § 52.

194

Rawls is sure follows from the definition of justice as fairness? I doubt anyone could make sense of this scrambled scheme, but let us move on.

Rawls' main position falls into two parts: there is the definition of justice as fairness, and there are the two principles. Before I discuss the two principles let me take up another point. Rawls claims that the two principles follow from his definition of justice as fairness. But nowhere has he shown in what way the definition of justice as fairness leads to his two principles, they are merely stated after it. For of course it can be admitted that the prospect of justice invokes feelings of fairness without admitting also that either of these constitutes a definition of justice. Either justice is a matter of principles or a matter of fairness, it cannot be both. Psychological attitudes, fairness included, are not principles, and principles are not attitudes. There are alternating references throughout the essay to justice as principles and to justice as fairness; clearly they have not been brought together.

Rawls asserts that "justice as fairness can be understood as saying that the two principles previously mentioned would be chosen in the original position in preference to other traditional conceptions of justice."[26] But do they follow? What is the evidence? I admit that Rawls has claimed for his definition a great deal more than most careful students would be able to elicit from the term, but even if we accept the deductions which Rawls claims, namely, the first virtue of social institutions and the contract theory, it is still difficult to see how even these necessarily imply the two principles.

Like the definition of fairness the two principles can also be traced to Aristotle, the first principle being derived from his commutative or "universal" justice, and the second from his "distributive" justice,[27] although in the earlier essay cited Rawls himself credits Kant and Mill. The first principle covers the similarities to which the laws of the land are to be applied, and the second covers the differences. Both principles have been recognized in English common law but not necessarily everywhere and always.

When Rawls comes to apply his theory of justice we begin to see the flaws in it. To assume that a given society is "nearly just," he tells us "implies that it has some form of democratic government" with the "willing cooperation among free and equal persons."[28] Plato outlined his ideas of a republic as an essay on justice, yet it was hardly democratic. It would seem however to answer to Rawls' two principles quite well.

26 pp. 49-50.
27 *Eth. Nic.*, Book V, 1-2.
28 p. 382.

His second principle, as a matter of fact, might conceivably appeal to both the western nations in which capitalism is practiced and the eastern nations which have adopted communism, since each needs to defend on principle the social and economic inequalities which prevail in his type of social organization. One might ask, however, whether the second principle does not to some extent contravene the first. The first seems to call for a kind of equality which does not exist in the second except as an end. As a means the first is egalitarian, the second not.

Rawls says that he will "try to bypass the dispute about the meaning of liberty"[29] but then he explains what he intends to assume by the term. His explanation is given in terms of function: "the agents who are free, the restrictions or limitations which they are free from, and what it is that they are free to do or not to do."[30] Quite apart from the fact that we still do not know from this what the essence of liberty is, it is difficult to see how it follows from the understanding of justice as fairness.

Liberty as a first principle of justice has not been universally recognized in practice. It has been recognized in western societies since Locke and the French Revolution, but it has not been recognized elsewhere, and especially it has not been recognized by the Soviet Union or by Communist China. The freedoms mentioned in chapter X of the New Soviet Constitution of 1936 for instance are not nearly so broad. They would seem to include Rawls' second principle but not his first.

Since Rawls argues for the social contract theory and against utilitarianism, let me do the opposite. I shall argue against the social contract, at least as it has been understood, and for utilitarianism. That approach will, I hope, bring out the weakness in Rawls' position.

Let me say at the outset what I suspect. The revival of the social contract theory in recent years may stem from the fact that it seems to be verbal. A philosopher of ordinary language would want to argue that the social contract is a matter of language, whereas the utilitarian principle refers to a material state of affairs, and the analyst would opt for the reference to language every time.

The origins of society are as everyone knows matter of conjecture, but they probably involved loose associations including gradually accumulated customs and traditions which settled down to being communities when decisions were called for exigently and the consequent procedures made into precedents to be followed by enforcement. The

29 p. 201.
30 p. 202.

196

"social contract" in the sense intended is a fiction. When was one ever freely drawn up and agreed to? There is a meaning according to which every organized and going society can be said to operate under a social contract if it be possessed of a charter or constitution and a set of laws. But this operation is seldom entirely formal and never altogether complete.

Although we are told that men "are to decide in advance how they are to regulate their claims against one another,"[31] the fact is that this has not always been done. The French Revolution of 1789 and the Russian Revolution of 1919 were conducted by relatively small numbers of citizens and the types of government adopted by them were imposed on the majority. The French and Russian farmers who at the time constituted the bulk of the citizenry were not consulted as to what kind of state they would like to have installed. No "social contract" for them! Nor was there in either case a formal surrender of individual rights to the state. There was no expression of a "general will," no laws which the people imposed on themselves, no popular vote.

Most societies today see the necessity of appealing to judge-made law to fill in the cracks and crevices and to take up the slack introduced by exigencies in the social situation. Since we have no evidence of men living outside of a society of some sort, the theory is truistic and trivial, in addition to being a proposal which can never be checked out. It amounts to saying that there are socially established laws which men agree to obey either tacitly when they come of age or when as immigrants they take formal steps to acquire citizenship, little more.

The social contract is the legal side of a social order read backwards to its supposed beginnings thousands of years ago. If we were to assume that the social contract is indeed an historic fact even though there is no evidence to support our doing so, we would still have the problem of how to justify it as a binding force on present society, unless it is ratified by the formal adoption of a constitution in each particular instance.

Now for utilitarianism. A social contract admittedly applies to all members of a society, but not all will honor it equally. The criminal cares nothing for the social contract and neither does the traitor. Therefore the good of all while an acceptable goal does not strike anyone with a practical knowledge of human affairs as being attainable. All that we can hope to do is to make the greatest number happy, a majority, and if the society is moderately successful, a large majority. The total

31 p. 11.

happiness of all in any society is unlikely. Yet it could be the goal, even for a society living under the dispensation of utilitarianism. It is a modest proposal put forward in the light of what we know about human nature.

There is no reason to suppose a conflict between the social contract theory and the theory of utilitarianism. Both it seems to me, can stand as operative principles. We hold each and every member of society responsible for working toward the good of all and we expect at the same time to settle for the good of most. If a man is not one of the greatest number and therefore not in possession of the greatest happiness at least he has no complaint, for his very existence in the society means that he has covertly if not overtly accepted its principles and so become a party to the social contract even if not as a voluntary act of surrender of his power.

I fail to see therefore why an advocate of the social contract theory could not also be a utilitarian. A contract between ruler and ruled which imposes obligations upon them both is obviously intended to serve as a method of working toward a goal. The greatest happiness of the greatest number of individuals is the description of a goal held to be the best that can be hoped for under the circumstances that a population subject to human frailty and given to self-seeking imposes. Where then is the inconsistency between a method intended to reach a goal and a goal intended for a method to reach?

Now let me put together some more general criticisms. I think Rawls can fairly be charged with having fathered an eclectic theory of justice. Yet he does not refer to any legal theorists. For example, there are no references to Grotius, Pufendorf, or the earlier Austin. They had some ideas about the social contract which Rawls might have found relevant. The lines between philosophers and writers on legal theory are not so tightly drawn that either can be ignored by the other. Rawls' theory is, looked at in the round, one put together by selecting ideas taken from the history of philosophy without gaining a synthesis in which the parts fit and together make up a whole which is more than their sum. Instead he has chosen such doctrines as please him from various sources without regard to whether or not they can be integrated. For example, if his theory is as Kantian as he thinks it is, then how does it come about that social institutions play so large a role in it? The man who recognizes that people "know that they are subject to the conditions of human life," that "they are situated in the world with other men who likewise face limitations of moderate scarcity and competing claims"[32] can

32 p. 257.

hardly call himself a Kantian. Kant was a relativist for whom society in particular and culture in general were little more than the sum of self-seeking individuals for whom duty is the moral *a priori*. For Kant "nothing can possibly be conceived in the world, or even out of it, which can be called good without qualification, except a Good Will."[33] No good institutions, no good societies.

Kant would in this way put ethics ahead of law, whereas Rawls does no such thing. For Rawls the right is prior to the good,[34] and they are equal under practical reasoning.[35] For Kant the principles of law could be deduced from the principles of *individual* human conduct, whereas for Rawls social justice is the "basic structure of society," "or, more exactly, the way in which the major social institutions distribute fundamental rights and duties."[36] Not morality, only a "public system of rules."[37]

Rawls is not faithful to Kant in many other respects. Kant holds the external world of matter to be essentially unknowable. Knowledge is locked irrevocably in an internal world of concepts, and reality is concealed from view behind space, time, and a choice of the categories. There is in accepting Kant's view a deep scepticism as to what really exists, and this is sure in the end to prove an obstacle to the solid grounding of any theory.

It is difficult to see how the entire case for justice, which presumably applies to all human situations, can be made without a thorough treatment of laws! The mention of justice as fairness was connected by Aristotle with the notion of law. "The just," he wrote, "is the lawful and the fair, the unjust the unlawful and the unfair."[38] Can justice be adequately treated without reference to the law and its function in society? Such an understanding would seem to be required by all full dress treatment of justice.

I revert to the criticism implied in the charge of eclecticism. There is no way to render compatible the dissident elements in Rawls' scheme. The reason why it is not is chiefly that the elements are drawn from a kind of Aristotleian objectivity and a kind of Kantian subjectivity. The former was concerned with society, the latter only with the individual. It is possible of course to imagine a conception of justice which would

---

33 *Critique of Practical Reason*, 9 (trans. Abbott).
34 Rawls, *op. cit.*, pp. 31-2.
35 *Ibid.*, p. 109.
36 *Ibid.*, p. 7.
37 *Ibid.*, p. 55.
38 *Eth. Nic., loc. cit.*

include in a consistent fashion both the individual and society; indeed any acceptable theory of justice would have to do just that. But it is what Rawls' theory fails to do. His treatise does not present any deep or original insight around which the traditional views can be arranged in some order of subordination. It is more like an argument in the history of philosophy. How else could one hope to select a definition of justice from Aristotle and a social contract theory from Rousseau, and put them together in a framework provided by Kant in order to refute the utilitarianism of Mill?

It must be admitted that Rawls has made out the best case that could be made out for his position. I submit that it will not stand up under examination and I have sought to demonstrate this. Even if I am right, however, a great deal of credit must still accrue to Rawls for compelling many people to take seriously the fundamental issues in the philosophy of law and to see them not only as theoretically valuable but also as having the most crucial practical consequences. He has revived controversy in a field which has for years been neglected, and for having done so he has put us all in his debt.

2. Hart

Hart and Rawls represent for the most part the same philosophy applied to questions of justice. There are of course important differences. Hart is more concerned with the practice of the law, and Rawls' theory is on the whole more subjective; but the basic outlook is very similar.

The similarity is primarily concerned with the criterion of fairness and with Rawls' two principles. Hart evidently considers justice and fairness synonyms.[39]

Fairness, as both Rawls and Hart understand the term, is a description of a conscious process; it is a question of how something strikes one: it seems fair or it does not. This conception allows for no deep structures of belief held in the unconscious mind. And if there are correlates in the society, such as established laws and the machinery for their administration, they have their source in a psychological feeling, nothing more logical than that. One could suppose that there are structures of belief which are isomorphic with the structures of a legal system which society has established; but such a theory would downgrade the importance of the psychological feeling of fairness though allowing

39 H.L.A. Hart, *The Concept of Law* (Oxford: Clarendon Press, 1961), p. 154.

it to remain. In such a case, it would exist but not so much would hang on it.

As a matter of fact Hart differs from Rawls in that Hart sees the two principles in terms of a logical structure.[40] His natural bent toward objectivity (not shared with Rawls) leads him to think of justice not as a psychological term, as his previous definition would imply, but rather as a matter of general rules and judicial application.[41] He is concerned not only with the concept of justice but also with the whole legal system which in fact he sees as a system.[42] Justice is not as with Rawls a primarily individual affair but applies to classes of individuals.[43]

In a later book Hart retreats several times from his earlier position, once in terms of an increase in subjectivity and another time with respect to the independence of justice from all other considerations. The first has to do with a notion which, Hart tells us, is "very central to the notion of justice" and it has to do with the "claims of the individual as a *choosing being*, and distributes its coercive sanctions in a way that reflects this respect for the individual".[44] Does justice really depend upon the conscious choice of an individual? If so it has lost all objectivity.

The second has to do with the introduction of morality to the idea of justice. Justice this time is "the ideal of treating morally like cases alike and morally different ones differently".[45] But is this not untenable without a further statement identifying the specific morality referred to? And would that not rob the definition of all universality, since there is no recognized universal morality? Surely this represents a weakened position with respect to the definition of justice.

Hart in this book retreats further from the austere requirements of definition and describes justice in terms of what sounds more like a working rule. "Justice", he says, "consists simply of principles to be observed in adjusting the competing claims of human beings which (i) treat all alike as persons by attaching special significance to human voluntary action and (ii) forbid the use of one human being for the benefit of others except in return for his voluntary actions against them."[46]

40 *Ibid.*, p. 156.
41 *Ibid.*, p. 202.
42 *Ibid., E. q.* pp. 100, 107.
43 *Ibid.*, p. 163.
44 *Punishment and Responsibility* (New York 1968, Oxford University Press), p. 49.
45 *Ibid.*, p. 80.
46 *Ibid.*, p. 22.

Here is that "choosing being" again, this time represented by the phrase "human voluntary action". There is no more objective definition left, and as if to remind us that in a sense there never was he repeats the old equation used by Aristotle and after him by Rawls: "fairness or justice to individuals".[47]

---

47 *Ibid.*, p. 77.

INDEX

Absolute Idea, 179
Absolute monarchy, 28
Abstract thought, as response, 112
Actuality of justice, 26
Afghanistan, 51
Aggression, and sex, 82
 need for, 81
Aggressive behavior, types of, 77 f.
Allen, Sir C.K., 137
Ambivalence of drives, 19
Ambulance chasing, 133
Amendment V, 75
Anaximander, 141
Anglo-American law, 131 f.
Antony, 93
Aristotle, 25, 111, 190, 194, 201
 on justice, 174 f.
Aristotle's *Rhetoric*, 136
Artifacts, 178
 and personal relations, 44
 influence of, 51
 in institutions, 100
Aryans, 52
Athens, 54, 106
Atmosphere of culture, 107
Attic Nights, 57
Aulus Gellius, 57
Austin, J.L., 42, 45, 70, 191, 197
Authority, in natural society, 109
Axiomatic assumptions, 62
Axiomatic events, 62
Ayres, R.U., 133

Background, ideology of law, 125
Behavior as response, 94
Belief, and action, 82
 df., 128
 in the law, 128
 of majority, 128
Beliefs, institutions, artifacts, 67 f.
 two schemes of, 32

Bentham, J., 45, 60, 70
Bergson, H., 108
Boer War, 104
Bureaucrats, 13
Butler, S., 75

Cairns, H., 17
Cannibalism, 75
Capacities of legal systems, 64
Cardozo, B., 68
Carnegie, Dale, 22
Case law, 64
Categoricity, 24
Catholic outlook, 107
Centrality of contract, 166
Champerty, 45
Change in law and morality, 68
Charter, 103
 of institution, 100, 102
Choice, human, 21
Christian Middle Ages, 67
Christians, 52
Church of England, 160
Cicero, 57
Cities, origin of justice in, 51
Civil Aeronautics Board, 12
Civilization, 53
 beginnings of, 48
Codification, 55
 of laws, 123 f.
Coke, 40
Collective will, 177
Communist China, 54, 71
Communisty state, rulers of, 121
Commutative justice, 183
Completeness, 24
 of laws, 60
Concrete events, as theorems, 62
Concrete ontology, 101 f.
Conflict between laws, 68
Conscience, 32, 81 f.

and social norms, 87
Conservatism, effects of, 118
Consistency, 24
  of laws, 60, 124
Constitution, 74, 116
  of the United States, 68, 78
Continental law, 132
Contract, 161 ff.
  character of, 151
Control by leading institution, 105
Corporation as contract, 151 f.
Corpus Juris Civilis, 17
Corruption of juries, 148
Corrupt judges, 146 f.
Cortez, 106
Cosmic rights and duties, 76 f.
Courts, as social bulwark, 148
  atmosphere of, 131
Crime, and punishment, 137 f.
  problem of increase in, 138
Criminal law, 29, 137
Criminals, 18
Cultural conditioning, 85
Culture
  as binding force, 127
  as men and artifacts, 122
  in society, 82
  in the individual, 82 f.
Culture-makers, 108

Declaration of Independence, 68, 75
De Gaule, C., 115
Delaney Amendment, 122
Del Vecchio, 186 ff.
Demaratus, 56
Democracy vs. communism, 69
Descartes, R., 61
Destiny, category of, 165, 169
Deuteronomy, 6
Dialectical materialism, 164
Dialectic vs. eristic, 144
Dicey, 14
Dicey's rule of law, 74
Dickens, C., 148
Direction of justice, 26
Disraeli, B., 12
Distributive justice, 175, 183
Dravidian peoples, 52
Dreyfous Case of 1894, 185
Drives
  ambivalence of, 19
  of individuals, as unlimited, 77
Duties, df., 72
Dworkin, R., 73 f.

East Germans, 70
East India Company, 12
Eclecticism, 197 f.
Economic democracy, 69

Egypt, 28, 73
  novelty vs. conventions, 93
Eighteenth Amendment, 68, 78, 118, 121
Empedocles, 109
Empirical systems, 63
Enforcement of contracts, 152
Engels, F., 6, 69, 159
English Common law, 61
English Turnpike Act, 104
Equality, principle of, 103
Equity, 176
Eristic vs. dialectic, 144
Essence, category of, 165, 168
Established system of laws, 26 f.
Establishment, described, 121
  how it functions, 102
  of institutions, 98
  of laws, 121
  requires metaphysics, 101
Ethics, 31
  as issue, 94
  between ontology and practice, 33
  df., 65
Ethos, as force of culture, 106-107
Evasion of law, 143 f.
Evolution, role of, 89 f.
Existence, 166 f.
  category of, 164

Facilitative laws, 42
Fairness, 189
Falsity and truth, 129
Feelings, prepared by reasoning, 126
First Christian centuries, 107
Food and Drug Administration, 69
Force of culture, provided by ethos, 107
Forensic eristic, 144
Formal procedures, 131 f.
Fourteenth Amendment, 42
Fourth-century Greeks, 34
Freedom, 55, 114, 178
French Civil Code, 124
French legal procedures, 132 f.

Gaius, 104
God, 55
Gogarty, O. St. J., 104
Good, as source of right, 108
Grades of obligation, 72
Greek justice, 54
Greek law, 55
Greek logic in Roman law, 57
Grotius, H., 197
Group life, 156

Hart, H.L.A., 199 f.
Hebrews, 52
Hegel, G.W.F., 111, 157, 179 ff.
Helsinki Accords, 70

Henry IV, 106
Herodotus, 56
Hierarchy of needs, 80
Hindu outlook, 107
Hindu Scripture, 52
Hitler, A., 27, 115
Hobbes, T., 40, 48, 177
Holmes, O.W., 40
Horizontal logical systems, 62
Human culture, 53
Human individual, relations of, 154
Human needs, and ecological behavior, 94
    morality and law, 79 f.
Human rights, 75
Human societies, components of, 31
Human species, as plastic medium, 111
Hume, D., 26

Ideal legal theory, 36
Ideal of individual, 86
Ideal of justice, 26
Ideal of law, 90
Ideal of natural society, 88
Ideals, choice of, 92
    competition between, 86
    in social sphere, 80
Implicit dominant morality, 65, 74
Implicit dominant ontology, 101, 163
Increases in population, effects of, 116
Indian Independence Act, 168
Individual, needs, 49 ff.
    needs and social limits, 87
    rights and duties, 73 f.
Injustice, 20, 141
Institution, and legal framework, 117
    as system, 97
    df., 97
Institutions, between societies and cultures,
    108
    needs of, 98
Interpretation of justice, 166
Interpretation of laws, 124, 124 f.

Judge's decisions, influence on, 146
Juries in Constitution, 147
Juristic act, 152
Justice, as abstract deal, 187
    as fairness, 189, 192 ff.
    df., 23, 25
    meaning of, 1 f.
    Plato's theory, 173 f.
    requirements of, 11
    two principles of, 175
    value to criminal, 22
Justinian, 17
Justinian's Code, 104

Kant, I., 48, 111, 114, 160, 177 ff., 186, 190,
    198

Kant's Shaving Bowl, 12
Kant's will theory, 153
Kelsen, H., 45, 55, 117, 156
King Solomon's decision, 136
Kinsey Report, 85

Laetrile, 69
Language, and law, 42
    meaning and reference, 42
    role of, 69
Law, and sexual morality, 84
    and social development, 158
    as captive institution, 104
    as guide to behavior, 68 f.
    as institution, 103
    as permeating cultures, 53
    as theological, 71
    df., 39, 40
    ideal of, 90
    in practice described, 142
    properties of, 18
    reality, morality, 163 f.
    utilitarian aims of, 118
Law-abiding citizens, 148 f.
Law and morality compared, 65 ff.
Law-congener, 140
Law-makers, as answerable, 116
Laws, as extra-linguistic, 45
    as guide-lines, 134
    as index to beliefs, 85
    as norms, 45
    as objectified rationality, 112 f.
    as positive, 46
    as social contracts, 61
    as vertical systems, 61 f.
    confined to state, 39
    df., 121
    difficulties with, 46
    effects of, 42
    kinds of, 41
    need for, 41
    result from practical exigencies, 122
    serve society, 64
    strategy of, 113
Lawyers corrupted, 144
Lawyer's task, 145
Leading institution, 101 f.
    as society's ideal, 105
    properties of, 104 f.
Legal framework, and political system, 117
    as institution, 117
    of state, 113 f.
Legality, as enforced morality, 67
Legal personality, 153 f.
Legal procedures, 129 ff.
    as essential, 113
Legal relations, as material, 44, 123, 157
Legal sanctions, 139
Legal system, as logical growth, 62

206

built-in structure of, 63
df., 24
follows morality, 54
requirement of changes in, 91
Legal systems, capacities of, 64
validity of, 55 f.
Leibniz, G., 61
Lenin, V., 6, 115
Limited rights, 161
Litigation, 130
as end, 146
Litigations, 62
Locke, J., 69, 114, 190, 195
Lord Denning, 5
Louis XIV, 115

Macedonia, 54
Mafia, 19, 148
Maine, Sir H., 152
Maintenance of cultures by laws, 53 f.
Malinowski, B., 100
Mannheim, K., 101, 102
Mao, Chairman, 115
Marxism outmoded, 159
Marxist states, 75
Marx, K., 6, 69, 102, 159, 179
Master, myth and ethos, 107
Material culture, inheritance of, 82 f.
Materialism, new, 8
Material relations, 165 f., 166
of society, 123
Matter, and forms of energy, 157
kinds of, 157
Meaning, theory of, 191
Mendenhall, Liet., D.L., 32
Metaphysical assumptions, 7
Metaphysics, 163 f.
df., 100
Middles Ages, 48, 71
and divine authority, 55
Mill, J.S., 190
Miscarriage of justice, 141
Money as contract, 167 f.
Monogamy, 83 f.
Montesquieu, Count de, 69
Moors, 102
Moral integrative levels, 72
Moral strategy, 92
Morality, 31
and law compared, 65 ff.
as decision criterion, 200
df., 65
made concrete, 44
national variations in, 70
shifts in, 33
Morality vs experience, 33
Moses, 52
Mussolini, B., 115

Napoleon, 116
Natural and artificial, 155
Natural laws, 55, 119
and positive law, 35
Natural rights, 76
Natural society, df., 89
laws of unknown, 56
pictures of, 108 f.
Nazis, 27, 32, 107, 119
Needs, hierarchy of, 80
New materialism, 164
Nicholson, A., 145
Nietzsche, 107
Nizon, R., 115
Nuclear Regulatory Commission, 12
Nurenberg trials, 119

Objective morality, 67
Objectivity of justice, 184
Olivecrona, K., 42
Ombudsman, 140
Ontology, character of in law, 168
described, 100 f.
df., 101
Open system, 14
Oral sex, punishable, 119
Order, demand for, 14
Ordinary language, 191
Organization of institutions, 99
Origins of law, 47 ff.
Origins of society, not contractual, 195 f.
Ownership, 160 f.
of land, 158

Pandects, 59 ff.
Partially-ordered systems, df., 26
Partial orderings, 61 ff.
Partial truths, 129
Parts, as agents of wholes, 89
"Path of due process", 112
Pax Britannica, 21
Peirce, C.S., 13, 129
Penalties for non-compliance, 39
Peregrines, 60
Perfect society, in future, 88
Performatives, 42
Persia, 51
Personality, as contract, 155
Personal relations, and artifacts, 44
Persons, 153 ff.
Pervasive social morality, 169
Philosopher vs. man of action, 91
Philosophical systems, 61
Philosophy of law, requirements, 8
Plato, 5, 20, 26, 28, 141, 144, 173 f., 186
Plato's Apology, 74
Plutarch, 60
Political office, corruption in, 86

Pollution of environment, 139
Pope Gregory VII, 106
Positive law, 34, 41, 118
Positive law and natural law, 35
Positive morality, 66
Post ergo melior, 34, 54
Pound, Roscoe, 6, 76, 136
Practice, as life of law, 125
Preservation of order, 28
President Carter, 70
Presuppositions, search for, 164
Prevalence of crime, 139
Principles and practice, 2
Private retention schema, 67
Properties of belief, 129
Property, as contract, 157
   as personality, 178
   laws to regulate, 71
   not absolute, 160
   power over, 71
Public opinion, 74
Public retention schema, 67
Pufendorf, 197
Purpose of law, 40 f.

Quality of experience, 131
Queen Elizabeth, 12
Queen Victoria, 12

Radbruch, G., 183 ff.
Rawls, J., 189 ff.
Reality, of whole as exclusive, 179
   residence of, 66 f.
Reason, among the emotions, 93
   and nature, 178
Reasoning, among nomads, 50
   as fallible guide to practice, 126
   as human, 111
Regulative laws, 42
Religious law, 53
Religious life, 52
Renard, C., 103
Republic, 20, 28
Respect for law, decline in, 138
Retention schemata, 81
Rewards for obedience, 140
Riggs vs. Palmer, 68
Right instead of justice, 179
Rights, and duties, 72 ff.
   df., 72
   restrictions, duties, 77 f.
Robin Hood, 18
Roman Empire, 54
Roman law, 55, 61
   as institution, 56 f.
Rousseau, J.J., 48, 60, 114, 177, 190
Rule of law, 14, 117
Ruling community, 114

Russell, B., 61
Russian imperialism, 71

Schindler, O., 32
Settlement to community, 50
Sexual morality, and the law, 84
Sexual needs and social properties, 90
Sexual practices, 83
Shakespeare, W., 93
Sherman Anti-Trust Act, 12
Smith, A., 190
Smuts, General J.C., 104
Social aims, as deliberate, 169
Social complex, 66
Social context of behavior, 155
Social contract htoery, 177, 195
Social exigencies, 49
Social ideal, 87
Social injustice, df., 35
Social life, condition of, 77
Social order, and justice, 25
Social rhythm, dynamism and quiescence, 88
Social rights and duties, 74
Social stability of laws, 54
Social violence, 20
Societies, as changing, 89
   as partial system, 50
Socrates, 74, 119, 133
Solon, 60, 104
Soviet Union, 18, 35, 70, 71, 115
Spain, 102
Sparta, 54
Spartans, 56
Species' rights and duties, 75
Spinoza, B., 61
Stability of laws, 113
Stalin, J., 115
Stare decisis, 127
State, as coercive power, 114
   as legal custodian, 77
   as legal framework, 113 f.
   from needs of people, 116
   of nature, 48
   structure of, 115
   two aims of, 78
   vs. ruling community, 115
States, latitude of, 21
Status to contract, 152
Statutes dealing with perjury in England, 126
Strategy, biologically presented, 92
   moral, 92
   requirements on, 94
Structure of legal system, 63
Subjective morality, 67
Substance to function, 159
Supreme Court, 33, 68
System, df., 24
   of order, 18

Systems, of ideas, 102
  of laws in operation, 63
  of morality, individual, 83

Taft Court, 33
Taft, W., 29
Task of judges, 147
Ten Commandments, 52
Theorematic consequences, 62
Theory of meaning, 191
Tobacco, inconsistent actions toward, 22
Toynbee, A.J., 28
Traffic laws, 121
Transparent facilitation, of laws, 104
Trans-subjective standard, 187
Trial court and scientific method, 134
Trial lawyer, 134
Trial procedures, 143 f.
Trials, difficulties of, 135
Tribal customs, 47
Truth vs. truths, 70
Twenty-First Amendment, 78, 118
Two-story world, 163

Tyranny, shortcomings of, 28

Ultimate purpose vs. ultimate question, 52 f.
Unimproved land, 161
Universal justice, 175
Urbanizating, effects of, 51
Utilitarian aims of law, 118
Utilitarianism, 196 f.

Variety, needs for, 81
Vedic Hymns, 52
Visigoths, 102

Warren Court, 33, 145
Weber, M., 35, 109
Welfare state, 69
Western culture, 122
Wittgenstein, L., 43, 191

Xerxes, 56

Zoroastrian, 51 f.